On the Design of a Middleware for Super-Peer Desktop Grids

Vom Fachbereich Informatik der Universität Kaiserslautern
zur Verleihung des akademischen Grades
Doktor-Ingenieur (Dr.-Ing.)
genehmigte

Dissertation

von

Diplom-Wirtschaftsinformatiker

Matthias Priebe

Tag der wissenschaftlichen Aussprache
10. März 2010

Dekan
Prof. Dr. Karsten Berns

Vorsitzender der Promotionskommission
Prof. Dr. Stefan Deßloch

Berichterstatter
Prof. Dr. Peter Merz
Prof. Dr. Paul Müller

Zeichen der Universität im Bibliotheksverkehr
D 386

Bibliografische Information der Deutschen Nationalbibliothek

Die Deutsche Nationalbibliothek verzeichnet diese Publikation in der
Deutschen Nationalbibliografie; detaillierte bibliografische Daten sind
im Internet über http://dnb.d-nb.de abrufbar.

ISBN 978-3-8325-2453-1

Logos Verlag Berlin GmbH
Comeniushof, Gubener Str. 47,
10243 Berlin
Tel.: +49 (0)30 42 85 10 90
Fax: +49 (0)30 42 85 10 92
INTERNET: http://www.logos-verlag.de

Abstract

The combined resources of desktop computers can exceed the power of today's fastest supercomputers by large margins. Similar to a Computational Grid but departing from fixed components and significant administrative overhead, a *Desktop Grid* leverages the idle CPU time provided by online desktop computers. As they permit every participant to submit arbitrary jobs, Desktop Grids enable individuals and organizations to give computing power to others and request it on demand. Besides filesharing, Desktop Grids represent a second major type of application which can be built on top of Peer-to-Peer structures. This thesis concentrates on the algorithmic aspects of a middleware of which one instance is executed on every peer of a Peer-to-Peer-based Desktop Grid.

An analysis of the requirements of Desktop Grids indicates that super-peer topologies are particularly suitable as communications infrastructures for Desktop Grids. Two distributed algorithms that construct such topologies are presented. The benefit of network coordinates for the purpose of topology optimization is investigated, and various network coordinates-generating algorithms are examined, two of which are improved. In addition, with respect to the Chord topology, improvements to Chord's forwarding and identifier assignment procedures are introduced that can work in a pure Chord topology but perform best in a super-peer environment as proposed by this thesis.

In a reciprocity-based Desktop Grid, participants are expected to return favors. Then again, some users may act selfishly by exploiting the cooperativeness of others without providing resources of their own. Such free-riding behavior disturbs the desired reciprocity. To counteract free-riding, a distributed reputation system is presented that makes free-riding substantially less harmful to cooperative peers.

The findings compiled in the course of this thesis culminate in a middleware concept for a novel Desktop Grid blueprint, PEERGRID, which is fully distributed on the basis of a super-peer topology and can handle a wide variety of jobs. The PeerGrid concept has been implemented in a middleware prototype whose performance is evaluated on three testbeds. Experiments with four distinct jobs which represent the vast majority of problems likely to be submitted to a Desktop Grid show that unless the network is a severe bottleneck, the PeerGrid middleware prototype succeeds in accelerating distributed computation by tapping otherwise unused resources.

Zusammenfassung

Moderne PCs in großer Anzahl können eine kumulierte Rechenleistung bereitstellen, welche diejenige der schnellsten verfügbaren Großrechner wesentlich übertrifft. Ein solcher Verbund von PCs, die über das Internet miteinander kommunizieren und sich ohne zentrale Instanz koordinieren, wird als *Desktop Grid* bezeichnet. Desktop Grids ähneln Computational Grids, stellen aber die vollständige Verteiltheit und den Verzicht auf administrative Komplexität in den Vordergrund. Sie ermöglichen es, lokal ungenutzte Rechenleistung mit anderen zu teilen und im Gegenzug verteilt lösbare Probleme (Jobs) von entfernten Ressourcen berechnen zu lassen. Neben Filesharing bilden Desktop Grids einen weiteren Anwendungstyp, der auf der Grundlage von Peer-to-Peer-Strukturen realisiert werden kann. Die vorliegende Dissertation widmet sich vor allem den algorithmischen Aspekten einer Middleware, von welcher jeder teilnehmende Rechner eines auf einem Peer-to-Peer-Netzwerk aufgebauten Desktop Grid eine Instanz ausführt.

Eine Analyse der Anforderungen von Desktop Grids zeigt, dass sich Super-Peer-Topologien als Kommunikationsinfrastrukturen für sie besonders eignen. Es werden zwei verteilte Algorithmen vorgestellt, die solche Topologien erzeugen, einer davon auf Chord-Basis. Mehrere Verbesserungen für Chord reduzieren Übertragungsverzögerungen deutlich. Zudem werden Netzwerkkoordinaten und ihr Nutzen für die Topologieoptimierung vorgestellt sowie zugehörige Erzeugungsalgorithmen diskutiert.

In auf Gegenseitigkeit beruhenden Desktop Grids wird von den Teilnehmern faires Verhalten erwartet. Egoistische Teilnehmer, welche die Kooperationsbereitschaft anderer Teilnehmer ausnutzen, können diese Erwartung unterlaufen. Ihr Egoismus stört die erwünschte Fairness. Ihm wird durch ein verteiltes Reputationssystem entgegengewirkt.

Die gesammelten Erkenntnisse münden in ein Konzept für ein Desktop Grid-Schema, PeerGrid, welches verteilt auf der Grundlage einer Super-Peer-Topologie operiert. Dieses Schema wurde in Form eines Prototypen implementiert und der Prototyp auf drei Testplattformen evaluiert. Hierzu wurden vier Jobs entwickelt, die gemeinsam die große Mehrheit der Jobs, welche sich für die verteilte Berechnung in einem Desktop Grid eignen, repräsentieren können. Experimente mit diesen Jobs zeigen, dass der Prototyp die verteilte Berechnung von Jobs unter Verwendung ansonsten brachliegender Ressourcen erfolgreich beschleunigen kann.

Acknowledgements

I wrote this thesis during my time as a PhD candidate in the Distributed Algorithms Group at the University of Kaiserslautern's Department of Computer Science. Now that it is complete, I am much obliged to the giants on whose shoulders I had the honor to stand.

First and foremost, I wish to express my gratitude to my advisor, Prof. Dr. Peter Merz, for the opportunity to pursue my PhD goal, for his advice that helped me to focus on the essential aspects of the subject matter, and for his guidance and feedback all along. I also wish to thank Prof. Dr. Paul Müller for his interest in my work and for his effort to review it.

I have highly valued the kindness of my co-workers. Steffen Wolf and Thomas Fischer were marvelous company, and I remember stimulating discussions time and again. In addition, the two of them provided the best LaTeX assistance I could have wished for. I have appreciated the friendly environment created by Prof. Dr. Jens Schmitt and the remaining DISCO staff, and the supportive atmosphere all around my place of work.

I would like to thank my co-authors for the cooperation on joint publications. Prof. Dr. Peter Merz, Steffen Wolf, Dennis Schwerdel, and Florian Kolter contributed code that facilitated my experiments. Thanks to Steffen Reithermann, I never had to worry about the access to PlanetLab.

I am grateful for everyone's patience while I was working on this thesis. My friends ensured I did not lose touch with life outside the university. The encouragement, care, and support of my family have made it all possible in the first place. I would certainly not have gotten to this point without them.

This work is dedicated to Felix. We all miss you.

Contents

List of Abbreviations

API	Application Programming Interface
APSP	All-Pairs Shortest Paths
AS	Autonomous System
CAN	Content-Addressable Network
CP	Connected Problem
DHT	Distributed Hash Table
EC2	Elastic Compute Cloud
FLOPS	FLOating point operations Per Second
GA	Genetic Algorithm
GNP	Global Network Positioning
GPU	Graphics Processing Unit
ICMP	Internet Control Message Protocol
IP	Internet Protocol, also: Integer Program
ISP	Internet Service Provider
ITA	Independent-Task Application
LP	Linear Program
MIP	Mixed-Integer Program
MFLOPS	MegaFLOPS (millions of FLOPS)
NPS	Network Positioning System
P2P	Peer-to-Peer
PKI	Public-Key Infrastructure
RTT	Round-Trip Time
SPSA	Super-Peer Selection Algorithm
SPSP	Super-Peer Selection Problem
TIV	Triangle Inequality Violation
TTL	Time To Live

List of Figures

List of Tables

1

Introduction

The availability of solutions to a considerable number of problems depends on the availability of massive computational power. Examples of such computation-intensive problems are as diverse as combinatorial optimization, raytracing, and parameter-sweep studies. For decades, problems like these have been the exclusive domain of supercomputers. They provide computational resources to an extent which exceeds that of an ordinary desktop computer by orders of magnitude. However, they are costly to build and maintain, and there may be considerable lead time until one becomes available.

On the other hand, desktop PCs are occasionally idle, spending unused processor cycles for no return. This is particularly true for multi-core CPUs in which one or more cores may become underloaded or idle for considerable periods of time. MOORE'S LAW suggests that the number of transistors contained within integrated circuits doubles approximately every two years [205]. This rate of growth permits modern desktop computers to perform tasks beyond ordinary office work. Harvesting idle cycles from these desktop resources to form a virtual supercomputer that offers its cumulative computation potential to the general public represents an alternative to conventional supercomputing. Inside this virtual computation engine, a self-organizing system would interconnect the participating machines, splitting large jobs into small tasks, distributing the tasks among the desktop machines, and reassembling the individual results into a single one as it would have been computed had the job been processed by a supercomputer in the traditional way.

The notion of distributed computing has grown into an established concept. Among other forms, it has assumed shape as cluster computing and Grid computing, connecting resources on a local and a global scale, respectively. In both variants, resources are supervised by one or a group of trustworthy administrators, and they have been acquired with the intention of being accessed from the outside to handle distributed work.

On the contrary, desktop PCs operated by scientific institutions, companies, and private households are purchased for the purpose of performing work locally. The remote utilization of idle cycles from these devices has been facilitated by the widespread availability of Internet access. It has begun as *volunteer computing*, asking computer owners to voluntarily donate CPU idle time. In this model, a user would run problem-specific software that receives a job of a well-known kind from a fixed, pre-defined server, computes it, and returns the results to the server. A prominent example for this client/server-style approach to distributed computing is SETI@home [7] which analyzes radio signals from outer space for traces of extraterrestrial life. [1] SETI@home has pioneered the effort of tapping a wealth of computational power that has not been leveraged before on a global scale. The potential of this approach led Shirts and Pande to conclude that the "world's supply of CPU time is very large, growing rapidly, and essentially untapped" [211]. All volunteer computing projects pursue the economically sensible utilization of otherwise wasted CPU cycles on desktop computers.

Besides volunteer computing, another recent development concerns the way computers are interconnected. For a number of applications, Peer-to-Peer (P2P) networks have emerged as a viable alternative to client/server approaches. In their fully distributed form, P2P networks contain no single point of failure, scale to millions of participants, and include properties of self-organization that improve their robustness. Distributed computing in a P2P setting enables everyone to act as a job owner, asking other participants to join the computing effort. In the context of this thesis, because of its focus on desktop resources, a distributed system that handles a dynamic set of participants and enables everyone to submit arbitrary jobs for distributed computation is referred to as a *Desktop Grid*.

The described model is based on reciprocity: users contribute idle resources to the system in exchange for enormous cumulative computation power available eventually when the need arises. However, this approach may be exploited by individuals whose goals are selfish rather than cooperative. A selfish participant may join the Desktop Grid, submit its job, wait for its completion, and once finished, leave the system. That particular individual does not contribute any resources to the system but exploits it for its own good: it is a *free-rider*. While a certain extent of free-riding might be tolerated, the system breaks down when there is too much. Honest users might not want to support those unwilling to reciprocate. Hence, a Desktop Grid needs measures to counter free-riding.

In a P2P system, there is no hierarchy as in a client/server setting. A middleware may be deployed on every participant to manage the P2P network and enable jobs to be computed in a distributed way. The scope of this thesis is to define design goals, identify issues and propose solutions for a Desktop Grid middleware that minimizes dependencies on

[1] Section 2.5 will provide a compact account of SETI@home.

centralized components. It focuses on the algorithmic aspects of such a middleware, and its contribution is threefold. First, it develops a way to create and manage an efficient interconnection structure that links the participating machines. It is shown that a particular kind of P2P interconnection structure offers substantial advantages in the face of Desktop Grid requirements. The addition of network coordinates enables the proposed approach to scale well. Second, the impact caused by selfish behavior is assessed and a mechanism to counter free-riding is described. The resulting concept represents a blueprint for a middleware that may serve as the essential building block of a distributed, self-organizing, selfishness-aware Desktop Grid, PEERGRID. Third, a prototype of such a middleware has been developed to prove the concept's viability. With this prototype, various jobs of different kinds were distributed in live settings and their performance measured. The results confirm that considerable acceleration can be experienced by suitable jobs while at the same time, the underlying P2P structure maintains a high degree of connectivity.

1.1   The Peer-to-Peer paradigm

The term *Peer-to-Peer* designates a particular class of computer networks and the style of interaction between their participants [18, 27, 49, 51, 59, 85, 88, 120, 137, 139, 140, 152, 210, 212, 217, 224]. Unlike client/server systems, participants of P2P networks act autonomously as both client and server at the same time, and communicate with each other. They are called *peers* due to the absence of a hierarchy. An early definition for the term *Peer-to-Peer*, proposed in 2001 by [210], is

> Peer-to-Peer is a class of applications that takes advantage of resources – storage, cycles, content, human presence – available at the edges of the Internet. Because accessing these decentralized resources means operating in an environment of unstable connectivity and unpredictable IP addresses, peer-to-peer nodes must operate outside the DNS and have significant or total autonomy from central servers.

This definition permits compositions of the client/server and P2P paradigms to exist as special cases of P2P systems. In *centralized P2P* systems, a server as a fixed coordinator is present, yet the peers provide the predominant portion of resources and communicate with each other. The server provides services such as a directory service or message queuing for temporarily absent peers, as in the instant-messaging application ICQ or the file-sharing system NAPSTER [59, 74, 75, 137, 152, 210]. Centralized P2P systems inherit the dependency on a centralized component that client/server models possess, creating a single point of failure and a potential bottleneck. In contrast, pure P2P systems do not assign a fixed role to any participant. Every peer may fail without endangering the system's existence. A P2P system's scalability greatly benefits from the removal of central components [217]. Also, in pure P2P systems, all infrastructure is contributed by the peers. The peers self-organize in order to perform routing and forwarding, and to fix their interconnection structure when failures or departures occur [49]. A more sophisticated approach is to assign a server-like role dynamically to a number of peers, yielding a *hybrid* P2P architecture [62, 74, 191]. Hybrid architectures include *super-peers* which form a network of equals among themselves. The selection of super-peers is a key aspect of hybrid P2P systems and will be elaborated in Section 4.4.

P2P architectures are superior to client/server approaches in terms of scalability, cost of maintenance, and fault tolerance [27, 174]. Departing from the client/server paradigm, they move "from coordination to cooperation, from centralization to decentralization, and from control to incentives" [217]. They are built to deal with a high level of dynamics as peers may join or leave the system all out of a sudden, a phenomenon known as *churn* [1, 74, 151]. It is for this reason that peers cannot be entrusted with maintaining any important piece of system state exclusively on their own; P2P structures are made to account for this fact [59]. Besides featuring the capabilities for implementing distributed storage and sustaining high dynamics, P2P structures are designed to exhibit a low administrative overhead [239].

Due to the typical underutilization of clients in client/server settings, peers have idle resources that can be leveraged by P2P applications [100, 140]. The cumulative amount of peer resources suffices to compete with supercomputers. For example, on a day in 2001, the cumulative storage space of all Napster clients exceeded 7 TB [193].

1.1.1 Peer-to-Peer overlay networks

The network connecting the peers on the application-layer level is called *overlay network*, with *overlay* being a common shortcut [212]. P2P overlays are built on top of an existing network which is used for low-level communication, commonly the Internet. Besides, a P2P overlay may additionally deploy its own addressing scheme and offer additional communications services not available from the underlying network, in particular application-layer multicast. The provision of dedicated addresses (identifiers, IDs) is a necessity for persistent identification as IP addresses may change. In ICQ, a client connecting to the system might have a different IP address than during the previous session, but its ICQ ID remains constant, allowing others to correctly identify the peer.

To be able to participate in the P2P system, a peer needs to be connected to one or more other peers in the overlay. Hence, peers create connections to other peers which they then consider to be their *neighbors* [139]. The actual structure of an overlay is determined by its *topology* which influences performance, flexibility and efficiency [137]. A topology can be single-layered (flat) or multi-layered (hierarchical). Another substantial distinction differentiates *structured* from *unstructured* topologies [152, 191, 217]. In structured topologies, every newly joining peer is assigned an ID in a decentralized way. The ID's value determines the position which the peer is supposed to assume, hence defining its set of neighbors. In unstructured topologies, a new peer is free to pick any existing peers as its neighbors.

The first widespread fully distributed P2P system built on an unstructured topology was GNUTELLA [59, 75, 126, 152, 224]. As peers are both clients and servers at once, Gnutella refers to them as *servents*. Gnutella serves as the communication medium for a number of clients that speak the Gnutella protocol, a simple protocol that centers around a flooding mechanism which is constrained by a time-to-live (TTL) measure. Because of this, Gnutella servents will usually not find all other servents as their discovery broadcasts have TTL bounds too low to travel across the entire overlay, causing the servents beyond the TTL horizon to remain undiscovered. The major shortcoming of Gnutella is its failure to scale due to the high overhead incurred mainly through a flooding-based content search mechanism [59, 152, 217]. In addition, Gnutella is unaware of the underlying network's properties, a fact that adversely affects its routing performance [74, 200].

A structured topology provides the foundation for a *Distributed Hash Table* (DHT) [92, 152, 217, 228]. DHTs are tailored to support a swift access to data stored in decentralized P2P systems. A DHT represents a hash table whose values (data items) are distributed across the peers of a P2P overlay. It is commonly associated with means to route a unicast *lookup* message to the peer responsible for performing the actual key→value mapping. In a DHT, it is assumed that content can be addressed with a unique key, and that every peer keeps track of a portion of the hash table's key→value mappings. Every peer has a unique ID to which a key can be mapped using a hash function which is common knowledge among all peers. For content retrieval using a DHT, there is no need for a broadcast message to be sent as in Gnutella. When a peer wants to find content and has the associated key, the hash function is applied to the key. The hash value is then mapped to a peer ID that defines the peer responsible for the key. Since every peer has only a limited number of connections to other peers, the peer forwards the query to its most suitable neighbor, determined by the characteristics of the particular topology, in order to move the query message closer to its actual destination. This step is repeated iteratively until the peer responsible for the key has received the query and replies to the query's originator. Unlike the flooding mechanism used in unstructured topologies, DHT lookups are generally efficient [228]. Lookups are of particular interest in storage-related applications (e. g. filesharing, registry and directory services) where an efficient retrieval mechanism is desirable. For the purposes of Desktop Grids, the distributed lookup mechanisms of DHTs operating on structured topologies are adapted in particular for routing arbitrary unicast, multicast and broadcast messages, a facility on which Chapter 4 will elaborate.

In summary, a P2P topology and its associated maintenance mechanism are characterized by six key properties [1]:

1. The choice of an identifier space

2. The mapping of resources and peers to the identifier space

3. The peers' management of the identifier space

4. The structure of the logical network

5. The routing strategy

6. The overlay maintenance strategy

Due to its inherent benefits, in particular scalability, robustness, and the renouncement of a fixed infrastructure besides the underlying network, the P2P paradigm has gained significant momentum. Internet Service Providers (ISPs) are quoted with P2P traffic fractions of 50 % and more [217]. In 2004, it was determined that nearly 80 % of all traffic flowing on a FRANCE TELECOM IP backbone network stemmed from P2P applications [17].

To provide a common ground for P2P applications, SUN has introduced JXTA, a specification for P2P applications, in 2001 [1, 62, 88, 100, 140, 202, 224]. While it does not depend on a particular programming language or platform, the major implementation supports the JAVA language. JXTA abstracts from the underlying network by creating a number of entities: peers, peer groups, messages, and pipes (unidirectional communication channels). These resources are tagged with *advertisements* that can be discovered by other peers. JXTA adds a hierarchy of peers, enabling the concept of super-peers and proxy facilities to include peers behind firewalls, but it offers no dedicated topology optimization. JXTA uses the XML format for its advertisements by default but can operate with other container formats, too [100].

1.1.2 Summary of properties

P2P systems are characterized by the following properties:

- Every node is a peer.

- Peers communicate with each other.

- Every peer may be both client and server at the same time.

- Peers contribute their own resources.

- Peers enjoy considerable autonomy, in particular through independent administration by their respective owners.

- Peers are interconnected by an overlay network which is based on another communication network, typically the Internet.

- There is an additional addressing scheme at the application layer.

- Peers may join and leave at any time.

In addition, present-day P2P topologies are commonly pure P2P topologies characterized by adding the following properties:

- There is no centralized component: no single point of failure, no bottleneck, no censorship, and no directory service.

- Identities are inexpensive: a node can obtain an identity (a P2P address/ID at the application layer) at virtually zero cost.

The P2P paradigm offers significant benefits to applications that can make use of its properties such as massive scalability, robustness, and self-organization [152]. The aspect of self-organization is an essential part of decentralized P2P topologies. The next section will discuss this aspect at length.

1.2 Self-organization

Occurring in nature such as in bird flocks and ant colonies, *self-organization* is also a property of decentralized P2P systems [2, 112, 161, 162, 212]. Self-organizing systems distribute control, exploit locality, and provide the foundation for the emergence of global structures through local interactions without the need for intervention or coordination from the outside or by a central component [2, 161]. Since these systems are highly adaptive, scalability and fault-tolerance rise.

The evolution of self-organizing systems is based on the transition from one state into a subsequent state due to local interactions of the participants. The state space is explored until the system arrives at an equilibrium state that features a desired global property [2, 112]. There may be more than one equilibrium state. Any of these equilibria may attract the system into moving towards it, hence each of these states is an *attractor* which designates a state that the system wants to reach but not to leave once reached [112]. An attractor is commonly surrounded by a *basin*, a set of states that, once reached, will lead the system towards the attractor [112]. A second concept is *noise* which captures the idea of undirected influence from the outside that makes the system traverse its state space. The more noise, the swifter the movement through the state space. Hence, noise provides the energy to let the system move towards an attractor [112].

In P2P systems, the persistent properties of the infrastructure are not predefined but emerge over time [85]. The maintenance procedures of structured topologies such as Chord exhibit aspects of self-organization. A check list to determine the extent of self-organization in P2P systems contains the following criteria [162]:

- *Boundaries:* The P2P system itself should decide about accepting new peers.

- *Reproduction:* The P2P system should reproduce its structure (peers, connections, and data), in whole or in parts.

- *Mutability:* The P2P system should be able to change its structure, in particular by modifying the connections linking the peers.

- *Organization:* The P2P system exhibits some form of organization (e. g. a hierarchy).

- *Metrics:* The P2P system can detect perturbations triggered by its environment, such as connection failure, DoS attacks, and overload.

- *Adaptivity:* The P2P system can adapt to perturbations appropriately.

- *Feedback:* The P2P system reacts upon reception of feedback (positive or negative).

- *Complexity reduction:* The P2P system attempts to reduce overall complexity by hiding details from its environment, e.g. by forming clusters or creating entities from sets of other entities.

- *Randomness:* The P2P system uses randomness as a prerequisite for creativity.

- *Self-organized criticality*: The P2P system moves towards a state in which the system components are sufficiently reactive such that chain reactions can be triggered by single events.

- *Emergence:* The P2P system exhibits properties unknown to a single peer.

The first six criteria are related to general self-organization aspects while the latter five criteria are relevant for establishing *autonomy*, meaning that a system can act and adapt autonomously [162]. The importance of self-organization for Desktop Grids is stressed in [39] which asserts that in settings where centralized servers are unavailable, "peers must be capable of staying in the infrastructure by their own means." Thus, an algorithm that permits peers to self-organize is required. Chapter 4 will present two such algorithms for use with super-peer topologies.

1.3   Middleware

The term *middleware* designates an application-neutral software that provides common services to distributed applications and hides complexity from application developers [25, 77, 157, 224]. Typically, a middleware is placed between an operating system and applications based on its interface. It is deployed to bridge the heterogeneity of distributed systems in an application-transparent fashion, is reusable due to its inherent application neutrality, and provides an abstraction from underlying mechanisms to facilitate application development.

By distinguishing between the cardinal means of communication employed by middleware-running nodes, conventional middleware can be classified into four broad categories [77]:

- *Transactional middleware* uses transactions as the standard means of communication between two components that do not run on the same host.

- *Message-oriented middleware* provides a publish/subscribe and/or a message queue mechanism for asynchronous communication.

- *Procedural middleware* is built around the paradigm of synchronously invoking remote methods, the most prominent example being REMOTE PROCEDURE CALLS (RPC) [214].

- *Object-oriented middleware* extends procedural middleware with object orientation. Well-known examples include the COMMON OBJECT REQUEST BROKER ARCHITECTURE (CORBA) [202] and Java's REMOTE METHOD INVOCATION (RMI) [140, 202].

In a P2P context, a middleware that is run on every peer creates and maintains the overlay, communicates with other peers, and provides applications with an API [137, 157]. Among the abstractions provided by P2P middleware, the abstraction from the P2P topology is most important for applications [137].

There is a peculiar relationship between Web Services and P2P platforms. Both address distributed computing, and both rely on middleware for their respective implementation [113]. Web Services offer service orchestration and defined quality of service, features that P2P systems commonly lack. However, as Web Services typically rely on centralized components, their approach is not further explored for the purpose investigated here.

1.4   NetSim

A number of simulators for P2P overlay networks have been proposed. To address a large number of needs and demands, these simulators exhibit a broad range of individual properties, however researchers occasionally still conclude that no existing simulator properly fits their requirements [177]. For this reason, the NETSIM simulation framework was developed by Prof. Dr. Peter Merz. It has been extended to handle the experiments presented in this thesis. It deliberately focuses on the discrete event-based simulation of P2P topology construction and maintenance processes with the aid of inter-node delay information. NetSim has been designed to be convertible into a real distributed application, implementing a previously simulated protocol, with comparatively little effort, meaning that simulation results can be verified in a real setting. [2] NetSim concentrates on the overlay itself and generally abstracts from lower layers except for the message delay (alternatively on the round-trip time, RTT) between two nodes. By construction, it requires node-to-node delay information to be available. NetSim has been developed in the Java language, featuring a modular, object-oriented structure.

NetSim is based on the message concept, hence all communication is asynchronous. Nodes in the overlay exchange messages and act upon reception of a message. The reception of a message generally affects the recipient's local state, possibly resulting in the creation of additional messages sent to other nodes. NetSim can handle arbitrary P2P topologies and protocols. A protocol is implemented by inheriting from given generic Java classes that model individual node behavior such as sending messages and joining or leaving the overlay. NetSim features a number of overlay supervision functions, including a snapshot facility that may be called in regular intervals to perform arbitrary tasks with global view.

Messages contain their expected time of arrival (ETA) based on the communication delay. NetSim centers around an ETA-ordered message queue which distributes messages to individual nodes. When a node transmits a message, the message will be placed in the queue according to its ETA. The event-based simulation proceeds in time in a stepwise manner, removing the foremost message from the queue which is due to be the next message received by a node in the simulated network. Also, nodes may trigger local events by inserting messages into the queue that are addressed to themselves. These messages constitute a special kind of queue element; in particular, their ETA is set to the desired point in time when the local event should be triggered. Simulation stops when a pre-defined point in time or a desired event has been reached.

NetSim's design goal of being easily transformable into a real distributed application has influenced its mechanisms. Once a protocol has been implemented with NetSim and simulation yields promising results, NetSim's message queue may be removed, and send/receive operations may be replaced by counterparts which perform live message handling. Local events may be handled by timer-triggered callbacks. Along with a bootstrapping mechanism, this is already sufficient to make the implemented protocol

---

[2]The benefit of re-using code in this way has been pointed out in [177].

work in a practical distributed environment. Bootstrapping is generally handled by having a new node contact an arbitrary node which already belongs to the simulated network. Actual node behavior and subsequent actions depend on the respective protocol implementation.

NetSim integrates facilities to deal with two different kinds of node-to-node delays. One kind is the actual round-trip time or one-way delay between any two nodes, given by a squared matrix read from a file. Another kind of delay taken into account by NetSim is a delay estimate provided by network coordinates that are established at simulation run-time. [3] The simulated protocol is supposed to generally rely on the delay estimate, while the actual delay for a link will be available to nodes adjacent to that link only.

General criteria for the evaluation and differentiation of P2P overlay simulators were presented in [176, 177]. Using these criteria, NetSim can be characterized as follows:

- *Simulation architecture:* NetSim is event-based, designed for both structured and unstructured P2P topologies, and possibly enhanced by super-peers, with a special focus on the integration of network coordinates.

- *Usability:* NetSim is based on the Java platform, with no dedicated scripting language. Simulation parameters are defined in a configuration file.

- *Scalability:* Constrained only by the limitations of delay data integration, scalability is fostered through NetSim's lightweight approach to simulation.

- *Statistics:* NetSim provides both general, event-based and protocol-dependent statistics from an individual peer's point of view. A snapshot mechanism provides a global view on a regular basis for arbitrary purposes.

- *Underlying network:* Discarding details from lower layers except for the communication delay, NetSim concentrates on the overlay.

A recent survey related to P2P research revealed a number of simulators currently in use [177]. The survey's authors found none of these simulators to fit all requirements. Regarding the platform, 8 out of 9 major P2P overlay simulators investigated were based on Java. All were free software, however different kinds of license policies applied.

When compared to other event-based P2P simulators that concentrate on the actual overlay rather than also considering the layers below, NetSim proves to be different. OVERSIM is a P2P simulator based on OMNET++ with a focus on scalability [20]. As with NetSim, code re-use for practical applications has been a design goal. However, OverSim's model of node-to-node delays is too simplistic; it is based on either a single constant value or a placement of the nodes in a two-dimensional space. Simulators

---

[3]Network coordinates will be introduced in Chapter 3.

limited to structured topologies include P2PSim [144] and OverlayWeaver [20, 176]. Like NetSim, PlanetSim and PeerSim both support structured and unstructured topologies, and both run on the Java platform, however they have other shortcomings with regard to the requirements: PlanetSim offers no support for gathering statistics, while PeerSim focuses on epidemic algorithms which are outside this thesis' scope, and disregards latencies [176]. In [135], delays between hosts were modelled using network coordinates to circumvent the need for node-to-node delay matrices. This approach permits the consideration of large numbers of nodes but prevents the estimation of embedding errors due to the lack of actual measurements. NetSim differs from other simulators in the emphasis that it puts on coordinates-based delay estimation and the requirement for a node-to-node delay input matrix.

The methodology of the NetSim simulation framework has been published in [167].

1.5   Testbeds

Three testbeds served as platforms for evaluating the mechanisms presented in this thesis. All nodes in these testbeds were running Linux 2.6 kernels and Java 6 virtual machines.

To gauge the performance of individual processors, the Linpack benchmark has been deployed. The Linpack benchmark captures the currently available computational power with a focus on floating-point performance, and returns this value in units of millions of floating-point operations per second (*MegaFLOPS, MFLOPS*). [4] A Java version of Linpack was executed on the respective resource to assess the extent of its computational potential. [5] The benchmark was executed 30 times in sequence on every node with a randomly generated system of 500 linear equations per run. The elapsed real time per run was recorded and the mean over 30 runs per unit computed.

A first testbed was a local 6-node cluster run by the University of Kaiserslautern's Distributed Algorithms Group, henceforth referred to as DAG Cluster. Each node carried a dual-CPU Intel Xeon E5420 configuration with 4 cores per CPU clocked at 2.5 GHz each, yielding 48 CPU cores overall. The first node was equipped with 16 GB RAM, the remaining five with 12 GB RAM each. The nodes communicated via a switched Gigabit Ethernet LAN. The mean floating-point output of a single core was estimated with Linpack at 940.552 MFLOPS with a standard deviation of 3.61 MFLOPS.

In addition to this cluster system, two WAN testbeds were used which will be introduced in the remainder of this section.

---

[4] A description of the Linpack benchmark is provided in Section 6.2.5.

[5] http://www.netlib.org/benchmark/linpackjava/ provides the original Java Linpack port. For the experiments documented in this thesis, the refined version available from http://www.jeckle.de/freeStuff/jLinpack/ has been preferred.

1.5.1 PlanetLab

PLANETLAB is a global platform that serves as a testbed for experiments in the field of distributed systems [50, 201]. PlanetLab consists of geographically dispersed computers interconnected via the Internet, exposing them to phenomena such as fluctuating transmission delays, congestion, link failure, and packet loss. Most of PlanetLab's computers are provided by scientific institutions. All are running a Linux kernel with virtualization capabilities provided by the PlanetLab administration. It is PlanetLab's policy to require every participating institution to donate at least two computers that meet or exceed specified minimum performance requirements. In exchange, the donors gain access to all machines donated by other PlanetLab members. In August 2009, PlanetLab featured 1,022 machines spread over 483 sites worldwide.

Users can access PlanetLab machines in their own virtualized environment. Thus, PlanetLab creates an illusion of isolation through virtualization, providing every accessing institution with one or more dedicated *slices* that, for a customizable set of nodes, encompass a portion of each node's resources. The particular resources given to a slice on a single PlanetLab node are referred to as *sliver*. PlanetLab nodes and the slivers they provide are not protected by firewalls, allowing unconstrained access to their ports.

The usage characteristics of PlanetLab nodes were investigated in [185]. In a 6-month study, it was determined that CPU and network resource usage on PlanetLab was both generally heavy and dynamic. The study found CPU speeds and main memory (RAM) size to be considerably heterogeneous. Since PlanetLab nodes often belong to scientific organizations, they have access to high-speed backbones. In [141], the average bandwidth available between two PlanetLab nodes was reported to be close to 64 Mbps.

Table A.1 in the appendix shows the CPU equipment of 509 PlanetLab nodes probed in March 2009. The table indicates that the major part (67.2 %) of the probed nodes features standard desktop-level processors including Intel Core 2, Intel Celeron, Intel Pentium family, and AMD Athlon units. Such processors are also likely to be found in office workstations and household computers. Approximately one third (32.8 %) of the queried PlanetLab nodes feature a server-class processor: Intel Xeon or AMD Opteron.

Minimum	25% percentile	Median	Mean	75% percentile	Maximum
3.8	54.5	129.5	306.5	520.9	1,346

Table 1.1: Results of the Linpack benchmark on PlanetLab nodes; units are MFLOPS

Both the hardware and the system's actual load influence the cycle resources available for distributed computation. The heterogeneity and dynamics of PlanetLab resources are extensive. Only those 412 PlanetLab nodes that were able to complete all 30 passes of the Java-based Linpack benchmark have influenced the outcome which is summarized by Table 1.1 and depicted by Figure 1.1. The figure shows a histogram with a class width of 20 MFLOPS. It is skewed to the left as the median (129.5 MFLOPS) is considerably less than the average (306.5 MFLOPS).

PlanetLab creates a challenging atmosphere for applications to operate within [32, 201]. Nodes occasionally fail abruptly, the resources available to slivers may vary suddenly, and the network may exhibit connectivity issues as not all PlanetLab nodes can send IP packets to all other PlanetLab nodes or resolve their symbolic addresses via DNS. Due to these circumstances, PlanetLab is an excellent platform to deploy and test P2P applications in an environment affected by harmful real-world phenomena.

1.5.2 Amazon Elastic Compute Cloud

The ELASTIC COMPUTE CLOUD (EC2) is a commercial platform operated and marketed by AMAZON since 2007 [109, 229]. It implements the paradigm of *Cloud Computing* [109]. In Cloud Computing, customers can lease cluster-like resources on demand. EC2 permits the exact volume of resources to be specified at order time, limited only by a bound that Amazon defines. Customers receive root access to the leased resources. They pay for lease time and traffic that has either its origin or its endpoint outside the cloud. Due to the payment process, anonymity is impossible – customers need to disclose their identities for billing and accountability purposes. With the help of virtualization, customers can create virtual images of their preferred operating environment and application software which is then uploaded to EC2. When the demand arises, customers can set up the desired number of nodes running these images within virtual machines that appear as if they were dedicated servers set up exclusively for the respective customer.

The inherent scalability of EC2 is bounded only by real node availability which Amazon oversees. EC2 customers initially receive up to 20 nodes. More are available on special request. Amazon offers EC2 resources in various configurations that differ in performance and storage capacity. For the experiments presented in this thesis, Amazon provided up to 250 nodes of the SMALL configuration.

Out of 332 nodes reserved with Amazon EC2, only 2 CPU types could be observed: AMD's DUAL-CORE OPTERON 2218 HE, running at 2.6 GHz, and INTEL's XEON E5430, running at 2.66 GHz. The AMD Opteron CPU powered 282 of the 332 nodes (84.94 %) while the Intel Xeon CPU powered the remaining 50 nodes (15.06 %). The Linpack benchmark was executed 30 times on each of 40 EC2 nodes with the Opteron CPU and on each of 40 EC2 nodes with the Xeon CPU. The Linpack performance of these CPUs, measured using the same procedure as in PlanetLab, is shown in Table 1.2. At the 95 %

CPU type	Mean	Std. dev.	95% confidence interval
AMD Opteron 2218 HE	102.053	18.883	$[100.984, 103.123]$
Intel Xeon E5430	128.593	39.098	$[126.379, 130.808]$

Table 1.2: Results of the Linpack benchmark on Amazon EC2 nodes; units are MFLOPS

confidence level, a Welch test revealed the floating-point performance of AMD Opteron and Intel Xeon CPUs to be significantly different. The Xeon unit is faster as the 95% confidence interval for the difference in means equals $[24.082, 28.998]$. Thus, there is some heterogeneity in EC2's resources, but it is less than what is observed on PlanetLab.

1.5.3 Sources of delay information

For the algorithms introduced and discussed in this thesis, cost is frequently expressed in terms of end-to-end communication delay (latency) or similarly through the round-trip time. It is for this reason that live delay information was necessary for meaningful simulation experiments. There is publicly available real-world node-to-node delay information from various sources that has been used for these experiments. One source was PlanetLab. Jeremy Stribling has conducted all-pairs RTT probes between PlanetLab nodes. From the outcome [6], the first measurement for each month in 2005 (denoted by mm-2005 where mm $\in \{00, 01, \ldots, 12\}$) has been picked. Those networks consisted of 70 to 419 nodes. Other data include a 1,740-node matrix from the King project (King) [104] [7] and a 2,500-node matrix from the Meridian project (Meridian) [233].

In some cases, input data from PlanetLab data, King and Meridian were flawed. Several measurements were unavailable or substantially distorted. Depending on the context, the issue of missing distance information has been dealt with either by computing a two-hop distance to the destination via a randomly selected intermediate hop or by excluding the link for which no information was available from the respective experiment's evaluation.

In all cases, the delay of a node to itself has been assumed to be zero even if a different value was provided from an external source.

---

[6] Jeremy Stribling's measurements are publicly available at http://pdos.csail.mit.edu/~strib/pl_app/.
[7] The King approach is described in Section 3.3.4.2.

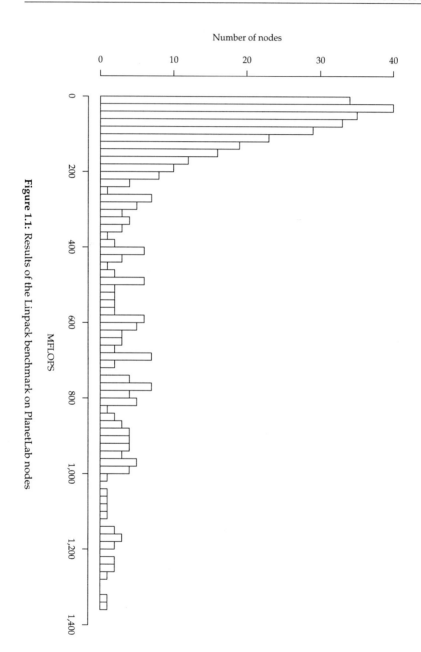

Figure 1.1: Results of the Linpack benchmark on PlanetLab nodes

1.6   Assumptions

A number of assumptions underlie the treatment of the various aspects covered in this thesis. Additional assumptions may apply for limited scopes within distinct sections. The assumptions valid throughout the thesis are the following:

- Communication networks are generally affected by non-negligible communication delays. Hence, optimizing communications structures for low delay is a permissible goal. Propagation delays between nodes are non-negative. A node always experiences zero propagation delay to itself.

- Delays unrelated to the transmission or propagation of messages are negligible. In particular, this concerns the processing delay in message forwarding.

- Modifications to standard components such as communication protocols (TCP/IP), operating systems, or the Java virtual machine are not permitted.

- When a job is distributed to a number of remote machines, the job may be assumed to be computation-intensive. Thus, it will occupy all available resources on the host computer until it terminates. Moreover, it is not migrated to another machine.

- Individuals participating in a Desktop Grid will not damage the system for irrational reasons (i. e. harming others without gaining a benefit from doing so).

- Message routing is safe in the sense that messages will not be discarded by those entities supposed to forward them. [8]

- There is no identity theft as in the *impersonation* attack.

- Traffic is distributed evenly among the node pairs.

For the sake of readability, non-negativity constraints in optimization models (linear, integer, and mixed-integer programs) have not been made explicit.

1.7   Thesis structure

The main content of this thesis is distributed over the upcoming five chapters. Chapter 2 outlines and compares major schemes of concurrent computing, including parallel, cluster, Grid, volunteer, and Desktop Grid computing, with a highlight on the properties and requirements of Desktop Grids. Chapter 3 introduces network coordinates, an important auxiliary to ensure scalability in network optimization processes that frequently require delay estimates between arbitrary nodes. The concept of network coordinates is laid out, and distributed algorithms that generate such coordinates are presented. Chapter 4

---

[8]Section 6.2.4 will elaborate on this aspect.

deals with the creation and properties of P2P topologies, both flat and hybrid, and their utility to Desktop Grid operations. A major part of that chapter is devoted to super-peer topologies and distributed algorithms to maintain them. Chapter 5 elaborates on the behavior of peers. Specifically, it addresses the inclination of selfish peers to exploit the cooperativeness of others, the phenomenon known as free-riding. The chapter discusses the value of reputation to distinguish free-riders from ordinary peers and presents a distributed reputation system to counter free-riding. Chapter 6 presents the PeerGrid middleware concept. The interplay between the components introduced in the preceding chapters is discussed along with implementation aspects generally relevant to Desktop Grids. Moreover, that chapter documents the experiments conducted with a PeerGrid middleware prototype. To this end, four jobs illustrate the performance gains attainable through distributed computing in a Desktop Grid. The thesis concludes with a summary and an outlook on possible future research in Chapter 7.

2

Parallel and distributed computing

The ever-increasing need for computational power has spurred the evolution of simultaneous computation. There, a number of processing units work on different segments of a given problem concurrently to increase the throughput per unit of time [58]. A substantial distinction between the various forms of concurrent computing is related to the inter-process communication infrastructure. The term *distributed computing* refers to all issues dealing with the network-based interconnection of autonomous computers and their use for remote computation, while the term *parallel computing* refers to single-computer multi-CPU configurations [58]. When a concurrent-computation system that interconnects computational resources equipped with dedicated memory is able to scale to thousands of participants, it is *massively parallel* [21, 58].

This chapter provides an overview of parallel computing and major distributed computing schemes, with a special focus on the loosest-coupled of them, the Desktop Grids.

2.1 Overview

Given a problem in need of substantial computational resources, there are two major requirements to be fulfilled for concurrent processing to work besides the availability of suitable resources. First, the problem at hand needs to be segmentable, i. e. the problem can be split into a number of tasks to be processed simultaneously. Second, a communication mechanism is required to permit the various tasks to transmit their individual results. Communication is an essential pillar in parallel and distributed computing. While the first requirement is determined primarily by the problem's nature, the second requirement largely depends on the properties of the chosen kind of concurrent processing. The development of distributed computing schemes and platforms is linked to the communications infrastructure that interconnects the resources involved. A network operating on a local scale is called *Local Area Network* (LAN), while a network that interconnects geographically scattered participants is a *Wide Area Network* (WAN) [221].

The various forms of concurrent computation can be classified along several criteria. With regard to the relationships between the computing resources, there are five major concurrent computation schemes [58, 192]:

- *Parallel computing* uses multiple CPU cores, multiple GPU cores, and/or multiple CPUs within one machine. Tasks can communicate via low-latency shared memory with data transfer rates on the order of gigabytes per second.

- *Cluster computing* uses two or more distinct computers, usually of a homogeneous type and under common administration, that communicate via a LAN and compute in parallel.

- *Grid computing* takes cluster computing to a global scale by interconnecting heterogeneous, geographically distributed resources via a WAN, usually the Internet.

- *Volunteer computing* is a client/server global-scale approach to distributed computing. A dynamic, potentially large set of clients can compute segments of work for a central entity and process them in a massively parallel fashion.

- *Desktop Grids* merge the benefits of Grid computing and volunteer computing by permitting every participant to submit a problem for joint computation. Moreover, in P2P Desktop Grids, there is no central entity.

The relationship between the job submitters and the resources that process the submitted jobs follows one of two paradigms:

- *Client/server computing* enables clients, commonly desktop workstations, to access servers and have them compute a task: "client/server computing is driven from the desktop computer" [214]. While both LAN and WAN settings are feasible, the system at large remains within the bounds of one organization [214]. Client/server computing is the paradigm underlying DCE's REMOTE PROCEDURE CALLS (RPC) [214], RMI [140, 202], and CORBA [202]. In addition to the computational servers, these architectures commonly deploy additional centralized infrastructure, e. g. a naming service. Client/server computing has superseded *host computing* where a powerful host was accessed by computationally weak terminals [214].

- *Peer-to-Peer computing* erases the hierarchy and permits every computer to become both client and server, while being connected to other peers via the Internet [202].

Each of the five concurrent computation schemes is leaned towards one of the two paradigms. In parallel computing, cluster computing, and Grid computing, the resources are typically accessed by clients that need powerful compute resources. In volunteer computing, the server hands out data for the clients to process, reversing the traditional client/server model. Only Desktop Grids enable true P2P computing as every participant can be a client now and a server later, or vice versa, or both at the same time. Since both volunteer computing systems and Desktop Grids invite the general public to participate, these approaches are subsumed under the term *public-resource computing*.

The strength of coupling manifests itself in the way computational resources are discovered. In parallel and cluster computing, the on-site administrator is aware of the number of computational resources. In Grid computing, other administrative domains may add resources at will, requiring a resource discovery service. In public-resource computing, clients can join without prior registration, allowing for substantial dynamics.

The ongoing shift from client/server computing towards decentralization has been recognized as early as 1992. In [214], it was noted that workstations could operate as clients in some instances and as servers in others. The same publication also defines the term *peer-to-peer computing*:

> A network of machines, each processor acting as both client and server, provides an opportunity for whole new classes of client/server computing. [...] Suddenly, [...] truly distributed, peer-to-peer computing is a reality.

For a number of applications, the advantages of loosely-coupled distributed computational systems outweigh the benefits of client/server structures. The remainder of this chapter will first discuss performance evaluation metrics, then continue with a more detailed examination of the various forms of distributed computing. For the sake of readability, the term *parallel computation* will refer to the process of simultaneously computing a partitioned problem notwithstanding whether parallel or distributed computing is the actual underlying paradigm.

2.2 Metrics for performance evaluation

Besides choosing a suitable scheme for concurrent computation, it is also worthwhile to consider metrics for performance evaluation. For a given computable problem, let t_{single} denote the time a single computer takes to solve it with the best available sequential algorithm, and let t_{parallel} denote the time a parallel computation takes to solve the same problem with the best available parallel algorithm on an arbitrary number of processors. Their ratio makes up the *speedup S* [192]:

$$S = \frac{t_{\text{single}}}{t_{\text{parallel}}} \qquad (2.1)$$

If $S > 1$, single-machine computation takes $(S - 1)$ times longer than parallelized computation, quantifying the benefit of parallelization.

In addition to speedup, the *efficiency* E of parallelization with p homogeneous processors is defined as [192]

$$E = \frac{S}{p} = \frac{t_{\text{single}}}{p \cdot t_{\text{parallel}}} \qquad (2.2)$$

For $E = 1$, there is linear speedup. $E \in (0,1)$ constitutes sub-linear speedup; this is a common case due to the administrative overhead of process synchronization, and the fact that some parts of the algorithm cannot be parallelized. If $E < \frac{1}{p}$, there is no factual acceleration as the single-machine computation takes less time than the parallel effort. In contrast, $E > 1$ constitutes super-linear speedup. In theory, this situation can occur when processors benefit from the work of other processors, e. g. by having loaded required data and/or code into shared caches, but it is rarely observed in practice.

When super-linear speedup is ruled out, the maximum achievable speedup through parallelization is governed by AMDAHL'S LAW [192]. Given a fraction $f \in [0, 1]$ of operations within a computation that must be performed in a sequential way, the maximum speedup with p processors ($p > 0$) is bounded in the following way:

$$S \leq \frac{1}{f + \frac{1-f}{p}} \qquad (2.3)$$

Asymptotically, for $p \to \infty$, the right side of (2.3) converges to $\frac{1}{f}$. Thus, the inverse of the fraction f of sequential operations determines a simple upper bound on the maximum speedup, provided that $f > 0$. For instance, if $f = 0.25$, the maximum attainable speedup S equals $\frac{1}{0.25} = 4$. This fact stresses the importance of every effort that reduces the degree of sequentiality in parallel algorithms.

In a fully parallelizable problem ($f = 0$), (2.3) yields $S \leq p$. Since I/O operations sometimes need to be performed sequentially until parallelized computation can continue or terminate, $f > 0$ holds in practice. However, f frequently decreases with the problem size. It is for this reason that the gains of parallelized computation, expressed through S, generally increase with growing problem size. This phenomenon is known as the AMDAHL EFFECT [192].

2.3   Concurrent computing on a local scale

When the computational resources are tightly coupled and geographically concentrated in a single location, they are said to be *local-scale*. In parallel computing, the implementation of parallelism is confined to the physical bounds of a single machine. Within these bounds, multiple CPUs or GPUs, multiple cores on one or more CPUs or GPUs, or the ability of a single core to process consecutive instructions concurrently enable parallel computing [58].

A classification of computational elements is provided by Flynn's Taxonomy [58, 192]. It distinguishes processors according to their capabilities in applying one or more instructions to one or more units of data at the same time. There are three practically relevant elements in the taxonomy:

- *Single Instruction, Single Data* (SISD) paraphrases the conventional way processors work. There is at most one instruction per clock, and it operates on at most one unit of data.

- *Single Instruction, Multiple Data* (SIMD) describes vector-processing units: a single instruction modifies an array of data concurrently. SIMD capabilities have been added to modern CPUs through multimedia-focused instruction set extensions (MMX, SSE, 3DNow) [108].

- *Multiple Instruction, Multiple Data* (MIMD) configurations commonly involve a number of processors that can dynamically handle threads of instructions and communicate via shared memory or message passing. MIMD represents the most sophisticated form of parallel computing.

The idea of parallel computing is taken to a larger but still local scale with cluster computing [21, 120]. In cluster computing, two or more machines, called *nodes*, are interconnected by a LAN. Nodes may be able to achieve parallelism on their own by implementing parallel computing features. As part of a cluster, they provide their capabilities and resources to all users of the cluster, and they may interact with other nodes via the LAN.

An example for a practical cluster computing scheme is the Beowulf project [21, 47, 199, 218]. Initiated in 1993 by the need for high-performance scientific computing resources, Beowulf's goal was to provide NASA with 1 GFLOPS output at a price of less than US$ 50, 000 [21]. In Beowulf, clusters of ordinary workstations are tightly coupled through a modified Linux kernel running on each workstation, and interconnected with an Ethernet LAN. Beowulf links the workstations' resources in a way that is transparent to the user, i. e. the process scheduler transparently migrates processes between cluster nodes, and the disk space is handled in a cumulative way. Thus, the Beowulf cluster appears to the user as a powerful single machine instead of distinct workstations. This scheme was shown to succeed in comparison to supercomputers when both performance and deployment cost are considered as criteria [218]. The original Beowulf cluster consisted of a 16-node cluster built with desktop CPUs for a total price of US$ 40,000; by 2001, 28 Beowulf-type clusters had made their way into the TOP500 list that keeps track of the world's fastest computers [21, 171, 199].

The introduction of the network to interconnect computational resources introduces a drawback over parallel computing. This drawback is inherited by all more loosely-coupled forms of distributed computing. Since conventional memory is substantially faster in both latency and transfer rate than Ethernet, problems that require frequent access to shared memory tend to perform poorly in LAN settings. Parallel computing better suits these problems due to the availability of potentially fast shared memory [21]. Still, for all other problems, cluster computing is a viable way to save on deployment time and total cost by replacing a supercomputer with a cluster of workstations or server-class machines, using off-the-shelf hardware for both computing and networking components.

2.4 Grid computing

Grid computing designates the infrastructure and interactions of geographically dispersed, heterogeneous, high-performance resources from various administrative domains [31, 85, 86, 87, 120, 158, 224]. From a number of Grid computing definitions in the literature, a survey has extracted the key aspects and compiled a common definition [31]. According to this survey, a Grid is

> a large-scale geographically distributed hardware and software infrastruc-ture composed of heterogeneous networked resources owned and shared by multiple administrative organizations which are coordinated to provide transparent, dependable, pervasive and consistent computing support to a wide range of applications. These applications can perform either dis-tributed computing, high throughput computing, on-demand computing, data-intensive computing, collaborative computing or multimedia comput-ing.

Basically, Grid computing takes cluster computing to a global scope. Resources which are not limited to computers but can also be storage, sensors, networking equipment, and peripherals, are distributed both geographically and over a number of administrative domains. They communicate using standardized protocols in a persistent infrastructure [244]. Their usage is coordinated to deliver nontrivial quality of service [86]. The resources are interconnected by a WAN, typically the Internet, and make up a potentially large-scale computing system. They are more loosely coupled and heterogeneous in nature than those in a cluster system. Resources are shared, while all participating organizations may be both consumers and providers, and there is no single centralized component that controls the organizations. Every organization participating in a Grid has its own administration and policies that regulate, among other things, the users' rights and access conditions of shared resources. Anonymous access is usually disallowed. While computational resources are distributed, centralized components that fulfill server duties e.g. for resource brokerage and discovery/naming services, are commonplace.

Grids serve *virtual organizations*: groups of individuals or organizations that have agreed on rules of Grid resource sharing [85, 87, 120, 224]. Virtual organizations are dynamic in that their membership composition is changing over time, and they are multi-institutional in that they accommodate various individuals and institutions.

Depending on their primary purpose of deployment, Grids can be divided into Data Grids, Service Grids, and Computational Grids [134, 224]. In the context of this thesis, Computational Grids stand in the focus of interest as Data Grids concentrate on distributed storage while Service Grids provide multimedia streaming and group collaboration facilities. Frameworks, toolkits and middleware such as the GLOBUS TOOLKIT [202] provide applications and users with the means to perform practical work, and resource brokers such as NIMROD-G provide cost-efficient scheduling of Grid tasks under customizable constraints [35, 134].

An extensive account of Grid computing history is provided by [202]. It sketches the evolution of Grid computing structures over time and also provides a list of vital components of Grids, including authorization, resource management, and naming services. [134] contains a taxonomy of Grid resource management systems and a compact account of selected approaches. A catalogue of application types suitable for Grid computing is provided by [31]. This catalogue includes, among others, applications that feature computation-intensive components.

2.5 Volunteer computing

There is a class of systems that enable client/server-based distributed computing with a large, dynamic composition of computational resources donors connected to the server via a WAN [6, 7, 28, 109, 206]. Since the participants volunteer to donate their idle CPU cycles, these systems are collectively referred to as *volunteer computing*. The most prominent representative is SETI@HOME [6, 7, 206, 211, 224]. There, a server distributes radio signal information received from outer space to be processed by the clients. Upon completion, the clients return their respective results to the server and receive a new task.

In volunteer computing systems, clients donate otherwise unused computational resources for altruistic reasons to projects they deem useful. The server acts as a coordinator only. Volunteer computing reverses the client/server paradigm: clients serve the needs of a central entity [56, 58, 214]. The clients are free to join and leave at any time. Also, clients do not know of each other's existence; there is no direct client-client interaction.

As in Grid computing, volunteer computing resources are geographically diverse and owned by various administrative domains. In the case of volunteer computing, an administrative domain typically does not encompass more than a single machine. In contrast to Grid computing and more tightly coupled forms of distributed computing, volunteer computing systems ask the clients to bring their own resources. A volunteer computing system's operator provides a server and software for the clients to run, and asks for the clients' idle cycles to be donated. In exchange, there is little guarantee for quality of service as resources may be volatile and heterogeneous.

The SETI@home project has broken ground for pioneering large-scale non-profit volunteer computing with a dynamic set of participants over the Internet. Every individual equipped with a desktop computer, an operating system supported by the SETI@home software, and Internet access is welcome to join. When the computer is idle, a screensaver starts that performs the relevant computations for SETI@home. User interaction with the screensaver causes the computation to be interrupted and the computer to be freed for the user's work. SETI@home has been exceedingly successful. In 2001, the world's fastest supercomputer was the U.S. Department of Energy's ASCI WHITE unit, peaking at 12.3 TFLOPS for a purchase price of US$ 110 million. At the same time, SETI@home peaked at 20 TFLOPS for an investment of $700,000$ US$ (including the operational cost for one year), using computers whose idle CPU cycles were harvested only if the respective owner did not need the computer himself [6]. With SETI@home, as in all volunteer computing systems, resource availability is subject to dynamics, but even in the average case, SETI@home has still managed to sustain 13 TFLOPS [21].

While SETI@home is a client/server application, its creator has found parallels to the P2P paradigm in that both approaches support a large number of participants which may drop out of the system at any time [6]:

> The huge number of computers participating in a P2P system can overcome the fact that individual computers may be only sporadically available (i. e. their owners may turn them off or disconnect them from the Internet). Software techniques such as data replication can combine a large number of slow, unreliable components into a fast, highly reliable system. The P2P paradigm [...] shifts power, and therefore control, away from organizations and toward individuals.

SETI@home's approach has been successfully adopted in similar projects. In 2005, a volunteer computing software was deployed to find drug targets for both cancer and anthrax. By proceeding in this manner, the anthrax research project identified $376,064$ candidates for novel anti-anthrax remedies, $12,000$ of which underwent close investigation, in less than a month [78]. [28] contains a list of popular volunteer computing projects.

Volunteer computing is the harbinger of Desktop Grids, a concept that takes the ideas of volunteer computing further to enable genuine P2P computing.

2.6 Desktop Grids

A *Desktop Grid* is a distributed computing platform that combines the essential properties of Computational Grids with the access to a large, dynamic set of clients and the aim of leveraging idle cycles from those clients as in volunteer computing [39, 46, 48, 133, 239]. Typically, Desktop Grids are designed to enable a large degree of scalability, high dynamics among the participants, and low administrative overhead. Primarily due to its scale and participants' fluctuation, a Desktop Grid acts as a "dynamic pool of resources" [39]. While server-augmented Desktop Grids exist [46], Desktop Grids are commonly based on fully distributed P2P topologies which favor self-organization over server-based coordination for scalability reasons [59].

Desktop Grids differ from volunteer computing systems in their decentralized nature regarding both the lack of a coordinating server and the right to submit jobs not being limited to a single entity. Thus, their focus is shifted from a donation-oriented to a reciprocal approach. Unlike server-oriented forms of distributed computing, the decentralized nature of P2P Desktop Grids precludes the existence of participants that could become single points of failure or bottlenecks for the entire system's performance [73]. In contrast to Grid structures, P2P systems are not created by the "collaboration between established and connected groups of systems" [152]. Existing Grids require dedicated resources to keep up their organizational structure and are usually smaller in scale than P2P systems [220, 240]. Another difference to Grid computing is that relationships between peers are mutually distrustful due to the peers' anonymity [59]. Moreover, similar to volunteer computing, the resources provided by the peers are inherently volatile [133].

From time to time, research facilities such as universities and laboratories need extensive computational resources to run benchmarks, simulations and scientific applications. This is a common use case for Desktop Grids. By sharing idle cycles from workstations, clusters and supercomputers during periods of low utilization, these facilities could request enormous cumulative power from a Desktop Grid in return when the demand arises [239]. Individuals with single computers could use a Desktop Grid for tasks that have low economic value but are nevertheless both useful to the individual and computationally intensive, such as ray-tracing.

Since the approach discussed in this thesis concentrates on P2P Desktop Grids, the term *Desktop Grid* shall refer to a P2P Desktop Grid unless noted otherwise. While the term emphasizes desktop-level resources, Desktop Grids may integrate all devices with a digital heartbeat that are connected to the Internet and can execute a Desktop Grid middleware's code. Besides desktop computers, this includes servers, supercomputers and clusters as well as smartphones, netbooks and video game consoles.

The following assertion was stated in 2005 with regard to a dynamic, decentralized form of Grid computing [202]:

> One very plausible approach to address the concerns of scalability can be described as decentralisation, though this is not a simple solution. The traditional client-server model can be a performance bottleneck and a single point of failure, but is still prevalent because decentralisation brings its own challenges. [...] In P2P computing, machines share data and resources, such as spare computing cycles and storage capacity, via the Internet or private networks. Machines can also communicate directly and manage computing tasks without using central servers. This permits P2P computing to scale more effectively than traditional client-server systems that must expand a server's infrastructure in order to grow, and this 'clients as servers' decentralisation is attractive with respect to scalability and fault tolerance [...].

Desktop Grids serve the purpose of best-effort large-scale resource sharing based on the principles of anonymity, reciprocity, and openness. In contrast, Grid computing has been motivated by the needs of professional communities that wish to collaborate and share resources using a predominantly fixed infrastructure [85]. Desktop Grids do not require the set-up of special infrastructure or policies, and they do not request users to register with an authentication service or to disclose their identity in other ways. They invite everyone to join and share resources as in volunteer computing. Desktop Grids link the ad-hoc, best-effort, large-scale approach of the P2P paradigm to the idea of globally distributed resource sharing promoted by Grid computing, but without the high administrative costs, centralized components, and otherwise indispensable user registration.

Primarily due to the limited abilities of the participating resources, the properties of jobs need to be taken into account as some problems are more amenable than others for the distributed computation on Desktop Grids. Some jobs apt for conventional Grid computing may therefore not be suitable for submission to a Desktop Grid. A job is well-suited for computation by a Desktop Grid if the following criteria are met [59]:

- *Computation-intensive:* The job requires substantial amounts of computational resources to be solved. When a Desktop Grid is unavailable, the job would be submitted to a supercomputer.

- *Little I/O:* The demand for computation substantially outweighs the demand for communication.

- *Divisible:* The job is decomposable into small tasks that can be received by desktop computers over standard Internet connections (e. g. DSL, cable). The results are returned via the same medium.

In contrast, a job is unsuitable for a Desktop Grid if one of the above criteria is not fulfilled, or if one or more of the following criteria are met:

- *Mission-critical:* The job must be completed until a given deadline.

- *Identifiable workers:* The job requires workers to be held accountable for their actions, or the job requires a proof of identity from each worker for other reasons.

- *Interactive:* The job requires user interaction.

- *Classified:* The job or the computed results contain confidential information.

Due to their low cost, Desktop Grids are ideal for users whose demand for extensive computational resources is rare. They also address those who cannot afford to invest in a fixed Grid infrastructure themselves or join an existing one [110]. Moreover, Desktop Grids offer a distributed way to leverage idle cycles that would otherwise go unspent. Most scientific computing is well suited for Desktop Grids, except for distributed applications with a frequent need for large-volume inter-worker communication [211]. Those applications are likely to experience network I/O as a bottleneck and are better served by tightly coupled shared-memory platforms. Section 6.3.2.2 will elaborate on an example for this phenomenon.

In summary, Desktop Grids are meant to be efficient, robust, secure, scalable, manageable, and to provide an easy-to-use API [47]. They especially honor the integration of heterogeneous resources and the ad-hoc nature of dynamic P2P networks. While conceptually close to Grid computing and volunteer computing, Desktop Grids constitute a distinct form of distributed computing.

2.6.1 The workflow in Desktop Grids

Desktop Grids permit every peer to submit a job for remote computation. In a first step, a job is split by the submitting peer into a number of *tasks* that may be processed by other peers [41]. A peer that processes a task is a *worker*, whereas a peer that submits a job is the *initiator* of that job. Jobs are assumed to contain all information necessary to compute the solution to a given problem, including code, parameters, data, and preparatory code that distributes the total workload among the registered workers.

The workflow model for the Desktop Grid proposed in this thesis assumes that initiators want to lease computation time on idle workers. An initiator generally wishes to minimize its job's total time to completion (referred to as *makespan* [91]). Following this approach, the time the slowest worker takes will determine the makespan. To assess a worker's performance, initiators may ask potential workers to first compute a *local power index* (LPI) benchmark based on a predefined task which may be distributed along with a Desktop Grid middleware. The computation of that task yields a benchmark number that eases the comparison of the peers' actual computing capabilities, similar to the *Horse Power Factor* in [195]. It captures both the system's general capabilities and its current load. To properly judge a peer's computational resources, the chosen benchmark's nature should reflect the computational requirements of typical jobs likely to be submitted to a Desktop Grid.

In this thesis, two kinds of jobs which are both instances of the master-worker paradigm are considered [24, 225]. The first kind is *independent-task applications* (ITA), also known as *bag-of-tasks* [9] or *embarrassingly parallel* problems [23, 211]. In this class of problems, the workers process their tasks independently and isolated from each other. Examples for ITA jobs include parameter-sweep applications that occur frequently in physics, biology, and computer graphics [40, 41, 91].

Moreover, there are *connected problems* (CP) [195] which benefit from the interaction of workers, requiring the participating workers to perform their computation efforts concurrently. For example, connected problems include evolutionary algorithms that address combinatorial optimization problems such as the bin packing problem that will be discussed in Section 6.3.2.3. There, workers communicate with others to indicate that they have found a new best known solution. That way, the best known solution is replicated among the workers, removing the strict need to replace a failing worker. Since the global optimum is unknown, a criterion to terminate the computation is required, e. g. a deadline. In the ITA case however, it is unknown how long a task will take to be computed by a worker, and a worker's failure implies that its assigned task must be computed again by another worker.

The model proposed here provides utmost freedom for the initiator to select a communication pattern. By supplying the appropriate code to the workers, it is free to create any communication topology between the workers, provided that a subset of the workers is reachable from the outside. The default topology assumes the simplest case, a client/server setting which treats the initiator as a central component and the workers as being directly connected to it. The client/server model can serve jobs with an arbitrary number of workers up to the initiator's capacity, and if more workers are required than the initiator can handle directly, the initiator can select the most suitable topology.

A potential initiator first determines its job requirements which encompass the minimum and maximum numbers of desired workers, a worker's minimum acceptable local power index, the job type (CP or ITA) and a deadline until which all workers must have finished their computations. The initiator then broadcasts a request for worker participation with the job requirements attached, and waits an arbitrary timespan for replies to arrive. After this timespan has elapsed, the initiator holds a list of worker candidates which it sorts according to local power index, reputation and availability, and picks a sufficiently large set of workers which shall perform the distributed computation. The workers start computing upon reception of task code and task data transmitted by the initiator. Each worker returns a partial result to the initiator. The workflow ends with the initiator validating the partial results and merging them into the complete outcome that would have resulted had the job been computed on a single machine in a non-distributed way.

The implementation of workflows is eased by middleware support. A Desktop Grid can be built by executing a Desktop Grid middleware on every participating peer. The middleware instances enable the peers to interact with each other. The middleware needs to address the requirements of Desktop Grids:

- *Abstraction*: Like all middleware, a Desktop Grid middleware needs to export an API to application developers that hides all complexity not related to application development.

- *Minimum configuration*: To enable a wide level of acceptance, the middleware should attempt to minimize the need for human intervention to handle configuration issues.

- *Platform independence*: Peers generally feature heterogeneous hardware architectures and operating systems. The middleware should be able to run on as many platforms as possible, or even be entirely independent from the underlying platform through the use of a virtual machine.

- *Topology maintenance*: The middleware needs to construct and maintain a communication overlay on top of underlying WAN structures.

- *Scalability*: Due to the potentially huge size of P2P overlays, efficient communication patterns and low overhead are important aspects.

- *Code handling*: Since jobs can be of arbitrary nature, a middleware instance needs to be able to send and receive arbitrary code. In particular, it needs to be able to dynamically load code, send code to remote peers, and execute received code in a sandbox environment.

The PeerGrid middleware satisfies all listed requirements.

2.6.2 Related work

The relationship between conventional Grid computing and Desktop Grids was explored in [59, 85, 120, 220]. Desktop Grids accommodate larger numbers of users but offer less elaborate security provisions and resource management services. The most comprehensive comparison between P2P-based Desktop Grids and Grid computing is provided in [85] which examines target communities, incentives, resources, applications, scale, and services. According to this investigation, P2P systems have originally focused on integration while Grid computing has originally focused on performance, but with time passing, the two approaches are closing in on each other. This is also due to the fact that both approaches have the common goal of sharing pooled resources in a distributed way. Still, differences remain: Grids might require accountability, hence anonymity is not desirable, while P2P systems may thrive on their users' anonymity in order to prevent the creation of obstacles for new users [85].

A stepping stone on the way from Grid computing to Desktop Grids is CONDOR, a job and resource management system that harvests idle cycles from workstations [120, 134, 225]. The owners of participating workstations are free to decide about the maximum contribution of idle cycles, and they may also decide to withdraw from the Condor resource pool. In the Condor approach, there are fixed server components called *matchmakers* that align supply and demand of computational resources, with typically one matchmaker per organization. The set of resources overseen by a matchmaker is a *Condor pool*. A first extension to Condor, *gateway flocking*, enables one gateway node per Condor pool to communicate with the gateway nodes of other Condor pools to exchange supply and demand information, enabling Condor pools to interact with others in a way which is generally transparent to the users. However, Condor pools cannot automatically detect the presence of other pools, creating a need for administrative intervention. Due to its management complexity, gateway flocking has been superseded by *direct flocking* in which workstations apply with several matchmakers in parallel. Still, workstations need to be aware of the matchmakers' presence.

Contemporary research on Desktop Grids can be broadly divided into two streams: one that addresses building blocks for Desktop Grids, while the other considers the structure and experiences with tangible systems. The remainder of this section follows this division and starts with a summary of work that concentrates on the components of Desktop Grids.

2.6.2.1 Building blocks

The benefits of self-organizing P2P structures to Desktop Grids were pointed out in [44]. Decentralized control well suits Desktop Grids which can comprise millions of participants. The approach in [44], called ORGANIC GRID, is based on mobile agents forming a tree-like overlay. It considers altruistic behavior only, and its capability to deal with peer failures is limited. Tree-like dependencies are also considered by [68] which additionally considers building the tree in a latency-optimized, proximity-aware fashion. However, it does specify neither a scalable mechanism to reshape the tree according to fluctuating latency information nor a repair procedure that deals with the potential failure of the tree's inner nodes.

A comparable approach contrasts the large-scale, heterogeneous, volatile and distributed nature of self-organizing, open Grids to conventional, existing Grids which are found to be essentially multi-site supercomputer centers [240]. The suggested approach constructs a particular kind of topology, the MINIMUM-DELAY TREE (MDTree), for the purpose of creating an open Grid with heterogeneous components that are arranged in a proximity-aware fashion to facilitate the formation of variable-size worker clusters on demand. The MDTree topology is discussed in the context of hybrid P2P topologies in Section 4.4.3.2.2.

There is a vast body of work on scheduling. Scheduling can be performed both on a system-wide scale (initiators need to truthfully state the number of workers they require) or on a job scale (within the set of workers jointly computing a job, load can be migrated among the workers and more complex tasks can be assigned to more capable workers). The job-related scheduling strategy depends on the particular needs of a given job. Section 6.3.2.1 compares a random-assignment strategy to a heuristic that assigns more complex tasks to more powerful workers. Similar to the Desktop Grid concept presented in [39], PeerGrid pursues a best-effort approach to provide initiators with references to workers. Initiators are then free to schedule tasks to the selected workers as desired. Existing schemes include the APPLES adaptive Computational Grid project [24] which contains a comparison of various Grid scheduling strategies. The WAVE SCHEDULER assumes that computers are used less frequently at night. Thus, it migrates tasks to workers located in places around the globe where it is currently night, a unique approach

presented on the basis of a CAN overlay [246]. [9] A fault-tolerant scheduling regime for
ITA jobs is introduced in [11]. There, 8 scheduling policies (the combinations of four
machine-related with two task-related elementary policies) are evaluated in two simulated scenarios, Enterprise Desktop Grids and public-resource Desktop Grids (mainly
differentiated through the average fault time). The key result emphasizes the benefit
in prioritizing the task with the longest residual running time, however this requires
the running time to be known in advance which can difficult to realize with ITA jobs.
OMNIVORE is a tree-based scheduler which can be integrated into the Globus Toolkit
[110]. It uses a Pastry implementation for distributed storage and multicast. Its goal is to
transparently provide Grid users with computational resources from desktop computers
connected to the Grid infrastructure. Experimental results are available for a 22-node
setting only [110].

2.6.2.2 Existing Desktop Grid systems

There are several existing Desktop Grid systems.

VISHWA is a two-layered middleware for P2P distributed computing [195]. It incorporates
load migration, fault-tolerance, and a notion of proximity awareness as nearby peers form
clusters, but it is based solely on altruistic peer behavior and does not tap the benefits of
hybrid P2P topologies.

OURGRID is a P2P Desktop Grid that focuses on bag-of-tasks problems [10]. It does not
specify a topology maintenance mechanism; its authors suggest JXTA for this purpose.
OurGrid's peers participate in a NETWORK OF FAVORS: hosts sharing resources expect the
beneficiary to eventually return the favor. Peers whose demand for resources exceeds
their supply tend to accumulate debt with other peers, lowering the priority with which
other peers are willing to allocate resources for them. There is only local accounting in
OurGrid – peers do not exchange reputation ratings with other peers. This reputation-
related aspect of OurGrid will be revisited in Section 5.3.4.

P3 (short for PERSONAL POWER PLANT) is a middleware for P2P distributed computing that
resorts to JXTA for P2P overlay construction and maintenance. In P3, an initiator creates
a distinct peer group for its job. Every peer can discover the available job peer groups
through JXTA's group discovery facility. To act as a worker, a peer joins the group associated with the preferred job and starts exchanging messages with the initiator. Besides
star-shaped master-worker communication, P3 enables a message-passing interface for
parallel computing. False results are detected by a voting mechanism. In addition to
the drawbacks of Vishwa, P3's reliance on JXTA precludes middleware-driven topology

---

[9]The CAN topology is discussed in Section 4.3.2.

optimization. Also, the message-passing interface is slow: according to the authors of P3, the average message delay is estimated to be approximately 70 times as large as that of a standard TCP connection under Java.

CLUSTER COMPUTING ON THE FLY (CCOF) is a Desktop Grid that uses the wave scheduler outlined in the previous section [149, 245]. CCOF supports four kinds of jobs, one of which corresponds to the ITA type while another is similar to CP. A number of available methods for resource discovery in the overlay include expanding-ring search and random walks. CCOF features a verification mechanism for returned task results that occasionally transmits particular tasks of which the initiator already knows the results. The worker's honesty can be verified through these *quiz* tasks. They are contrasted to security through voting in Section 6.2.4.

ZORILLA is a Desktop Grid middleware in its prototype phase [73]. Like the PeerGrid prototype, it is based on the Java platform for portability and security reasons. [10] The Zorilla Desktop Grid is fully distributed. It is built on the BAMBOO P2P topology. [11] To discover workers, Zorilla performs FLOOD SCHEDULING, a more sophisticated variant of the Gnutella flooding mechanism adapted to the needs of Desktop Grids, resembling expanding-ring search. There are notable parallels between Zorilla and PeerGrid including the incorporation of a structured topology, proximity awareness, efficient broadcast, and complete decentralization. However, Zorilla does not tap the benefits of super-peers. Zorilla peers must be reachable from the outside to permit the construction of Bamboo topology links. Bamboo inherits the disadvantage from Pastry that in order to outperform other structured topologies in terms of the average path length, a large number of connections need to be kept up (cf. Section 4.3.1). Moreover, the Zorilla Desktop Grid is vulnerable to free-riding as all peers are implicitly assumed to be altruists.

The ENTROPIA system is a commercial Desktop Grid tailored for a corporate environment [36, 46, 47, 133]. While this does not necessarily limit the system to a LAN, in the enterprise context, several simplifications such as the absence of maliciousness and the presence of a common administration including common policies apply. Unlike the other Desktop Grids outlined in this section, an Entropia Grid is organized around a central component. Entropia goes to great lengths in ensuring the safety of a task's execution environment by putting it into a virtual machine. In [133], a 220-node network running the Entropia DCGRID commercial Desktop Grid software was found to be equivalent in overall performance to a 209-node cluster on weekends and a 160-node cluster on weekdays. The difference to the full complement of 220 nodes is explained through host volatility.

---

[10]Section 6.2 will discuss PeerGrid's relationship to Java in more detail.

[11]Bamboo is a descendant of the Pastry topology with improvements that increase the degree of topology stability in the face of high dynamics. The Bamboo topology is introduced in [198]. Pastry is discussed in Section 4.3.1.

The Desktop Grid architecture proposed in [239] is built on the Pastry DHT, and it assumes the majority of peers to be honest. Its facilities center around a monitoring component, GRIDCOP, which transforms code submitted for distributed computation by inserting beacons that notify the initiator once the respective beacon is reached. Every time a beacon-based notification is triggered, the initiator is supposed to transmit digitally signed currency tokens called *credits* to the worker as compensation for the worker's efforts. The worker would not continue if the credits are not issued. This incremental payment scheme attempts to evade the vulnerabilities of payment processes. If the initiator pays in advance, the worker may cheat by not working. Conversely, when the initiator is supposed to pay after computation has ended but refrains from paying, the worker has been exploited. Each credit represents a currency unit, is identified with a unique peer ID and a sequence number, and can be traded with others. Both credits and feedback that peers give to rate the behavior of other peers are stored in the DHT. When a peer receives a credit, it hashes the peer ID and sequence number to obtain a pointer to the DHT location where the credit is stored. Credits are given to other peers by relaying the pointer to the credit. Feedback is stored at the DHT location that is retrieved by hashing the rated peer's ID. A series of issues are not solved by [239]. For instance, a peer could give out a large batch of credits that are all stored at different DHT locations. Since DHT peers do not exchange information on a peer's credits, this gives rise to inflation. DHT peers are expected to reply honestly and to every query. Also, if a DHT peer suddenly fails or leaves, it takes its credit information with it. Finally, there is no protection against forged feedback.

Similar to a Desktop Grid, the event-driven NARADABROKERING system organizes and maintains a hierarchically organized network of cooperating resource brokers based on the publish-subscribe communication pattern [88]. The brokers oversee clusters of cycle providers. They keep up links to other brokers, creating a small-world network [130]. Like Entropia, NaradaBrokering depends on a central component for resource management and scheduling.

The Desktop Grid presented in [39] incorporates both desktop and cluster resources. It is based on an unstructured topology and a Gnutella-like flooding mechanism to discover workers up to a given TTL horizon. The assertion made in [39] that DHTs cannot be used for Desktop Grids as they offer only a unicast lookup operation becomes irrelevant with the constrained broadcast mechanism for structured topologies presented in Section 4.2.1. Moreover, while [39] focuses on connected problems and presents two demonstration jobs with large numbers of workers that interact with each other, neither peer behavior nor topology optimization are considered.

2.7   Summary

With a focus on Desktop Grids, this chapter has outlined various concurrent computation schemes. Table 2.1 provides a comparison of these schemes' key properties.

Scheme	Scale	Administration	Network	Dynamics	Job submission
Parallel	Local	Local	Internal	None	Known users
Cluster	Local	Local	LAN	None	Known users
Grid	Global	Trusted group	WAN	Limited	Known users
Volunteer	Global	All autonomous	WAN	Strong	Server only
Desktop Grid	Global	All autonomous	WAN	Strong	All users

Table 2.1: A comparison of distributed computing schemes. The columns contain the respective scheme's name, the scheme's scale, the administration of the processing units, the communication medium interconnecting them, the extent of computational resources' dynamics, and the group of users permitted to submit a job.

To leverage the idle resources of desktop computers connected to the Internet, both volunteer computing and Desktop Grids offer viable approaches. While volunteer computing requires a centralized component (a server) and is commonly focused on the one-way donation of resources by the clients, Desktop Grids foster reciprocity and can work in a fully distributed way. The following chapters of this thesis introduce the components of a Desktop Grid middleware that offers self-organized topology maintenance and optimization, free-riding prevention, efficient broadcasts, scalable delay estimation, and the inclusion of peers that operate from behind firewalls.

3

Network coordinates

Topology awareness [12] concerns the construction and re-organization of overlay networks in a way that takes the underlying topology into account [236]. When overlay networks can be established and maintained in a topology-aware fashion, their structures can operate more efficiently because the underlying topology's properties are observed [59, 152, 193, 194]. A major metric to quantify a communication link's performance is the communication delay, the time a transmitted bit takes to arrive at the link's remote end [194]. Observed link delays depend on the physical distance, the traffic volume on the respective link, the routing policies, and the link layer technology [244]. To integrate the communication delay into the process of overlay construction, nodes will need to estimate their communication delays to other nodes, and possibly change their overlay links according to the outcome. This makes for a frequent need to estimate delays between arbitrary nodes. In IP networks, a standard way to determine the link delay is to estimate the round-trip time (RTT) by sending an ICMP ECHO (*ping*) packet to the remote end and taking the time until the reply arrives [221]. Assuming that both directions of the link work with equal performance, the delay equals half the RTT. However, measuring link delays by sending messages can considerably increase the network load. Delay estimations of this kind may be substantially facilitated through the use of *network coordinates*, a concept which has attracted considerable attention in recent years [55, 57, 60, 122, 123, 139, 179, 180, 189, 209, 222]. Instead of probing all $O(n^2)$ links within an n-node network which is prohibitively costly [240], network coordinates mechanisms assign coordinates to nodes, and measure distances using these coordinates. A comparatively small amount of ping measurements, the exact number of which depends on the chosen generation scheme, suffices to set up network coordinates.

---

[12]In the context of this thesis, the terms *topology awareness* and *proximity awareness* are considered synonyms.

In this chapter, general properties of network coordinates are examined along with their benefits, drawbacks and limitations, and their relevance for the operations of Desktop Grids is explored. Moreover, various algorithms that generate network coordinates are discussed and compared.

3.1   Overview

Network coordinates mechanisms embed networks of nodes into continuous metric spaces for the purpose of node-to-node delay estimation. Every node in the network is assigned individual coordinates from the target space such that the spatial distance between any two nodes approximates the measurable delay between those nodes in the network. Once a node has learned of another node's coordinates, it may predict the delay to the remote node by evaluating the spatial distance using the space's metric at virtually no cost instead of sending ping packets over the network's links [139, 147].

3.1.1 Embedding a network

The core activity of network coordinates mechanisms is to infer coordinates from a small number of measured delays [222]. This process starts with a graph $G = (V, E)$ that represents the network to be mapped and ends with a continuous metric space into which G has been embedded. It may be formally cast as follows [153, 222, 244]. A *metric space A* is a space associated with a function d that fulfills four conditions:

- *Reflexivity:* $d(x, x) = 0$ $\forall\ x \in A$

- *Symmetry:* $d(x, y) = d(y, x)$ $\forall\ x, y \in A$

- *Positive definiteness:* $d(x, y) > 0$ $\forall\ x, y \in A,\ x \neq y$

- *Triangle inequality:* $d(x, y) + d(y, z) \geq d(x, z)$ $\forall\ x, y, z \in A$

Any function d that satisfies the specified conditions is a *metric* on A. The Minkowski distance L_k is a widely used family of metrics, parameterized with $k \in \mathbb{N}, k > 0$. It is defined as [128]

$$L_k(x, y) = \sqrt[k]{\sum_{i=1}^{n} |x_i - y_i|^k}   \forall\ x, y \in A \tag{3.1}$$

L_2 is the Euclidean norm [107]:

$$L_2(x, y) = \sqrt{\sum_{i=1}^{n} (x_i - y_i)^2}   \forall\ x, y \in A \tag{3.2}$$

In the context of network coordinates, the predominantly used target space is Euclidean: $A = \mathbb{R}^n$ for a fixed but arbitrary $n \in \mathbb{N}, n > 0$. Euclidean spaces use L_2 as their metric.

Network coordinates generation mechanisms seek a mapping $\phi : G \to A$ that minimizes an error function which the generation mechanism defines. The error function typically reflects the difference between the spatial distance of two nodes x and y, $d(x, y)$, and their true delay in the network.

The primary quantity considered by network coordinates mechanisms is latency, i. e. link delay [59]. Other quantities, such as bandwidth and jitter, are possible [139]. However, latency is less expensive to measure than the other quantities [194]. Moreover, it does not change until the link operates at its capacity limit, while an accurate bandwidth estimation requires exhausting the link's capacity to determine the bandwidth maximum. In addition, it was found that in a PlanetLab environment, latency is a good predictor for a link's bandwidth, with low latency implying high bandwidth and vice versa [139, 185].

3.1.2 Benefits

Delay estimation using network coordinates causes only a fraction of the network load which would be incurred with standard delay measurement methods [55, 122, 123, 139, 179, 189, 222]. Besides being able to estimate the delay to a remote node without sending a message, the provision of network coordinates yields additional benefits:

- With network coordinates, a node is able to estimate the delay between any two other nodes without sending extra messages [222]. This feature is useful for overlay construction. Furthermore, it can render sophisticated message forwarding procedures in structured P2P topologies possible as Section 4.4.2.3 will demonstrate.

- Network coordinates enable geometry-based algorithms that require coordinates to work by mapping discrete networks to continuous metric spaces [3, 55, 139]. With respect to Euclidean spaces in particular, since network coordinates mechanisms map a set of nodes to a set of points, the use of such spaces enables access to a wide range of algorithms for examining and manipulating point sets. This includes clustering and dimensionality reduction methods [222].

Nodes can learn of close neighbors without the need to directly communicate with them, using background gossip as their source of information [139]. In summary, network coordinates support all processes that frequently need to estimate the delay to remote nodes.

3.1.3 Drawbacks

Aside from the additional complexity and the need for appropriate parameter choices, delays generally fluctuate. For this reason, network coordinates need to be recomputed to match the underlying topology's properties [233].

Moreover, the accuracy of network coordinates suffers from embedding errors. Such errors may stem from two sources. First, algorithms that embed a network introduce an embedding error if they fail to locate an optimum solution. A potential second cause is related to the properties of the target space. Network coordinates mechanisms embed networks into metric spaces. In metric spaces, the triangle inequality holds by definition. In live networks however, the triangle inequality is frequently violated by routing policies. For this reason, error-free embeddings are practically unavailable [153, 233, 244]. On PlanetLab, a study found between 16.6 % and 23.8 % of all examined node pairs to violate the triangle inequality [244].

From an individual node's point of view, the embedding quality cannot be quantified unless all of the network is probed, a circumstance which network coordinates mechanisms explicitly wish to avoid [153]. The upcoming section will investigate the embedding quality of network coordinates with a particular focus on the effects of triangle inequality violations and the dimensionality of the target space.

3.2   Embedding quality

To applications, the utility of network coordinates grows with their accuracy. Accordingly, good network coordinates mechanisms are supposed to provide low-error distance estimates. Besides the choice of the type of target space (e. g. Euclidean, spherical), choosing the dimensionality of the space influences the embedding quality. More dimensions enable more opportunities to map peculiarities of node delays into the space, thus improving the coordinates' predictive accuracy, but also require more storage space and more computation time for the embedding.

The authors of VIVALDI [13] suggest two- to three-dimensional spaces as delays are dominated by geographical distance that could be captured by two-dimensional coordinates [60]. The addition of a third dimension provides an opportunity to capture additional properties including routing policies that do not forward packets along the shortest route. Beyond three dimensions, no significant progress in terms of predictive accuracy is recorded. Also, it is found that using a spherical distance function that takes the Earth's curvature into account does not prove beneficial. [14]

---

[13] The Vivaldi approach to network coordinates generation will be discussed in Section 3.3.2.

[14] A discussion of end-to-end delay estimation using geographic coordinates is provided in Section 3.3.4.4.

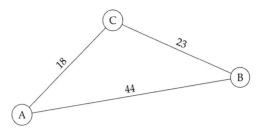

Figure 3.1: Example violation of the triangle inequality

Primarily due to routing policy regulations, violations of the triangle inequality occur frequently in the Internet [244]. The findings documented in [204] indicate a statistically significant difference between shortest paths and actually chosen paths. In [223], it is shown that on average, approximately 20 % of Internet paths are 1.5 times or more as long as the shortest path between the respective ends. Also, about 50 % of all examined paths could be shortened by routing via a detour node (i.e. the current path is split into two: first source→detour, then detour→destination, resembling the key step in the Floyd-Warshall algorithm [15]). In all cases where taking a detour reduces the path length, the triangle inequality is violated.

Let the measurable end-to-end communication delay between two arbitrary nodes X and Y be given by $d_{real}(X, Y)$. When the triangle equality holds, delays will satisfy the condition $d_{real}(X, Y) \leq d_{real}(X, Z) + d_{real}(Z, Y)$ for any combination of nodes X, Y and Z in the network. Figure 3.1 shows an example of a triangle inequality violation involving three nodes, A, B, and C. The edge weights are the delays experienced when sending a message across the respective link. As can be seen from the figure, $d_{real}(A, B) = 44 >$ $d_{real}(A, C) + d_{real}(C, B) = 18 + 23 = 41$. The triangle inequality could be restored by routing all traffic from A to B via C which would replace the edge weight of 44 with 41. However, this requires C to forward traffic going from A to B, and it also requires A to forward traffic to B via C. If local routing policies forbid C to accept traffic from A, or A to route traffic via C, the triangle inequality continues to be violated.

In addition to the unavailability of error-free embeddings due to violations of the triangle inequality, heuristics used to embed the network introduce an additional embedding error if they fail to locate an optimum solution. To measure the accuracy of a network coordinates generation mechanism and to compare two mechanisms with one another, a metric that quantifies the embedding error is required. In line with the definition above, let $d_{real}(A, B)$ denote the live delay experienced in the actual network when

---

[15] A discussion of the Floyd-Warshall algorithm is provided in Section 6.3.2.2.

transmitting data from A to B, and let $d_{\text{estimate}}(A, B)$ denote the estimate provided by the spatial distance between A's and B's respective network coordinates. Moreover, let $d_{\text{real}}(A, B) = 0$ iff $A = B$. Otherwise, if $A \neq B$, let $d_{\text{real}}(A, B) > 0$ and $d_{\text{estimate}}(A, B) > 0$.

Consider $A \neq B$. The *pairwise absolute embedding error* is defined as

$$error_{\text{abs}} = |d_{\text{real}}(A, B) - d_{\text{estimate}}(A, B)| \tag{3.3}$$

From this definition, one derives a relative error measure as [122, 123]

$$\frac{error_{\text{abs}}}{d_{\text{real}}(A, B)} = \frac{|d_{\text{real}}(A, B) - d_{\text{estimate}}(A, B)|}{d_{\text{real}}(A, B)} \tag{3.4}$$

This measure is flawed. If the actual delay $d_{\text{real}}(A, B)$ is underestimated by the network coordinates-based prediction (i. e. $d_{\text{real}}(A, B) > d_{\text{estimate}}(A, B)$), the relative error is bounded by 1. On the other hand, if $d_{\text{real}}(A, B) < d_{\text{estimate}}(A, B)$, there is no upper bound to the error. Due to this property, the proposed relative error measure is biased upwards. To fix the issue, the relative error measure's denominator may be extended in the following way to yield the per-edge embedding error which will be used in the remainder of this chapter [57, 117, 123]:

$$error_{\text{rel}} = \frac{|d_{\text{real}}(A, B) - d_{\text{estimate}}(A, B)|}{\min(d_{\text{real}}(A, B), d_{\text{estimate}}(A, B))} \tag{3.5}$$

With (3.5), the relative embedding error for a single pair can be computed. In addition to the error-free situation of $d_{\text{real}}(A, B) = d_{\text{estimate}}(A, B)$, it takes two cases into account. First, if the delay is overestimated, i. e. $d_{\text{real}}(A, B) < d_{\text{estimate}}(A, B)$, the results of (3.4) and (3.5) are identical. In the opposite case, when the delay is underestimated, (3.5) quantifies the fraction of the estimate by which it needs to grow to reach correctness.

As noted in [122], embedding systems try to minimize an overall error measure such as the mean square error. When the mean embedding error over all links is computed, a common observation is the presence of a very small number of severe outliers that bias the mean [153]. For this reason, the median embedding error as an outlier-robust measure is preferred [139].

3.3   Generation algorithms

There are various algorithms that generate network coordinates. A desirable solution for network proximity detection should be simple, fast, distributed, and scalable [194]. The algorithms that fulfill these requirements can be classified using two criteria:

- *Coordinate stability*: static algorithms compute coordinates which do not change over time unless the algorithm is re-executed. In contrast, dynamic algorithms have coordinates fluctuating in the course of time. In the case of a static network, coordinates provided by dynamic algorithms can ultimately converge to constant values if the respective algorithm enables convergence.

- *Hierarchy*: landmark-based algorithms pick nodes with a particular role, called *landmarks*, that help other nodes attain coordinates. This way, a hierarchy is established that contains landmarks and common nodes. On the contrary, simulation-based algorithms rely on the interaction of all nodes without any kind of hierarchy. Rather, approaches in this class imitate physical phenomena such as the relaxation of springs or the influence of force fields on particles to provide nodes with coordinates. This criterion has originally been suggested by [139].

Using these criteria, this section provides a summary of major network coordinates mechanisms and discusses their individual strengths and weaknesses. Furthermore, it reviews a number of procedures that estimate delays in alternative ways.

3.3.1 Global Network Positioning

With GLOBAL NETWORK POSITIONING (GNP), Ng and Zhang [179] have introduced a way to provide network coordinates using a landmark-based approach. GNP strives to solve a sequence of nonlinear unconstrained minimization problems of which there are two distinct types:

1. The *initial problem* ("Landmark operations" in [179]): a minimization problem which embeds an initial set of nodes at once such that all these nodes receive coordinates. They make up the set of landmarks.

2. The *individual problem* ("Ordinary host operations" in [179]): after the initial problem has been solved, this subsequent problem addresses the assignment of coordinates to a newly joining node. A joining node first measures the respective delays to a number of landmarks, then attempts to choose its coordinates such that the embedding error with regard to the landmarks is minimized.

The initial problem generally occurs only once and needs to be solved before any individual problem can be solved. In this context, there is a constraint on the minimum number of landmarks. Let n be the dimensionality of the target space. A minimum of $n + 1$ nodes will be required to participate in the initial problem [55, 179]. In the original

GNP formulation, the set of nodes picked as landmarks for any individual problem will exactly match the set of nodes that made up the initial problem [179].

GNP is the essential component of the NETWORK POSITIONING SYSTEM (NPS) which replaces the centralized, fixed-landmark infrastructure of GNP with a hierarchical system of landmarks [123, 180]. The modification to GNP proposed by [55] is most flexible. It allows a newly joining node to pick a sufficiently large set of arbitrary nodes that already have coordinates as landmarks. This approach fits the requirements of highly dynamic P2P environments best due to the inherent independence from fixed infrastructure nodes. With this modification, any node which has computed its coordinates will be able to serve as a landmark for all subsequent coordinate-requesting nodes, causing the landmark set to grow over time.

In line with [179], a generic objective function to evaluate a given solution for the initial problem is

$$f_{\text{initial}}(c_{L_1}, ..., c_{L_N}) = \sum_{L_i, L_j \in \mathcal{L}} \mathcal{E}(d_{\text{real}}(L_i, L_j), d_{\text{estimate}}(L_i, L_j)) \qquad (3.6)$$

where $\mathcal{E}$ defines an error function, $\mathcal{L}$ is the set of initial landmarks, c_{L_i} is the i-th landmark's coordinate vector, $d_{\text{real}}(L_i, L_j)$ yields the measurable delay between landmarks L_i and L_j, and $d_{\text{estimate}}(L_i, L_j)$ returns the estimated delay for this landmark pair. Also in line with [179], a similar function to address the individual problem is

$$f_{\text{individual}}(c_x) = \sum_{L_i \in \mathcal{L}^*} \hat{\mathcal{E}}(d_{\text{real}}(x, L_i), d_{\text{estimate}}(x, L_i)) \qquad (3.7)$$

where $\hat{\mathcal{E}}$ is an error function, x is the node to be embedded, c_x are its coordinates, and $\mathcal{L}^*$ is the set of chosen landmarks.

3.3.1.1 Algorithms

This section discusses Simplex Downhill, the algorithm which GNP uses to solve the optimization problems it creates. Moreover, it presents two improvements that deliver solutions which are substantially more accurate compared to those produced by the original Simplex Downhill algorithm.

3.3.1.1.1 Simplex Downhill

SIMPLEX DOWNHILL is the method of choice in [55, 179, 180] for heuristically solving
unconstrained optimization problems of continuous variables for arbitrary real-valued
objective functions. It was originally suggested by Spendley, Hext and Himsworth [215].
Given an objective function $f(v) : \mathbb{R}^n \to \mathbb{R}$ that is to be optimized, Simplex Downhill
works on a regular simplex consisting of $n + 1$ distinct vertices $v_i \in \mathbb{R}^n, i \in \{1, \ldots, n + 1\}$ in
an n-dimensional Euclidean space. The simplex represents the convex hull of these $n + 1$
vertices. Each vertex $v_i = (x_{i1}, \ldots, x_{in})^t$ corresponds to a solution for the optimization
problem and can be evaluated by computing $f(v_i)$. In a series of iterations, Simplex
Downhill transforms the current iteration's simplex into another by replacing one vertex
with a vertex which is not part of the simplex yet, or by shrinking the simplex if the
algorithm detects that it is closing in on a local optimum. A sequence of regular simplices
is generated until a termination criterion is met, e. g. when the vertices are sufficiently
close to the current simplex' centroid.

In every iteration, Simplex Downhill first determines the best and worst vertices according to f: v_{best} and v_{worst}, respectively. In a minimization problem, [16]

$$v_{\text{worst}} = \arg\max_{v_i}\{f(v_1), \ldots, f(v_{n+1})\} \tag{3.8}$$

$$v_{\text{best}} = \arg\min_{v_i}\{f(v_1), \ldots, f(v_{n+1})\} \tag{3.9}$$

Next, the centroid of the current simplex without v_{worst} is computed:

$$v_{\text{centroid}} = \frac{1}{n} \cdot \sum_{\substack{i=1 \\ v_i \neq v_{\text{worst}}}}^{n+1} v_i \tag{3.10}$$

All vertices of the simplex remain in their respective places except for the worst one
which becomes subject to *reflection* across the aforementioned centroid:

$$v_{\text{reflected}} = v_{\text{worst}} + 2 \cdot (v_{\text{centroid}} - v_{\text{worst}}) = 2 \cdot v_{\text{centroid}} - v_{\text{worst}} \tag{3.11}$$

In addition to reflection, *shrinking* contracts all vertices around the best vertex:

$$v_i = \frac{1}{2} \cdot (v_i + v_{\text{best}}) \; \forall \, i \in \{1, \ldots, n + 1\} \tag{3.12}$$

If only reflection is applied, the new simplex is adjacent to the previous one since only a
single vertex is exchanged. One common hyperplane remains. The iterated replacement

---

[16]Since GNP requires error minimization, this section focuses on minimization problems. The case of maximization
is handled analogously.

of the respective worst vertex moves the simplex through the solution space, away from areas perceived as poor by the current simplex, and terminates once an arbitrary convergence criterion is met.

This originally suggested form of Simplex Downhill was improved by Nelder and Mead [116, 136, 178], and it is now commonplace to refer to the Nelder-Mead method as Simplex Downhill (e.g. in [179]), a practice which this thesis adopts for the remainder of this chapter. Nelder and Mead lifted the requirement of the simplex to be regular. Their method works with arbitrary general (but non-degenerate) simplices. Besides reflection and shrinking as suggested by Spendley, Hext and Himsworth, Nelder and Mead presented two additional operations, *contraction* and *expansion*, both of which may create irregular simplices. Moreover, the Nelder-Mead method also considers the second-best vertex. In a minimization problem, the second-best vertex is

$$v_{\text{second-best}} = \arg\min_{v_i, v_i \neq v_{\text{best}}} \{f(v_1), \ldots, f(v_{n+1})\} \tag{3.13}$$

When reflection yields a new optimum ($f(v_{\text{reflected}}) \geq f(v_i), i \in \{1, \ldots, n+1\}$), Simplex Downhill performs an expansion step by moving the reflected vertex farther along the reflection's direction:

$$v_{\text{expanded}} = v_{\text{reflected}} + (v_{\text{reflected}} - v_{\text{centroid}}) \tag{3.14}$$

Contraction moves the worst-rated vertex closer to the centroid:

$$v_{\text{contracted}} = \frac{1}{2} \cdot (v_{\text{worst}} + v_{\text{centroid}}) \tag{3.15}$$

Reflection, expansion, contraction and shrinking are applied as specified by Algorithm 1 for a minimization problem to warp and move the simplex through the solution space towards a (presumably non-global) optimum where Simplex Downhill will eventually converge [116, with modifications]. While arbitrary convergence criteria can be applied, [116] suggests using the vertices' standard deviation with respect to the centroid. Given a minimum value $\tau > 0$ that the standard deviation needs to exceed in order to continue for at least one more iteration, this criterion terminates the computation if inequality (3.16) holds:

$$\sqrt{\frac{1}{n} \cdot \sum_{i=1}^{n+1} (f(v_i) - f(v_{\text{centroid}}))^2} \leq \tau \tag{3.16}$$

The geometric operations performed by Simplex Downhill, applied to an example simplex in two dimensions ($n = 2$), are depicted in Figure 3.2. A simplex in two dimensions has $n + 1 = 3$ vertices, hence it is a triangle as shown in Figure 3.2(a). It consists of

---

Algorithm 1 Simplex Downhill, Nelder-Mead variant, for a minimization problem

---

1   **while** convergence criterion not met **do**

2        $v_{\text{centroid}} = \frac{1}{n} \cdot \sum_{i=1, v_i \neq v_{\text{worst}}}^{n+1} v_i$

3        $v_{\text{worst}} = \arg\max_{v_i}\{f(v_1), \ldots, f(v_{n+1})\}$

4        $v_{\text{best}} = \arg\min_{v_i}\{f(v_1), \ldots, f(v_{n+1})\}$

5        $v_{\text{reflected}} = v_{\text{worst}} + 2 \cdot (v_{\text{centroid}} - v_{\text{worst}})$

6   **if** $f(v_{\text{reflected}}) < f(v_{\text{best}})$ **then**

7                $v_{\text{expanded}} = 2 \cdot v_{\text{reflected}} - v_{\text{centroid}}$

8   **if** $f(v_{\text{expanded}}) < f(v_{\text{reflected}})$ **then**

9   Replace v_{worst} with v_{expanded} in the simplex

10   **else**

11   Replace v_{worst} with $v_{\text{reflected}}$ in the simplex

12   **end if**

13   **else**

14   **if** $f(v_{\text{second-best}}) \geq f(v_{\text{reflected}})$ **then**

15   Replace v_{worst} with $v_{\text{reflected}}$ in the simplex

16   **else**

17   **if** $f(v_{\text{reflected}}) < f(v_{\text{worst}})$ **then**

18   Replace v_{worst} with $v_{\text{reflected}}$ in the simplex

19   **end if**

20                   $v_{\text{contracted}} = \frac{1}{2} \cdot (v_{\text{worst}} + v_{\text{centroid}})$

21   **if** $f(v_{\text{contracted}}) \geq f(v_{\text{worst}})$ **then**

22   **for all** v_i **do**

23                           $v_i = \frac{1}{2} \cdot (v_i + v_{\text{best}})$

24   **end for**

25   **else**

26   Replace v_{worst} with $v_{\text{contracted}}$ in the simplex

27   **end if**

28   **end if**

29   **end if**

30   **end while**

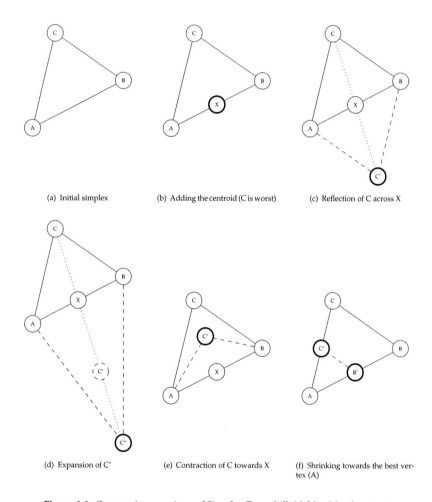

(a) Initial simplex

(b) Adding the centroid (C is worst)

(c) Reflection of C across X

(d) Expansion of C'

(e) Contraction of C towards X

(f) Shrinking towards the best vertex (A)

Figure 3.2: Geometric operations of Simplex Downhill, Nelder-Mead variant

vertices A, B, and C, and it is assumed for the example that the objective function, f, rates vertex A best and vertex C worst. As C is the worst vertex, the centroid X is computed from vertices A and B, located halfway between these vertices as shown in Figure 3.2(b). The reflection of C across X yields a new vertex, C'. Figure 3.2(c) shows this reflection and hints at the new simplex consisting of vertices A, B and C' through dashed lines. If the reflection can be improved by expansion as shown in Figure 3.2(d), the new simplex will be composed of vertices A, B and C''. On the contrary, if contraction is necessary, C is attracted towards X as shown in Figure 3.2(e). Finally, if the algorithm detects that no improvement can be attained through the other operations, shrinking moves all vertices toward the best one. This is depicted in Figure 3.2(f).

Simplex Downhill is widely accepted as a direct search method for unconstrained continuous nonlinear problems, especially when derivatives of the objective function are unavailable [138]. A detailed discussion of Simplex Downhill's properties is provided by [116, 138, 178].

The quality of solutions provided by Simplex Downhill strongly depends on the simplex' starting position in the solution space. Under unfavorable conditions, Simplex Downhill quickly converges in a local optimum which is substantially worse than the global optimum. To the end of countering this effect, coupling Simplex Downhill with a population-based evolutionary approach yields *Evolutionary Simplex Downhill*, a hybrid approach that resorts to a Simplex Downhill iteration as the equivalent of a GA's crossover operator [136]. Given a n-dimensional problem, the evolutionary algorithm draws $n + 1$ randomly chosen individuals from a population in each iteration and builds a simplex with these individuals as the simplex' vertices. On this simplex, it then performs a single iteration of the Nelder-Mead method. This step yields a point which replaces the worst individual in the population if it is superior. Evolutionary Simplex Downhill continues to iterate until the population does not improve any more. In this way, the population gradually moves towards more promising parts of the solution space. This evolutionary approach is expected to partially overcome Simplex Downhill's inherent problem of premature convergence in local optima.

3.3.1.1.2 The hypercube method

For the individual problem, a set of landmarks $\mathcal{L}$, their coordinates and measured delays to the joining node are known. Instead of solving this problem with Simplex Downhill, an alternative procedure is proposed in this section. The proposed procedure creates a sequence of shrinking-volume finite sections of an n-dimensional Euclidean space, each of which assumes the shape of a hypercube. While this approach behaves in a greedy fashion, it features a tendency to surmount local optima because its termination criterion does not depend on the comparison of current and best known solutions.

In this setting, hypercubes are not defined via labeled vertices. Instead, they are uniquely defined by centroid and edge length, an approach that better suits the application domain because the proposed procedure generally deals with points located inside the hypercube, not with the vertices.

For the individual problem, this approach may be translated into the following sequence of steps:

1. *Initial hypercube construction:* The centroid of all nodes in $\mathcal{L}$ becomes the centroid of the initial hypercube. The initial edge length equals twice the maximum delay measured between the joining node and any landmark from L.

2. *Splitting step:* The hypercube is split into 2^n equally-sized hypercubes referred to as *sub-cubes*. Next, the procedure computes the objective function for each sub-cube's centroid. All sub-cubes except the one with the best objective function value will be discarded. Only one sub-cube remains which replaces the old hypercube.

3. *Improvement check:* Should the objective function value for the surviving hypercube's centroid fall short of the previously known minimum, this new best known solution is memorized.

4. *Termination check:* If the new sub-cube's edge length falls below a previously defined threshold $\epsilon > 0$, the procedure terminates to return the best known solution. Otherwise, the procedure continues with step 2 for the next iteration.

In the splitting step, the edge length h' for the new sub-cubes will be determined based on their parent hypercube's edge length, h. Let $k \in (0,1)$ and $h' = k \cdot h$. For a split that lets the new sub-cubes occupy exactly the volume covered by their parent hypercube, the edge length needs to be halved, i.e. $k = 0.5$. In this case, points in the solution space outside the initial hypercube are unreachable. However, for $0.5 < k < 1$, sub-cubes will be able to wander around in solution space, eventually leaving the portion of space covered by the original hypercube if required. Since the termination criterion is based on edge length, choosing a larger k will make the algorithm create more intermediate sub-cubes and hence take longer to complete. With $k \geq 1$, the procedure will not converge because the sequence of edge lengths does not decline, while $0 < k < 0.5$ will render portions of the solution space within the initial hypercube unreachable. Hence, k can safely be restricted to the interval $[0.5, 1)$. If the hypercube is supposed to be able to roam in solution space, this restriction can be narrowed to $k \in (0.5, 1)$.

To derive sub-cubes from a given parent hypercube with edge length h and centroid z, one moves $\frac{1}{4} \cdot h$ from z along each axis in both directions. Formally, let $z \in \mathbb{R}^n$ be the parent hypercube's centroid and $h \in \mathbb{R}, h > 0$ its edge length. Let $D = \{1, -1\}^n$. The set

C_z of new centroids given z is

$$C_z = \left\{ z + \frac{1}{4} \cdot h \cdot a \mid a \in D \right\} \tag{3.17}$$

An objective function f may now be used to evaluate elements of C_z, picking $b^* = $ arg min $\{f(b) \mid b \in C_z\}$. All remaining centroids ($C_z \setminus \{b^*\}$) are discarded. The new hypercube is defined through its centroid b^* and its edge length $h^* = k \cdot h$.

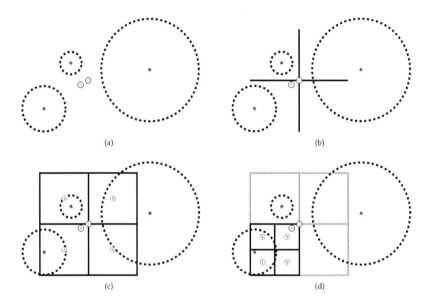

Figure 3.3: Hypercube example. (a) Three landmarks (solid grey dots with dotted circumference), their centroid, C, and the optimum, O. (b) Reaching out from the centroid. (c) The hypercube has four sub-cubes, with centroids numbered 1 to 4. (d) Exploring the bottom-left sub-cube which again features four sub-cubes with centroids 1 to 4.

Figure 3.3 depicts an example. It shows the embedding of a new node referencing three landmarks in a hypercube using $k = 0.5$ and $n = 2$. According to the delay information measured by the new node, it should be located a given fixed distance away from each landmark, but since the circles do not intersect, there is no perfect embedding. Instead, a minimum-error embedding is sought, marked in the figure by O. With the hypercube approach, this is accomplished using the landmarks' centroid, C, as a vantage point from which one extends the maximum delay in perpendicular directions. In Figure 3.3(d), it was assumed that centroid 1 from the sub-cube in Figure 3.3(c) proved best in the previous iteration so its surrounding hypercube became subject to intensified exploration.

The procedure will always terminate given $k \in (0,1)$. It does so once $i^* \in \mathbb{N}$, the number of iterations, is sufficiently large to make $h \cdot k^{i^*} < \epsilon$ hold. From that condition, one derives i^* as

$$i^* = \left\lceil \log_k \frac{\epsilon}{h} \right\rceil \tag{3.18}$$

The hypercube algorithm's complexity does not depend on the number of nodes in the network as it only interacts with a landmark set whose size does not exceed a predefined constant and is therefore on the order of $O(1)$. In each iteration, 2^n hypercubes are generated out of which $2^n - 1$ are eventually discarded. Thus, the hypercube algorithm has a runtime complexity of $O(2^n)$.

The initial hypercube's centroid z, its edge length h and the shrinking constant $k \in (0.5, 1)$ determine the portion of the solution space covered by a given hypercube. By moving strictly into the same direction until the termination criterion is satisfied, one will eventually encounter the farthest reachable point in that direction. Assuming an arbitrarily chosen but fixed direction, let i^* be the number of iterations available until termination as specified by (3.18). Furthermore, let $g_i \in \mathbb{R}^n$ be the centroid assigned to the respective hypercube created in iteration i, and let the distance $d(x, y)$ between two centroids x, y be given by (3.2). The difference between g_i and g_{i+1} amounts to

$$g_{i+1} - g_i = \left(\frac{1}{4} \cdot k^i \cdot h, ..., \frac{1}{4} \cdot k^i \cdot h \right) \in \mathbb{R}^n \tag{3.19}$$

Using (3.19) in conjunction with (3.2), the distance between two subsequently created centroids equals

$$d(g_i, g_{i+1}) = \sqrt{n \cdot \left(\frac{1}{4} \cdot k^i \cdot h \right)^2} = \frac{1}{4} \cdot \sqrt{n} \cdot k^i \cdot h \tag{3.20}$$

Essentially, this is a diagonal's length in an n-dimensional hypercube with edge length $\frac{1}{4} \cdot k^i \cdot h$. (3.20) bears the useful property that if centroids x, y and z are created in sequence, then $d(x, z) = d(x, y) + d(y, z)$ because x, y and z all lie on the same straight line. Furthermore, in contrast to (3.2), (3.20) no longer depends on centroid coordinates. If two centroids are adjacent in the creation sequence, their distance can be computed using (3.20). Otherwise, their distance equals the cumulative distance determined via the intermediate centroids. Ultimately, maximum reach corresponds to the distance between the first and the final hypercube centroid, i. e. the distance between g_0 and g_{i^*-1}, quantified by

$$d(g_0, g_{i^*-1}) = d(g_0, g_1) + d(g_1, g_2) + \ldots + d(g_{i^*-2}, g_{i^*-1})$$

$$= \sum_{i=0}^{i^*-1} \frac{1}{4} \cdot \sqrt{n} \cdot k^i \cdot h$$

$$= \frac{1}{4} \cdot \sqrt{n} \cdot h \cdot \frac{k^{i^*} - 1}{k-1} \qquad (3.21)$$

(3.21) contains a finite geometric series since i^* is finite. To examine asymptotic behavior, the assumption of infinitely many iterations makes the series infinite, causing maximum reach to converge at

$$d(g_0, g_\infty) = \sum_{i=0}^{\infty} \frac{1}{4} \cdot \sqrt{n} \cdot k^i \cdot h$$

$$= \frac{1}{4} \cdot \sqrt{n} \cdot h \cdot \frac{1}{1-k} \qquad (3.22)$$

Given infinitely many iterations, the result expressed by (3.22) means that a point farther away than $d(g_0, g_\infty)$ units from the hypercube's centroid z is out of reach for the hypercube procedure. For points that cannot be reached by traveling from z along a unidirectional sequence of sub-cube centroids, the reach is even smaller because in this case, the hypercube will intermediately need to change directions, shortening its effective range. Every reachable point in space represents a solution to the problem at hand, but points out of reach cannot serve as solutions. Thus, it is vital to pick a suitable site for the hypercube's initial centroid as a vantage point for the search. The hypercube method uses the landmarks' centroid for this purpose.

A hypercube encloses a portion of the solution space. Once there is a hint to the potential location of a good solution, a hypercube may be set up with its centroid at that site. The longer its edges, the larger the covered portion of solution space, but there is also a risk of being misled by greedily choosing the wrong sub-cube centroid. The extent of this risk primarily depends on the behavior of the objective function. With $0.5 < k < 1$, the risk diminishes because a sub-cube may leave the part of solution space covered by its parent hypercube, and it may also re-enter parts of the solution space covered by other sub-cubes in past iterations.

Both Simplex Downhill and the hypercube method belong to a family of heuristics that form geometrical entities in an n-dimensional Euclidean space. These entities iteratively change size and position, controlled by the respective algorithm. For both approaches, the objective function may be of an arbitrary type as long as it is based on all-continuous variables. In contrast to Simplex Downhill, the hypercube, by construction, cannot reach every point in solution space, and its volume steadily decreases. Since its termination criterion does not depend on relative improvements, it can surmount local optima.

3.3.1.2 Evaluation

Experiments were conducted with a single Intel Xeon E5420 core running Linux and a Java 6 virtual machine. Results were computed for Euclidean spaces with $n \in \{2, \ldots, 5\}$ dimensions. Landmarks were picked randomly, following the *random* rule introduced in [55]. The initial problem was solved with the minimum possible number of nodes $(n + 1)$. Nodes joining afterwards solved individual problems, respectively, picking up to 16 available nodes per problem as landmarks. As in [179], the initial problem's first solution was a random one, and it was improved using Simplex Downhill. Simplex Downhill, Evolutionary Simplex Downhill, and the hypercube method contended for solving the individual problem. The terminating edge length ϵ was set to 0.1. Evolutionary Simplex Downhill's population consisted of 100 individuals which were initialized with random solutions.

Various termination criteria for Simplex Downhill were considered. An adaptive solution was found to be best in terms of both accuracy and speed: according to it, Simplex Downhill ran for 15 iterations in the first place. If an improvement occurred – regardless of its extent –, the counter was reset for another 15 iterations. If no improvement was noticed after a batch of 15 iterations, execution was terminated. Increasing the number of iterations per improvement cycle beyond 15 did not improve accuracy. This scheme ensured that Simplex Downhill would run for 15 iterations at least. Besides the termination criterion, the initial simplex solution exerts influence on the final result. Again, various alternatives were evaluated. For every number of dimensions examined, the relative embedding error according to (3.5) for each edge in every network was computed. From the gathered data, the median relative error for each matrix was retrieved prior to computing the average median error for all probed matrices. Both the error and the average time required to embed a single node were recorded. The average median error value was weighted with the number of embedded node pairs because the error is computed on a per-edge basis, while the average embedding time was weighted with the number of embedded nodes since embedding time is relevant for nodes but not for edges.

For both the initial problem and the individual problem, a variety of objective functions were sampled to evaluate the error of attained solutions. The sampling yielded different results than [55] where squared relative error was preferred for the individual problem. First, for the initial problem's error as given by (3.6), the average of (3.5) for all participating edges quantified the error. With regard to the individual problem, [179] suggested both ordinary and normalized squared error, although that approach might erroneously prefer less desired solutions over more desired ones. This is because a squared error measure may shroud the fact that part of the embedding is excellent while a singular outlier causes a large error. To illustrate this phenomenon, two error-quantifying objective functions for a node x are compared. The first one is the absolute error with respect to the landmarks,

$$f_p(x) = \sum_{i \in \mathcal{L}} |d(x,i) - \delta(x,i)|^p \qquad (3.23)$$

The second one is the relative error with respect to the landmarks,

$$g_p(x) = \sum_{i \in \mathcal{L}} \left(\frac{|d(x,i) - \delta(x,i)|}{\min(d(x,i), \delta(x,i))} \right)^p \qquad (3.24)$$

Using (3.23), it was observed in preliminary experiments that for values of p around 1.1, the total median relative error will ceteris paribus drop substantially compared to other values of p, in particular $p = 2$. Apparently, $p = 2$ exposes exaggerated strictness when dealing with single outliers. Hence, a value of $p = 1.1$ has been preferred for all experiments as documented in the following section. For similar reasons, absolute error as defined by (3.23) has been maintained because of its observed beneficial effects on the total median relative error. Table 3.1 contains a summary of the experiments with absolute and relative error functions using Simplex Downhill and PlanetLab delay information.

The effect can be illustrated by an example where a node x is about to embed itself into a 4-dimensional Euclidean space with 5 landmarks, and its placement procedure needs to decide between two solutions offered by two landmark sets, A and B. According to A, the per-landmark embedding errors as given by (3.3) equal 1, 7, 12, 28, and 532, respectively, while those of B equal 144, 203, 163, 225, and 361. This corresponds to the situation that A represents a good solution with respect to 4 out of the 5 landmarks, while B refers to a mediocre solution with no outlier. One expects A to be more useful with respect to the purpose of network embedding because B features considerable errors for all landmarks while A does so only for one landmark. In the case of $\mathcal{L} = A$, $f_{1.1}(x) = 1,060.52$ and $f_2(x) = 284,002$, while in the case of $\mathcal{L} = B$, $f_{1.1}(x) = 1,890.55$ and $f_2(x) = 269,460$. In this example, x will prefer A over B for $p = 1.1$ but B over A for $p = 2$. In general, for $p = 1.1$, the penalty for large deviations is far less than that imposed by $p = 2$. It was observed that for $p = 1.1$ and all other parameters constant, the total median relative error will assume a minimum in the considered setting.

Table 3.2 captures the performance of various initial simplex construction methods, all of which use q, the maximum delay of any chosen landmark to the new node, as its parameter. The values shown in the table are averages of the median embedding errors of the PlanetLab networks for which delay information was available. *origin 1.0* has the

| | $p = 2$ | | $p = 1.1$ | |
Dimensions	absolute	relative	absolute	relative
2	26.94	45.04	21.54	37.44
3	20.47	30.44	13.88	25.46
4	16.88	22.16	11.76	19.17
5	18.07	28.46	11.94	22.42

Table 3.1: Median relative error (%) for 4 types of objective functions

simplex vertices' coordinates sampled from a uniform distribution, centered at the origin with random distance up to q. All remaining columns in that table used the landmarks' centroid as center, drawing uniformly random coordinates values limited by q, $0.5 \cdot q$, $0.25 \cdot q$, and $0.1 \cdot q$, respectively. Except for the 2-dimensional case, the origin performed best and hence has been preferred.

| | origin | | centroid | | |
Dimensions	1.0	1.0	0.5	0.25	0.1
2	21.54	23.67	19.29	17.68	19.97
3	13.88	16.09	13.14	14.09	18.05
4	11.76	18.58	13.88	14.04	17.15
5	11.94	25.93	13.77	14.87	18.83

Table 3.2: Median relative error (%) for various starting simplices

| | Dimensions | | | |
k	2	3	4	5
0.5	29.35	22.08	18.76	17.63
0.6	23.66	18.67	16.88	15.95
0.7	21.86	17.78	16.15	15.42
0.8	21.24	17.33	15.99	15.31
0.9	20.15	17.20	15.92	15.31
0.93	20.04	17.04	15.92	15.33
0.96	20.08	16.99	15.92	15.40
0.99	20.39	16.91	15.89	15.32

Table 3.3: Weighted average median per-edge error (%) for PlanetLab, King, and Meridian matrices embedded with the hypercube algorithm

Table 3.3 conveys the embedding accuracy of the hypercube algorithm. The accuracy generally improves with both increasing k and an increasing number of dimensions, except for the extreme cases of $k \geq 0.96$ in two dimensions and $k = 0.96$ in five dimensions where performance declines slightly. The same setting in the three-dimensional case sees continuous improvement with rising k and yields substantial improvements over the

k	|		Dimensions	
	2	3	4	5
0.5	1.52	2.93	5.69	11.54
0.6	2.07	4.06	7.47	15.10
0.7	2.77	5.43	10.30	20.67
0.8	4.46	8.38	16.07	31.81
0.9	9.44	17.43	33.03	66.32
0.93	13.67	25.18	47.80	95.99
0.96	24.21	44.79	84.72	170.35
0.99	97.51	179.95	344.12	695.87

Table 3.4: Weighted average per-node embedding time (in milliseconds) of the hypercube algorithm for PlanetLab, King, and Meridian matrices

Algorithm	Dimensions			
	2	3	4	5
Simplex Downhill (Nelder-Mead)	28.63	23.75	19.43	19.32
Evolutionary Simplex Downhill	19.97	17.23	16.52	15.92

Table 3.5: Weighted average median per-edge error (%) for PlanetLab, King, and Meridian matrices embedded with simplex-based algorithms

two-dimensional case. Table 3.4 contains the time the embedding of a single node took with the hypercube algorithm. Embedding accuracy and required time for the simplex-based approaches are captured in Table 3.5 and Table 3.6, respectively. All accuracy figures in these tables are weighted averages of median relative error numbers computed in 30 runs for all available PlanetLab matrices, the King matrix and the Meridian matrix. The weighted average median error is expressed in per cent, measured on a per-edge basis, to assess the embedding quality, while the weighted average embedding time is expressed in milliseconds, measured on a per-node basis to quantify the time a single node would take to embed itself.

The figures show that the hypercube algorithm performs best, and except for the extreme case of $k = 0.99$, it is also faster than Evolutionary Simplex Downhill. Still, Evolutionary Simplex Downhill is significantly more accurate than the original Nelder-Mead variant. The major advantage of Simplex Downhill is its speed. Embedding a node takes place on the order of few milliseconds even in 5-dimensional spaces. In addition, the recorded runtime shown in Table 3.4 empirically confirms the complexity-related analytical findings in Section 3.3.1.1.2. For instance, the observed runtime approximately quadruples

| | Dimensions | | | |
Algorithm	2	3	4	5
Simplex Downhill (Nelder-Mead)	1.57	2.37	3.20	4.10
Evolutionary Simplex Downhill	126.60	167.28	212.93	247.92

Table 3.6: Weighted average per-node embedding time (in milliseconds) of simplex-based algorithms for PlanetLab, King, and Meridian matrices

from $k = 0.96$ to $k = 0.99$, a result which is consistent with (3.18). In summary, Evolutionary Simplex Downhill and the hypercube algorithm trade computational resource usage for improved accuracy, but their embedding time per node still remains reasonable.

A special case of triangle inequality violations was observed with all probed procedures. In this special case, nodes are torn apart by the embedding procedure if they happen to be located close to each other according to the delay input matrix. This effect occurs because node pairs with measured delay 0 should have equal delay to all other nodes, but this is frequently violated in practice. If the triangle inequality held, either node of a pair with an intra-pair delay of 0 could forward messages to destinations closer to the other node at no expense in terms of delay to the other pair member (since the delay is zero). However, this is not the case in practice. As a result, affected edges can experience large embedding errors. Moreover, a tiny fraction of edges may suffer from substantial outliers. These rare but very large errors distort average relative error numbers, making median relative error a more robust error measure to quantify the overall embedding accuracy.

Since GNP benefits from the presented hypercube algorithm and the flexible choice of landmarks introduced in [55], experiments in upcoming sections will use the augmented GNP using both improvements and designate it GNP* to distinguish it from the original approach.

3.3.2 Vivaldi

Vivaldi [57, 60, 123, 139, 153, 190] is a distributed network coordinates generation mechanism that places nodes within an Euclidean space. Each node participating in Vivaldi contacts random other nodes in arbitrary intervals. The contact-initiating node measures the link's delay and computes the spatial distance to the target, then sets up a virtual spring between both nodes. Should measured delay and spatial distance be identical, the spring rests in a zero-energy state that represents the optimum. Otherwise, the spring is relaxed or compressed, applying a force to the nodes which either pulls them closer toward each other or pushes them apart in the space. This way, the energy contained in the spring reflects the mismatch between measured delay and spatial distance. Vivaldi will strive to reduce that energy for all springs to a minimum, preferably zero, level.

3.3.2.1 The Vivaldi algorithm

While a centralized variant of Vivaldi is available [57], the distributed Vivaldi algorithm better suits the nature of Desktop Grids.

Algorithm 2 Vivaldi

---
1 dir = remote_coordinates − local_coordinates
2 dir = dir · $\frac{1}{\|dir\|}$
3 d = dist(remote_coordinates, local_coordinates) - measured_delay
4 force = dir · d
5 δ = max(δ − 0.025, 0.05)
6 force = force · δ
7 local_coordinates = local_coordinates + force

Algorithm 2 contains the pseudocode for the distributed Vivaldi variant [57, 60]. The algorithm is executed after the network delay to a remote node has been determined and stored in the variable `measured_delay`. Its input is the set of coordinates for both the local and the remote node as well as the measured delay. The static variable $\delta \in [0.05, 1]$ is initialized with the value 1. Let `dist(x,y)` be the Euclidean norm (3.2) that returns the spatial distance between points x and y. With these prerequisites, the Vivaldi algorithm works as follows.

- In line 1, Vivaldi determines the vector `dir` that points to the remote host from the current local coordinates, then normalizes this vector in line 2.

- Line 3 contains the core idea of Vivaldi. Here, the algorithm computes the difference between the spatial distance and the actual delay, and stores the difference in the variable d. Thus, d contains the (directed) distance that the current node must move towards the remote node in the Euclidean space to attain a zero-energy state. If the coordinates are perfect with regard to the nodes involved, then d = 0: the virtual spring rests in the desired zero-energy state. If the spatial distance exceeds the actual delay, then d > 0. Otherwise, if the spatial distance is smaller than the actual delay, d < 0.

- In line 4, direction and spring state are combined in a single vector, `force`, that represents the virtual spring's force which is exerted on the current node.

- Lines 5 and 6 multiply `force` with the monotonously decreasing δ factor to dampen oscillation. By construction, δ will not drop below 0.05.

- Finally, in line 7, the force given by force is applied to the current node's coordinates.

The original Vivaldi algorithm initializes all nodes with coordinates equal to the origin, and moves two nodes away from each other in a random direction if they have equal coordinates. Preliminary experiments with Vivaldi in the context of this thesis have indicated that initializing the coordinates with random values from the start yields no worse, if not better median embedding errors.

When the number of dimensions is a constant, and n nodes perform m Vivaldi rounds with one randomly picked other remote each, Vivaldi's runtime complexity, measured for the entire network, is $O(n \cdot m)$. Every Vivaldi round requires two messages to be sent to determine the delay (or alternatively, the round-trip time) between the initiating and the contacted node, thus the message complexity is also on the order of $O(n \cdot m)$.

The authors of Vivaldi conducted a study on the effects of varying δ [57]. The study found that a very small value, 0.001, resulted in long convergence times while large values – as large as 0.5 – accelerated convergence at the expense of reduced accuracy. The maximum value, $\delta = 1$, caused a failure to converge because the coordinates oscillate. With $\delta = 1$, every Vivaldi iteration causes the probing node to adjust its coordinates in a way that reduces the embedding error with respect to the remote host to zero. This is because the probing node's coordinates are translated the complete way to the position required to meet the criterion dist(remote_coordinates, local_coordinates) = measured_delay. However, this neglects previous coordinate adjustments with other nodes, and makes the coordinates change erratically. The scheme that decreases δ over time until a minimum value of 0.05 has been reached was found to be a viable solution that takes both accuracy and convergence speed into account. More refinement can be added by incorporating the remote node's δ value as a measure of its confidence into its own coordinates, leading to a δ quantity which is not monotonously decreasing but adapts to both the local and remote error [60].

A simple yet effective improvement is to let the nodes participating in a Vivaldi cycle apply half the computed force to both nodes instead of updating the probing node's coordinates only. To this end, line 7 in Algorithm 2 is replaced by the two lines shown below:

1   local_coordinates = local_coordinates + $\frac{force}{2}$
2   remote_coordinates = remote_coordinates - $\frac{force}{2}$

Technically, to perform the remote coordinates change in line 2, a third message must be sent at the end of a Vivaldi cycle to notify the remote node of its new coordinates. To distinguish original Vivaldi from this improved version in the upcoming evaluation section, the improved variant will be denoted *split-force* Vivaldi.

Another way to modify Vivaldi is the addition of *heights* [60]. Besides the ordinary coordinates, every node maintains a positive height value $h \in \mathbb{R}$, $h > 0$. The Euclidean coordinate component models connections in a high-performance network backbone where coordinates largely represent geographical distances, while the height h captures the delay from a node to its access point to the backbone. This is particularly useful for users connected to Internet Service Providers (ISPs) via phone lines. The distance between two nodes equals their Euclidean distance in the backbone plus both nodes' heights.

Let $[z, z_h]$ denote a vector that contains Euclidean coordinates z and an associated height value z_h. To be able to handle heights, the Vivaldi algorithm undergoes a minor modification by having vector operations redefined in the following way [60]:

$$[x, x_h] - [y, y_h] = [(x - y), x_h + y_h] \qquad (3.25)$$

$$\left\| [x, x_h] \right\| = \|x\| + x_h \qquad (3.26)$$

$$\alpha \cdot [x, x_h] = [\alpha \cdot x, \alpha \cdot x_h] \qquad (3.27)$$

Adding heights enables nodes to move upwards along the height when spring forces would cancel out otherwise.

Finally, a different way to improve Vivaldi is the addition of filters. Live settings expose Vivaldi to jitter. Coordinate accuracy can be improved through the introduction of filters that preprocess raw delay information, reducing the influence of jitter [190].

3.3.2.2 Evaluation

Like the algorithms evaluated in conjunction with GNP in Section 3.3.1.2, Vivaldi's performance improves with higher dimensionality, and like the hypercube algorithm, more iterations generally yield better accuracy. While in the case of the hypercube algorithm, the number of iterations can be influenced indirectly by increasing k, Vivaldi directly depends on a parameter that specifies the number of rounds. The experiments with Vivaldi were conducted in the same setting as those with GNP documented in Section 3.3.1.2. They focused on the comparison of original to split-force Vivaldi as the addition of heights has already been evaluated in [60] and the use of filters on raw delay information in [190]. Table 3.7 shows the weighted median per-edge error, averaged over all PlanetLab matrices, the King matrix and the Meridian matrix. It can be seen from these results that only in the case of 500 rounds or more, Vivaldi can compete with the accuracy provided by the hypercube algorithm. Since two messages are sent per Vivaldi cycle, this causes a message load of 1,000 messages per node. The situation improves when the split-force improvement is applied. Table 3.8 shows the weighted median-per edge error, averaged over the same set of matrices, for the split-force Vivaldi variant. Operating under identical circumstances except for the additional message per cycle, split-force Vivaldi achieves hypercube algorithm-like accuracy at 200 rounds and comes reasonably close to that level already at 100 rounds. The improvements over original Vivaldi are most notable when the number of rounds is low. As shown in the table, only when performing large numbers of iterations can original Vivaldi catch up with the split-force improvement.

An iteration of the Vivaldi algorithm is computed quickly. On an Intel Xeon E5420 core, it took less than 0.01 ms to embed a node given the latency information. In live networks, the delay caused by the latency probe message dominates the computational effort.

Rounds	Dimensions			
	2	3	4	5
10	72.27	66.69	62.03	56.87
20	60.34	55.09	47.60	50.05
50	46.77	39.59	36.41	34.52
100	41.44	35.01	32.12	29.91
200	37.74	30.70	27.54	25.21
500	29.61	23.17	21.00	20.29
1,000	26.01	21.86	20.32	19.18

Table 3.7: Weighted average median relative error (%) for PlanetLab, King, and Meridian matrices embedded with the original Vivaldi algorithm

Rounds	Dimensions			
	2	3	4	5
10	53.53	46.30	44.97	40.94
20	49.74	41.30	37.84	36.87
50	40.54	33.77	30.14	29.01
100	36.36	29.44	26.32	24.64
200	31.13	24.77	22.39	20.78
500	24.72	20.73	19.13	18.14
1,000	22.89	19.74	18.16	17.82

Table 3.8: Weighted average median relative error (%) for PlanetLab, King, and Meridian matrices embedded with the split-force Vivaldi algorithm

In addition to the matrix-based simulations of Vivaldi, the algorithm was executed on 100 PlanetLab nodes and the development of the coordinates tracked. Figure 3.4 shows the modifications to the 2D coordinates of the PlanetLab nodes with time passing. The coordinates were provided by a distributed Vivaldi implementation running on each node. The implementation initiated a new Vivaldi cycle every 10 seconds. Between two subsequent plots shown in the figure, 75 seconds had elapsed. The figure shows that the seemingly random scattering of nodes in the first plot gradually shifts to a clustered setting in the final plot.

3.3.3 Big Bang

The BIG BANG SIMULATION (BBS) system is another dynamic approach that embeds networks into metric spaces [209]. Like Vivaldi, BBS is based on a natural phenomenon. However, BBS is considerably more complex and has a centralized component. It does not achieve substantially more accurate embeddings than Vivaldi or GNP*, so it has found less use in practical applications. In BBS, every node is represented by a particle in the target space. The embedding is performed by simulating a force field which influences the motion of these particles. Similar to the virtual springs in Vivaldi, to reduce the embedding error, a force induced betwen two particles either pulls them farther apart or pushes them closer to each other.

BBS is divided into a number of phases, and every phase is divided into a number of iterations. In the beginning, all particles are placed at the origin and moved into random directions during the first iteration. Subsequently, BBS models attraction, friction, and acceleration of particles. Since all particles' actions affect all other particles, there is $O(n^2)$ complexity per iteration with n particles and the need for a centralized component to supervise and simulate the force field's effects on all particles. This need makes BBS unsuitable for a fully distributed approach.

3.3.4 Embedding-free approaches

There are methods that estimate the pairwise delay between nodes without embedding the network. While these methods generally prove inferior to the embedding approaches, they may serve to aid comparisons in benchmarks and provide rough estimates of a delay if an embedding mechanism is unavailable. Additionally, other methods deliver a rank ordering between nodes without explicitly specifying the inter-node delays. The proponents of some of these methods argue that it is sufficient for the respective application domain to know an order of nodes sorted ascendingly by proximity. Although this may be true in some cases, knowing a reasonably accurate delay to arbitrary nodes enables additional features. For instance, geometry-based algorithms require spatial coordinates

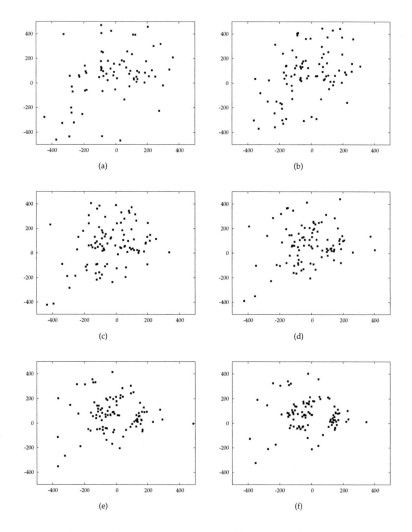

Figure 3.4: Vivaldi coordinates of 100 PlanetLab nodes adjusting over time

to work, and timeout values for remote nodes can be based on an estimate of the end-to-end delay. A number of embedding-free approaches are presented in this section for the sake of comparison.

3.3.4.1 XOR metric

The XOR METRIC assumes delays to be proportional to the distances of IP addresses [94]. Considering IPv4 addresses of 32 bit size, let i_v denote bit v of address i. The XOR metric defines the IP address-based distance of two nodes with respective IP addresses j and k to be

$$d(j,k) = \sum_{v=0}^{31} |j_v - k_v| \cdot 2^v = \sum_{v=0}^{31} (j_v \text{ XOR } k_v) \cdot 2^v$$

The XOR metric is a weighted HAMMING distance between j and k. Like other metrics, it satisfies the criteria of reflexivity, symmetry, positive definiteness, and the triangle inequality [152, 160]. However, when applied to binary representations of IP addresses, the XOR metric exhibits two severe downsides. First, no quantifiable delay information can be inferred from the IP distance. The metric may serve only to estimate a rank ordering that sorts remote nodes according to the IP distance. Moreover, the assumption of delays growing with the XOR metric may not be true. For instance, 173.252.88.31 might be farther away from 174.63.20.12 than from 178.225.16.38 in terms of end-to-end communication latency, yet the XOR metric would consider 174.63.20.12 to be closer.

The XOR metric is used by the KADEMLIA P2P system to measure the distance between 160-bit DHT peer IDs [160]. Without explicitly suggesting the XOR metric, the idea of using IP addresses for delay estimation was mentioned also in [79].

3.3.4.2 King

The KING method uses DNS servers to approximate delays [104]. Its general idea is to contact one DNS server to issue a recursive DNS query that resolves a destination host's address, and measure the amount of time the query takes to complete. Afterwards, the delay to the contacted DNS server is measured with a ping message and subtracted from the DNS query's time to yield the time it took the contacted DNS server to communicate with the other server. This approach makes a strong assumption as DNS servers are expected to be negligibly close to the hosts whose symbolic addresses they are supposed to resolve. Also, the authors estimate the King method to work approximately 94 % of the time due to the dependence on the availability of recursive queries; i. e. in a sufficiently

large sample, King fails to serve 6 out of 100 queries. The authors claim the delay
prediction error to be less than 20 % in three quarters of the measurements.

Unlike embedding methods, every King query creates network load, and it is more load
than would be generated through a simple ping request/response scheme. A portion of
the additional load incurred with King is shifted to the DNS servers. The measuring
host needs to send three messages (two DNS queries, one for preparation purposes and
one for the actual measurement, and one ping message) and receive three replies, one
for each message. Moreover, DNS servers will experience heightened traffic and CPU
load as they are used for delay estimation. The authors of King expect the extra load to
be insignificant compared to the load caused by Web-induced DNS queries but do not
provide any empirical data to support this claim.

The King approach has several advantages. It requires no extra infrastructure beyond
DNS, faithfully incorporates violations of the triangle inequality as there is no embedding
into a metric space, enables the estimation of delays to nodes that do not respond to ping
queries, and does not require cooperation among nodes. On the contrary, there are
a number of disadvantages. It is questionable if DNS server operators agree to having
their systems used for a purpose they have not been deployed for. The nature of recursive
queries being forwarded from one DNS server to the next might not match the sequence
of IP forwarding hops that ping messages cover. In addition, DNS servers need to be
very close in terms of delay to the hosts to which the actual delay should be estimated.
The authors found that in Napster, up to 70 % of link-disjoint paths to Napster clients
and their respective name servers had a delay difference of 10 ms or less. At the same
time, this means that at least 30 % of disjoint paths to Napster clients and their respective
name servers experienced a delay difference of more than 10 ms, with no upper bound
available. The most severe disadvantage, however, is that actual network load is caused
by every measurement. Each probe requires three messages to be sent and three messages
to be received by the probing host. Additionally, there is extra load on the DNS servers
and their communication links.

3.3.4.3 Binning

The CAN DHT [193] [17] deploys the BINNING method introduced in [194] where nodes
first measure their network latency to a fixed set of landmarks, then assign themselves
to virtual bins which each represent one particular ordering of the landmark latency
results. Two nodes belonging to the same bin are expected to be close in terms of
proximity because both of them have obtained the same order of landmarks. This way,
binning performs a simplified form of clustering: nearby nodes are likely to be put into

---

[17] A discussion of the CAN topology is provided in Section 4.3.2.

the same bin. For instance, if three landmarks named A, B, C exist, a node X might measure the delays to the landmarks, resulting in $d(X, A) = 74[\text{ms}]$, $d(X, B) = 92[\text{ms}]$ and $d(X, C) = 35[\text{ms}]$. X will order the landmarks according to their measured proximity as C, A, B and assign itself to the bin CAB.

The concept is refined through the addition of aggregated delay information to the bin's name. This works by dividing the range of delay values into intervals ("levels" [194]), and adding the index of the respective interval to the bin's name according to the selected landmark ordering. For instance, in the C, A, B sequence above, if intervals are chosen as $0 - 49$ ms for level 0, $50 - 99$ ms for level 1 and $100 - \infty$ ms for level 2, the bin will be designated "$CAB : 011$". The authors of binning suggest that in the case a landmark is lost, existing bins will remove that landmark from their designation [194]. To determine their degree of relative proximity, nodes compare their own bin to another bin on the basis of the common set of landmarks occurring in both bin designations. Binning is shown to be beneficial to overlay routing in the CAN DHT [193, 194]. Given a fixed ordering of the landmarks, the CAN virtual space is divided into portions (zones) in the landmark ordering. A nascent node, after having assigned itself to the proper bin, joins the zone associated with its bin. This ensures that all nodes in the same zone have the same landmark ordering while nodes in different zones have different landmark orderings. When nodes are placed in the CAN space using binning instead of being placed randomly, substantial savings in end-to-end message delay follow [194].

With n landmarks, there are $n!$ orderings for bin designations (notwithstanding class-partitioned delay information), allowing for a sizable number of bins. However, binning's suitability for a self-organized, large-scale Desktop Grid is limited for several reasons. According to the authors, binning was designed to provide "simple topological hints to solve certain application-level problems" [194] because the authors found that significant performance improvements in server selection and overlay construction could be obtained already with approximate delay information. As such, the simple approach of binning does not provide quantified delay estimates, just rank orderings of landmarks. Moreover, the few landmarks need to sustain elevated levels of ping messages: the authors of binning estimated that with a suggested landmark set size of 8 to 12 landmarks, 1 million nodes in the network, 10 pings to a landmark to obtain an accurate delay estimation, and every node refreshing its bin once per hour, a landmark will need to handle $2,700$ ping queries per second. While the authors argue that an AMD Athlon 800 MHz machine could handle this load, it adds substantial network traffic and CPU load to a server that handles other duties, too.

3.3.4.4 Geographical coordinates

Another way to estimate the delay between two hosts is to consider it proportional to the geographic distance between the hosts. While this approach does not provide delay information in time units, it permits imposing a proximity-sorted order on a set of nodes whose geographical coordinates are known.

Delay estimation based on geographical coordinates is a special kind of a static mechanism. While both Vivaldi and GNP are based on latency measurements, implicitly incorporating link capacity and utilization, a geographical approach assumes the distance of any two nodes to strongly correlate with their round-trip time, focusing on location only. Concisely, the distance between any two points on the Earth's surface with known latitude and longitude equals a great circle's section running through both points. The authors of GNP have examined the aspect of geographical coordinates in their work [179] and found GNP's distance measurement to go beyond mere geographical relationships.

Assuming that nodes do not move, geographical coordinates never change, so no extra network load is incurred as no messages for delay-estimation purposes need to be sent. However, using geographical coordinates for delay estimation has several shortcomings. First, a reliable source for geographic coordinates is required; either every node knows about its coordinates or they are retrieved from a database on demand. Moreover, the assumption of delay being proportional to geographical distance is a very strong one. For example, the US–Europe link is generally a short-delay one compared to the Europe–Asia link; packet routing decisions are not taken into account when using geographical coordinates. Finally, no delay prediction can be inferred from the geographic distance. Like binning, it permits the ordering of a number of nodes according to their geographic distance (given in units of length) but does not provide tangible delay estimates (given in units of time).

Since geographic coordinates do not predict a quantifiable delay, the coordinate quality assessment has been based on the cumulative communications delay value of a P2P topology optimized for minimum cost. The associated experiments are described in Section 4.4.1.4.

3.4 Related work

A general overview of network coordinates and their applications is given in [139]. The authors stress the importance of constructing overlay networks in a way that is sensitive to the properties of the underlying topology, and highlight the benefits of network coordinates.

The topology maintenance approach introduced in Chapter 4 relies on network coordinates providing sufficiently accurate inter-node delays in a scalable way. For applications that need only know the relative ordering of nodes sorted ascendingly by the estimated delay, [153] proposes a measure, RELATIVE RANK LOSS, that quantifies the number of misorderings caused by imprecise network coordinates. This measure requires full probings and is therefore best suited to simulations and practical environments that can provide all-pairs node delays ex post.

Generally, with the exception of GNP-based NPS [180], network coordinates mechanisms assume cooperation among the nodes to exchange truthful information with each other. This creates a loophole for malicious participants to disrupt the proper operations of such mechanisms. In particular, attack strategies include the introduction of disorder to lower the overall accuracy of delay estimates, the forgery of coordinates to trick nodes into moving away from their correct spatial positions, and the isolation of specific nodes through collusion [123]. The options of malicious nodes in this context are discussed in [122]. Implementations of these strategies were deployed in a simulation-based study to assess their impact on Vivaldi and NPS [123]. The study concludes with finding that

- larger systems are less vulnerable than smaller ones,

- under certain conditions, systems with fixed infrastructure suffer more from these attacks than others,

- a trade-off between accuracy and vulnerability exists, and

- an ongoing attack can severely degrade the benefit network coordinate systems provide to applications.

A solution to the problem is proposed by [122]. It requires an infrastructure of honest, trustworthy nodes called *Surveyors*. Surveyors know each other and exclusively use coordinates from other Surveyors to compute their spatial positions. This way, Surveyors are immune to the attacks of malicious nodes. The dynamic coordinates of a node, varying as time progresses, are modelled as a stochastic process with linear dependencies. The evolution of a node's coordinates is tracked in a distributed way to the end of estimating model parameters with which future coordinate adjustments can be predicted. The null hypothesis of a remote node's coordinates having been faithfully acquired may be rejected by a hypothesis test if the difference between the observed and the expected coordinate adjustment is statistically significant. It is estimated that 1 % to 8 % of all nodes are required to assume Surveyor roles for the system to work.

Surveys of mechanisms that generate network coordinates are available in [139, 153].

3.5   Summary

This chapter has discussed the concept and utility of network coordinates along with algorithms that generate them. With network coordinates, every node is embedded into a position in a continuous metric space such that the spatial distance between two nodes approximates the true, measurable delay in the live network. Provided that a distribution scheme enables the dissemination of coordinates in a network, a node which learns of other nodes' coordinates can estimate both its own delay to remote nodes as well as the delay between two remote nodes at virtually zero cost. Practical embeddings are not error-free due to frequent violations of the triangle inequality in the Internet and the common inability of coordinates generation heuristics to escape local optima, however the median embedding error is usually sufficiently low to permit the computation of meaningful estimates.

Network coordinates generation mechanisms can be divided into landmark-based and simulation-based algorithms. The major landmark-based mechanism is GNP which can be augmented through flexible landmark selection and alternative optimization algorithms that include the hypercube method and an evolutionary variant of Simplex Downhill, GNP's default optimization algorithm. In contrast, the major simulation-based mechanism is Vivaldi which can be augmented through heights, filters, and the split-force procedure.

Among other advantages, network coordinates can relieve algorithms that frequently need to estimate inter-node delays from causing excessive network load, contributing to their scalability. In particular, this benefit concerns P2P topology optimization mechanisms which will be introduced in the next chapter.

The hypercube method has been published in [166].

4

Peer-to-Peer topologies

The performance of Desktop Grids varies with the properties of the particular P2P topology they resort to. While all contemporary P2P systems can deal with dynamics and provide their own identifier scheme apart from DNS, some topology types satisfy the needs of Desktop Grids better than others. In addition, since end-to-end delay is a major performance-impacting factor as perceived by applications, proximity-aware routing mechanisms are frequently superior to the standard hop count metric employed by numerous structured topologies. This chapter compiles the topology-related requirements of Desktop Grids and discusses algorithms that create and maintain suitable P2P topologies with a special focus on proximity awareness.

4.1   Overview

A Desktop Grid faces an environment which typically exhibits the following properties:

- *large*: it accommodates potentially millions of peers
- *heterogeneous*: peers have varying capabilities
- *dynamic*: peer composition and message delays change over time

Moreover, scalability and robustness benefit if no central component is present. Besides the removal of a single point of failure, an anonymous, ad-hoc way of participation without a form of registration at a server exhibits no obstacles for individuals to join. These properties are generally fulfilled by decentralized P2P systems. Hence, a first major requirement is that a Desktop Grid should be constructed on the basis of a pure P2P overlay with no central component whatsoever.

A general list of requirements regarding P2P topology design and maintenance contains the criteria shown below [1]:

- *Efficiency:* the effort to minimize the average path length and the bandwidth usage in routing helps conserve resources and accelerates message delivery.

- *Scalability:* the ability to sustain large number of peers without performance deterioration is essential for P2P overlays as an upper bound to the practically feasible overlay size would otherwise exist.

- *Self-stabilization:* in the absence of central control and in the presence of extensive dynamics, the overlay should be able to stabilize itself regardless of its current state.

- *Fault-tolerance:* since any peer can fail at any time, a reasonable level of service by the overlay should be maintained even in the face of a partial outage.

In addition to these requirements, facing substantial dynamics, resource heterogeneity, and large numbers of peers, a P2P topology that underlies a Desktop Grid and the mechanism that maintains it should be able to cater for the specific requirements that Desktop Grid operations entail. The topology should attempt to remain connected for the maximum period possible to permit broadcast messages to reach all participants, and strive towards connectivity when it is partitioned. Furthermore, apart from the general requirement that the overlay should adapt to its environment in a self-stabilizing way, it should also change its organizational structure depending on the number of participants, and account for fluctuating message delays.

Besides self-stabilization, topology formation and re-organization benefit from the guidance provided by an optimization objective. Possible objectives include criteria as diverse as balanced load, minimum path length (in terms of hops traveled), or minimum end-to-end delay. The topology maintenance process needs to pick suitable criteria and see to it that they are implemented.

To preserve scalability and to conserve as many resources as possible for the work on actual jobs, topology maintenance procedures should treat resources with care. In the context of message primitives, since peers wishing to distribute a job need to ask a potentially large number of peers for participation, there needs to be an efficient broadcast mechanism. Since a Desktop Grid is supposed to integrate a vast range of heterogeneous resources, the load on individual participants must remain reasonable. In particular, they should not be required to handle plenty of connections at once. Moreover, it is desirable to allow the majority of peers to remain behind firewalls.

Centralized and unstructured P2P architectures cannot satisfy these requirements due to their inherent lack of scalability, and in the former case, also due to the presence of a single point of failure. Thus, structured architectures remain. Structured topologies with a network diameter on the order of $O(\log n)$ are particularly interesting as they provide a viable tradeoff between a low number of connections per peer and reasonably swift message delivery [59]. Out of all structured topologies, ring-shaped topologies are preferable due to their robustness when compared to topologies with other geometries [103].

The first portion of the remainder of this chapter, Section 4.2, is devoted to CHORD, a structured topology that fulfills most of the aforementioned requirements [219]. Subsequently, a selection of alternatives is presented, including PASTRY which is discussed in Section 4.3.1. Structured topologies can be fitted with an additional layer of hierarchy, yielding a hybrid topology. The remainder of this chapter will discuss the benefits and construction of such hybrid systems by introducing the concept of super-peers, and explore how they can be used to augment Chord such that all the requirements imposed by Desktop Grids are satisfied.

The experiments whose setup and results are discussed in this chapter were conducted in the following way unless noted otherwise: With regard to network coordinates, a 4-dimensional Euclidean space for both Vivaldi and GNP* was used. With Vivaldi, the peers were initially placed at positions drawn from a uniform random distribution where each coordinate was contained in the range $[0; 500]$, such that in a 4-dimensional space, the initial distance between any two peers did not exceed $1,000$.

4.2   Chord

A major representant of structured, ring-shaped topologies with logarithmically growing network diameters is Chord, a decentralized, fault-tolerant, scalable and adaptive system [18, 101, 152, 219]. Chord exhibits some properties of self-organizing systems, including feedback, reproduction, adaptivity, and organization [162]. In Chord, each of the n peers in the logical ring assigns itself an ID drawn with uniform probability from $\{0, 1, 2, \ldots, 2^k - 1\}$ with $k \in \mathbb{N}$ upon entry. The peers are arranged on the ring by clockwise increasing IDs modulo 2^k.

In a fully populated ring, a peer maintains a number of links to other peers. With one exception, these links are used in a clockwise direction only. They are called *fingers* due to the peculiar way Chord chooses the link targets. There are k fingers. Let x be the current peer's ID. The i-th finger targets the ID $(x + 2^{i-1}) \mod 2^k$ and is designated finger $i - 1$. If no peer on the ring bears that ID, the peer that follows next on the ring in clockwise direction is chosen as the destination for finger $i - 1$. The first finger ($i = 0$) points to the peer that is next in clockwise direction; this peer is designated *successor* of the current peer. [18] All finger data is recorded in the *finger table*, a Chord peer's routing table. [19] The single exception to links being used in a clockwise direction is an additional link to the *predecessor* which is the peer closest to the current peer in the counter-clockwise direction. In original Chord, the predecessor link is not used for routing purposes but for ring stabilization only [101]. The remainder of this section uses the following notation. successor(p) denotes peer p's successor, while predecessor(p) denotes peer p's predecessor. Analogously, successor$_{ID}(p)$ returns the ID of peer p's successor, and predecessor$_{ID}(p)$ returns the ID of peer p's predecessor.

With n peers in a fully populated Chord ring ($n = 2^k$), a Chord peer maintains k fingers and an additional link to the predecessor, yielding $(k+1) \in O(k) = O(\log 2^k) = O(\log n)$ outgoing links per peer. Additionally, a peer has $k + 1$ incoming links from other peers. In total, there are $2 \cdot (k+1) \in O(\log n)$ unidirectional connections per peer. This can be reduced if connections are used bidirectionally: the connection going to the successor can serve the successor to send data to the current peer which is its predecessor, reducing the number of overall connections per peer by 1.

The unidirectional ring that arises when all peers use their respective successor finger only is called *successor ring*. The successor ring is sufficient to route all messages with $\frac{n}{2} \in O(n)$ hops per message on average if all destinations are equally likely. To speed up message delivery by reducing the average path length and also to make the Chord ring more resilient in the face of link failure, additional fingers are used as shortcuts to distant peers.

The clockwise ID distance dist(a, b) between two peers a and b with IDs ID(a) and ID(b), respectively, is given as

$$\text{dist}(a, b) = (ID(b) - ID(a) + 2^k) \mod 2^k \tag{4.1}$$

If $ID(b) \geq ID(a)$, the distance computation from (4.1) can be simplified to dist$(a, b) = ID(b) - ID(a)$. Assuming the destination peer exists and the ring is not partitioned, Chord routing is based on the invariant that every hop decreases the remaining distance to the destination. Message forwarding in Chord uses a greedy rule: a peer that has a message to forward picks the finger target from its finger table which is closest to but not beyond the destination. If the message's destination ID lies between its own ID and its successor's ID, the peer concludes that the destination peer does not exist. An exemplary Chord ring with an identifier space size of 32 elements ($k = 5$) and 10 peers is depicted

---

[18]In Chord, the term *successor* is also used to designate a peer that occupies a given ID z, or if z is unoccupied, the first peer to follow z in clockwise direction [219].

[19]Throughout the remainder of this chapter, the finger table is assumed to be sorted clockwise, starting with the ID of the finger table owner's successor.

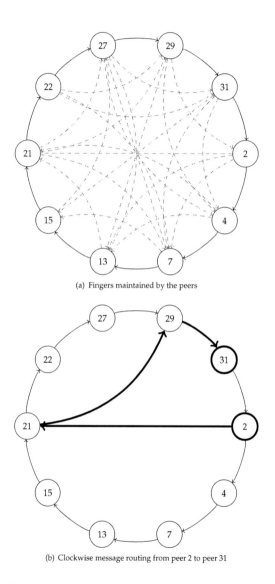

(a) Fingers maintained by the peers

(b) Clockwise message routing from peer 2 to peer 31

Figure 4.1: Exemplary Chord ring with 10 peers and $k = 5$

in Figure 4.1. Figure 4.1(a) shows all fingers maintained in this ring, while Figure 4.1(b) shows the fingers along which a message travels that is sent by peer 2 to peer 31.

When the finger tables of all peers are intact, every finger hop along which a message is forwarded covers at least half the remaining distance to the destination peer [101]. The case in which the ring is fully populated is equivalent to routing in a hypercube [14]. In this case, a message traveling over a finger connection reduces the remaining distance by the highest set bit since it represents the finger over which the message is to be forwarded. Each set bit in a distance value therefore represents one more finger that the message will be required to use until it arrives at the destination peer [219]. Distances are composed of k bits, i.e. there will be a maximum of k hops. Assuming that the number of messages transmitted between every pair of Chord peers a, b is a constant, a bit in $\text{dist}(a, b)$ will be set with a probability of 0.5. Thus, the number of set bits in a distance value, equivalent to the number of hops to travel, follows a binomial distribution with mean $0.5 \cdot k = 0.5 \cdot \log n$. It is for this reason that in an intact Chord ring, a message travels $O(\log n)$ hops on average from its source to its destination. This result has been empirically verified [219]. The performance can deteriorate to $O(n)$ if all fingers besides the successor are unavailable, requiring Chord to use the successor ring to route the message.

If the ring is not fully populated, let $n' = 2^j$, $j < k$, $j \in \mathbb{N}$ be the actual number of peers. Assuming that the present peers are spread over the ring such that the ID distance between adjacent peers is constant, there are $\frac{n}{n'} = \frac{2^k}{2^j} = 2^{k-j}$ units of the identifier space per peer. Equivalently, the gap between two peers is $2^{k-j} - 1$ units of identifier space wide, and distances between peers are multiples of 2^{k-j}. Since the i-th finger covers 2^{i-1} units of identifier space, the lowest $k - j$ fingers are not used as they point to unoccupied locations in the identifier space. In a fully populated ring, the maximum distance in clockwise direction exists between a peer and its predecessor: $\text{dist}(a, \text{predecessor}(a)) = 2^k - 1$, so all k bits of the distance value are set. In a partially populated ring, since distances are multiples of 2^{k-j}, only combinations of the upper 2^j bits are set, hence only j fingers are used for routing purposes. When each bit is set with a probability of 0.5, the average path length in a ring with 2^j members is $0.5 \cdot j$, equivalent to the average path length of a fully populated ring with an identifier space size of $n = 2^j$.

Chord was designed to deal with churn [219]. A new peer x joins the ring in a sequence of steps, given a bootstrap peer y which is already in the Chord ring and known to x. First, x draws a random ID $ID(x)$ or hashes its IP address with a cryptographic hash function such as SHA-1 [152]. In the next step, it asks y to determine x's predecessor and successor by routing messages to the IDs $ID(x) - 1$ and $ID(x) + 1$. If these destination IDs are not populated by peers, the queries are answered by the respective peer that is closest in counter-clockwise direction from the destination ID. When the replies have arrived, y can forward them to x, and x can join the ring by connecting to the announced predecessor and successor peers. To update the finger table, x can retrieve a copy of its successor's finger table as a starting point, then successively update its own table by routing messages to the theoretical finger IDs [219]. An alternative way for x to join replaces y's message routing with x iteratively connecting to existing peers. First, x queries y for the closest directly known predecessor y' of x's position (retrieved from y's finger table), then queries y' and continues to iterate until the queried peer y' replies with its own ID, meaning that it itself is the sought predecessor. In this case, the current successor of y' will become x's new successor while x becomes the new successor of y'. As in the case described above, x can copy the finger table of y' as an initial configuration.

A Chord peer improves its finger table by periodically performing a *stabilization* procedure [101, 219]. When executing its stabilization procedure, a peer x asks its successor to return a reference to its predecessor, predecessor(successor(x)). Should the situation arise that predecessor(successor(x)) $\neq x$, x sets predecessor(successor(x)) as its new successor and notifies it of having x as its predecessor. Additionally, Chord updates the remaining finger table by picking a random finger from the table, then routing a message to the finger's ideal destination ID ($ID(x) + 2^{i-1}$ for the i-th finger) to determine the peer which is actually responsible for that ID [101]. When a peer crashes or leaves the ring, the peers once connected to it update their finger tables by replacing the gone peer with its successor in the finger table. Since overlay routing depends on the correct knowledge about one's successor, Chord also maintains a *successor list* that contains a peer's first r successors [18, 101, 152, 219]. When its successor crashes, a peer simply replaces it with the next entry from its successor list. With high probability, a join or leave event causes $O(\log^2 n)$ messages to be transmitted by the surviving peers to update their finger tables [219].

Chord is oblivious to the underlying topology. Finger peers can be arbitrarily distant in terms of network delay [139, 152]. Section 4.4.2.3 will introduce three modifications to Chord that enable topology awareness.

4.2.1 Handling multiple recipients

Chord can be stripped of DHT-related facilities which are irrelevant to distributed computation. Then again, Chord may be augmented with an efficient broadcast mechanism that is vital to Desktop Grids. A broadcast mechanism has not been envisaged in the original Chord concept but invented later [76, 163]. It is based on the notion of a *limit* that specifies a particular ID up to which the broadcast message should be spread.

The procedure demonstrated below requires no termination detection or other coordination. Its basic working principle is based on *ranges* that define the portion of the Chord ring for which a message is destined. Ranges wrap around zero. Let the range $< a, b >$ be

$$< a, b > = \begin{cases} \{a, a+1, a+2, \ldots, b-1, b\} & \text{if } a \leq b \\ \{a, a+1, a+2, \ldots, 2^k - 2, 2^k - 1\} \cup \{0, 1, \ldots, b-1, b\} & \text{otherwise} \end{cases} \quad (4.2)$$

The method proposed here is based on ranges instead of limits because ranges can be used to address portions of a Chord ring through *constrained broadcast*, a feature useful for requesting workers in large-scale Desktop Grids. In constrained broadcast, the sender does not care about the identities of the receivers as long as it can estimate that its message reaches a certain number of arbitrary peers in the overlay. When the overlay size can be estimated [20] and it turns out to be very large, an initiator might want to address only a portion of the overlay's peers if its demand for workers is limited. Under the assumption that the peers are uniformly distributed across the identifier space, a constrained broadcast from peer p covering the range $< \text{successor}_{\text{ID}}(p), (ID(p) + \frac{2^k}{b} - 1)$ mod $2^k >$ is likely to reach $\frac{1}{b}$ of the overlay's peers.

The following description refers to the broadcast case but can be used analogously for constrained broadcast. The initial range for a broadcast initiator p is $< ID(p) + 1, ID(p) - 1 >$. [21] Since the initiator does not know any peers between itself and its successor in clockwise direction, it is safe to narrow this range to $< \text{successor}_{\text{ID}}(p), ID(p) - 1 >$. It can be narrowed even further to $< \text{successor}_{\text{ID}}(p), \text{predecessor}_{\text{ID}}(p) >$ if the same assumption holds for the predecessor, but since the message is forwarded in clockwise direction, a peer joining the ring with an ID in the range $< \text{predecessor}_{\text{ID}}(p) + 1, ID(p) - 1 >$ while the broadcast message is propagated would be excluded from receiving the broadcast. Hence, it is advantageous to stick with the range $< \text{successor}_{\text{ID}}(p), ID(p) - 1 >$. The broadcast initiator partitions this range into several disjoint ranges split at the finger ID boundaries, and sends the broadcast message along with the respective range to each finger. The finger peers, after having received the message, split the received range at their own finger ID boundaries and forward the message over their fingers along with the range information. The procedure terminates at a peer when the received range refers to only one peer (the receiver itself). In an overlay that has n peers, this method requires $n - 1$ messages as every peer, in addition to the initiator, receives the broadcast message exactly once. Every peer sends or forwards $O(\log n)$ broadcast messages, including the range information. Since Chord's network diameter is $\lceil \log_2 n \rceil$ with an intact, fully

---

[20] Besides the coarse approach of raising two to the number of distinct fingers in the finger table, a method to estimate the overlay size in the context of super-peer topologies is to use particular information disclosed by the super-peers. Section 4.4.1.2 discusses this aspect in more detail.

[21] In this context, addition and subtraction of absolute values from IDs are performed modulo 2^k. Thus, the result is always contained in the set $\{0, \ldots, 2^k - 1\}$.

populated Chord ring, all peers will have received the broadcast message after that many rounds.

Algorithm 3 Message forwarding in Chord broadcast and constrained broadcast

---

1   **if** $a == b$ **then**
2   return
3   **end if**
4   lastID = b
5   **for** $i = |f| - 1$ downto 0 **do**
6   **if** $ID(f[i]) \in < a, b >$ **then**
7   send($f[i]$, *message*, $< ID(f[i]), lastID >$)
8   lastID=$(ID(f[i]) - 1 + 2^k) \mod 2^k$
9   **end if**
10 **end for**

The mechanism for message forwarding in Chord broadcast and constrained broadcast is formalized in Algorithm 3. It expects a number of parameters: a and b describe the first and the last ID of the destination range, respectively, assuming that a refers to the ID of an actual peer that is a finger target referred to by the caller's finger table. *message* contains the actual message to be sent. f refers to the forwarding peer's clockwise sorted finger table with $f[i]$ referring to the $(i + 1)$-th finger. It calls a send(t, m, r) primitive which transmits a unicast message m to a finger target t, requesting t to forward the message within the range r.

A broadcast example that uses the Chord ring from Figure 4.1 is depicted in Figure 4.2. Time is divided into discrete rounds for this example, and peers that have received the broadcast message have a thickened circle around their respective ID in the figure. The broadcast is performed as follows:

- In the example's round 1, shown in Figure 4.2(a), peer 15 wishes to initiate a broadcast. Its finger table contains peers 21, 27, and 31. The initial broadcast range $< 16, 14 >$, narrowed to $< 21, 14 >$ as peer 15's successor is peer 21, covers the complete identifier space except for peer 15 itself since it is assumed to have received its own message before the actual broadcast mechanism starts. Peer 15 splits the broadcast range at the boundaries of its finger table, and sends the broadcast message to the respective peer along with the associated portion of the complete range. Hence, peer 21 covers the range $< 21, 26 >$, peer 27 covers the range $< 27, 30 >$, and peer 31 covers one half of the identifier space with the range $< 31, 14 >$.

- In round 2, shown in Figure 4.2(b), these ranges and the broadcast message are received by peers 21, 27, and 31. These peers proceed as if they had initiated the broadcast, but they limit themselves to the broadcast range they have received

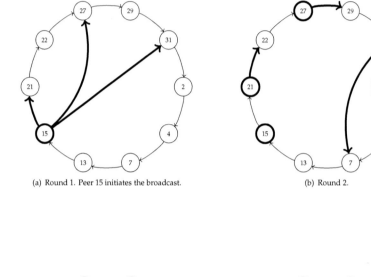

(a) Round 1. Peer 15 initiates the broadcast.   (b) Round 2.

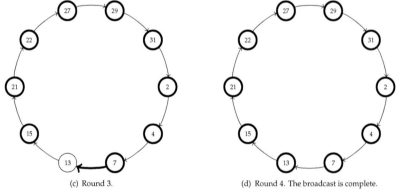

(c) Round 3.   (d) Round 4. The broadcast is complete.

Figure 4.2: Exemplary Chord broadcast in a ring with 10 peers and $k = 5$

from the initiator. Thus, peer 21 forwards the message to peer 22 with the range
< 22, 26 >. Peer 27 is a finger target of peer 21, but peer 21's broadcast range
< 21, 26 > does not cover peer 27. The same holds for peer 21's other fingers, so
the message to peer 22 remains the only one sent by peer 21. For similar reasons,
peer 27 forwards the message only to peer 29. Peer 31 needs to cover one half of
the identifier space as it is peer 15's farthest finger target. It forwards the message
over all its fingers within the range < 31, 14 >: to peers 2, 4, and 7.

- In round 3, shown in Figure 4.2(c), peer 13 is the only peer not to have received the
  message. This is made up by peer 7 transmitting the broadcast to its only finger
  target, peer 13, within the broadcast range < 7, 14 > which was assigned to it by
  peer 31.

- In round 4, shown in Figure 4.2(d), peer 13 receives peer 7's message. The broadcast
  is complete.

The broadcast scheme can be supplemented by a gossip phase that follows the broadcast
[163]. It can also be extended to perform ordinary multicast with known recipient
IDs: instead of a single range, messages carry lists of ranges, and the above broadcast
procedure is applied to every range in the list. The multicast scheme is the general case
for both broadcast (a single range) and unicast (a single range containing a single ID).

4.2.2 Discussion

Chord fulfills many of the requirements specified in Section 4.1. It is completely decentralized, scalable, and fault-tolerant. Chord's optimization objectives include a comparatively low number of connections per peer ($O(\log n)$ in a n-peer overlay) and the
minimization of the average path length. However, Chord is not proximity-aware in
its original form which hampers topology optimization for delay-oriented goals. Chord
peers cannot operate from behind firewalls as they must be reachable from the outside for
other peers to be able to create finger connections. Moreover, the failure or departure of a
peer always causes the ring to reorganize, forcing peers to update their finger tables and
set new finger connections. All cited issues can be overcome through the introduction of
super-peers as Section 4.4 will show.

4.3   Other structured topologies

4.3.1 Pastry

Pastry is a structured topology that shares a number of properties with Chord [101, 203]. Like Chord, Pastry is fully decentralized, self-organizing and scalable, and features an average path length on the order of $O(\log n)$ hops with n being the number of participating peers. The peers have random self-assigned 128-bit IDs which are assumed to be unique. Pastry routes a message with a given destination ID to the peer which is numerically closest to that ID. There is no strict dependence on a fixed forwarding direction as in Chord.

In Pastry, identifiers are sequences of digits with base 2^b, where $b \in \mathbb{N}$ is a configuration parameter with a default value of 4. When a peer selects another peer for the next hop in message forwarding, it chooses a peer whose ID's prefix has at least one more digit in common with the destination ID than the current peer's ID. If no such peer is available, the message is forwarded to a peer whose ID's prefix has the same number of common digits as with the current peer's ID, but is numerically closer to the receiver.

A Pastry peer stores and maintains three distinct structures: a routing table, a neighborhood set and a leaf set. Let x be the current peer, and let $ID(x)$ be its ID. x's routing table has $\lceil \frac{128}{b} \rceil$ rows and $2^b - 1$ columns. Like Chord's finger table, Pastry's routing table is built according to the principle that a peer should have detailed knowledge of peers close by in the identifier space but coarse knowledge about distant peers [101]. In Pastry's routing table, every column represents a distinct digit, while row i (with $i \in \{0, ..., \lceil \frac{128}{b} \rceil\}$) contains IDs of peers whose IDs have the first i digits in common with $ID(x)$. When filling a particular cell, there may be more than one peer with a suitable ID. If the application provides Pastry with a metric that quantifies the delay in the underlying network, Pastry chooses the ID of the closest peer in terms of network proximity, thus enabling locality. Pastry also replaces an entry in the routing table with another peer's ID if it finds a peer with the same ID prefix as the replaced peer to be closer [139].

Table 4.1 shows an example routing table for a Pastry peer with ID 10233102. In addition, Pastry maintains two sets within a peer's local state. The leaf set $\mathcal{L}$ accelerates routing to peers whose IDs are close by. $\mathcal{L}$ contains the IDs closest to $ID(x)$. It is split into two: there are $\frac{|\mathcal{L}|}{2}$ IDs of those peers whose IDs are less than $ID(x)$ and another $\frac{|\mathcal{L}|}{2}$ IDs of those peers whose IDs exceed $ID(x)$. The third item is the neighborhood set, $\mathcal{M}$, that helps to incorporate locality with Pastry. $\mathcal{M}$ contains the IDs and IP addresses of those peers that are closest to x in terms of network delay.

A peer x routes a message to a destination ID D in the following way. If $D \in \mathcal{L}$, the

02212102	1	22301203	31203203
0	11301233	12230203	13021022
10031203	10132102	2	10323302
10200230	10211302	10222302	3
10230322	10231000	10232121	3
10233001	1	10233232	
0		10233120	
		2	

Table 4.1: An example Pastry routing table for peer ID 10233102 (from [203]). Each column represents a digit while row i contains IDs of peers whose prefixes match at least i digits with the routing table owner's ID.

message is forwarded directly to the destination peer. Otherwise, the routing table is used. The next hop is determined by the particular row/column combination that is found through longest prefix matching, with row and column indices starting with 0. x determines the longest prefix that $ID(x)$ and D have in common. The length l of this prefix indicates the row of the routing table. The column index equals the $(l+1)$-th digit of D. Should no peer ID be stored in that particular cell of the routing table, the message is forwarded to the peer specified by the entry in row l which is numerically closest to the destination ID. Should the entire row be empty or the available peers farther away from the destination than x, x can resort to its leaf set, $\mathcal{L}$, and pick the peer numerically closest to the destination as the next hop.

In the context of the example shown in Table 4.1, the peer with ID 10233102 might want to forward a message destined for the ID 10131120. The longest common prefix is 10, its length $l = 2$. The $(l+1)$-th digit of the destination ID is 1. Hence, for the next hop, the peer will select the peer whose ID is given by the third row and the second column of the routing table (10132102).

On average, Pastry requires $O(\log_{2^b} n) = O\left(\frac{\log_2 n}{b}\right) = O(\log n)$ hops when routing a message, provided that routing table information is accurate. Every hop chosen through the routing table narrows the subset of the identifier space considered for routing by a factor of 2^b. If the destination peer is in the leaf set, there is only a single hop left.

Pastry's local state is considerably larger than Chord's. It is beneficial to keep up TCP connections to all peers in the routing table and in the leaf set in order to enable message delivery without a connection setup penalty. Pastry's average path length per message equals Chord's if $b = 1$. When the overlay is fully populated (2^{128} peers), a Chord peer would maintain 128 finger connections to remote peers, and a Pastry peer would keep up 128 connections (with $b = 1$) to the peers in the routing table plus $|\mathcal{L}|$ connections to the peers in the leaf set. In this case, both Chord and Pastry have the same routing table size (128 entries), but Pastry additionally has to maintain links to the peers referenced by the leaf set. In the case of $b = 4$ and 10^6 peers, a Chord peer would maintain 20 fingers while a Pastry peer had 75 routing table entries on average (with one TCP connection each) plus local state and connections to the peers in the leaf set [203]. When maintaining connections is potentially expensive, Chord's lightweight finger table is better suited to the requirements of peers in a live environment. Pastry's inherent notion of locality can be compensated by the improvements to Chord presented in Section 4.4.2.3.

4.3.2 CAN

The CONTENT-ADDRESSABLE NETWORK (CAN) is a scalable, fault-tolerant and fully de-centralized topology [18, 101, 152, 193]. In CAN, peers are placed in a d-dimensional Cartesian coordinate space which is organized as a torus in every dimension, i. e. there is a coordinate wrap-around [152]. Every peer covers a hypercube-shaped portion of the space that surrounds it. CAN calls this portion a peer's *zone*. When a peer joins a CAN overlay, it assigns itself random coordinates within the coordinate space. The zone which contains the new peer's coordinates is eventually split. One part of the zone is occupied by the original occupant of the original zone, while the other part is occupied by the new peer. If a peer leaves, its abandoned zone is merged with the zone of its closest neighbor.

The random assignment of IDs can be replaced by a topology-aware assignment. The binning scheme lends itself to this end [193, 194]. [22] Since there are $n!$ bins given n landmarks, CAN partitions the coordinate space into $n!$ zones. Peers join a random location within the zone assigned to them through their landmark ordering which binning has yielded. Thus, peers within the same zone have the same landmark ordering and are therefore likely to be close to each other in the underlying network, too. Additionally, with the help of network coordinates, CAN peers are able to adopt their network coordinates to determine their position in the overlay.

Routing is performed greedily by forwarding a message to the neighbor which is closest to the destination's coordinates. In a CAN overlay with n peers, routing takes $O(d \cdot \sqrt[d]{n})$ hops on average [152, 219]. Every peer maintains routing state in the form of references to its neighbors. Since every peer has two neighbors per dimension, the routing state encompasses $2 \cdot d \in O(d)$ entries. While the size of the routing state a peer must store does not depend on the network size, n, message routing takes more hops on average as

---

[22] The binning mechanism is discussed in Section 3.3.4.3.

in Chord [219]. By setting $d = \log_2 n$, message routing in CAN takes

$$(\log_2 n) \cdot \sqrt[\log_2 n]{n} = (\log_2 n) \cdot \left(2^{\log_2 n}\right)^{\frac{1}{\log_2 n}} = 2 \cdot \log_2 n$$

hops on average. This number is on the order of $O(\log n)$, the same as with Chord. To enable this equivalence, a CAN peer's local state grows with the overlay size. However, since the overlay size is considered to be highly dynamic, $d = \log_2 n$ would need to be adapted whenever n changes, creating the necessity for CAN peers to perpetually modify their coordinate vectors and neighbor information depending on the current value of d. Thus, in comparison to a realistic CAN configuration with fixed d, Chord has the lower average path length.

4.3.3 Meridian

MERIDIAN is a framework designed for scalable proximity-based node selection based on live measurements [233]. Meridian's authors describe the system as a loosely-coupled topology that can be used for leader election, closest-peer discovery and finding peers that fulfill specified maximum-delay constraints, with a methodical approach similar to GNP in combination with CAN for proximity-aware node selection. In a Meridian overlay with n peers, every peer has $O(\log n)$ neighbors which it assigns, according to the delay measured to the respective neighbor, to concentric rings with exponentially increasing radii. The number of stored rings and tracked peers per ring are bounded upwards to enable a low memory footprint for the individual peer. Membership and node discovery are handled stochastically with a gossip protocol.

While Meridian is a sophisticated approach, its delay measurement process is insufficient for the purpose pursued here. By construction, a Meridian peer cannot accurately estimate the delay between two arbitrary other peers, or the delay to a peer with which it has not communicated yet, without sending additional messages. The deployment of a stochastic component (gossip membership management) disables the provision of deterministic performance guarantees. Queries for proximity-aware server selection incur a considerable overhead [139]. Moreover, Meridian assumes that peers possess an estimate of n.

4.4   Super-peer structures

Hybrid topologies featuring *super-peers* combine the advantages of client/server and fully distributed P2P networks [191, 234, 237]. They introduce a hierarchy among peers, distinguishing between common peers and *super-peers*. Super-peers perform server-like roles. However, there is no single point of failure as the super-peer role may be assigned to a common peer at runtime when the need arises. Since every peer, in theory, can become a super-peer, and super-peers can downgrade to common peer level, this approach maintains the flexibility which is required to deal with large-scale, dynamic peer populations.

The introduction of super-peers has a number of benefits:

- Super-peers bring server-like facilities to a decentralized topology.

- Super-peers can serve as proxies for peers operating behind firewalls.

- Super-peers can act as multiplexers, combining messages forwarded via the same link to save overhead.

- Super-peers are selected such that only peers that are reachable from the outside may become one; hence, super-peers can be used for bootstrapping purposes or as the target of a Vivaldi cycle.

- Super-peers can enable locality by clustering edge peers that are close to each other in terms of the underlying network's communication delay.

Possible disadvantages include increased traffic on inter-super-peer links, the inability to properly forecast a super-peer's load, and the requirement to cater for sudden departures or losses of super-peers [14].

The term *super-peer topology* shall refer to a P2P topology that includes super-peers. In its original form, it is a generic term, leaving the relationships between peers and the rule according to which common peers become super-peers and vice versa unspecified. Thus, various kinds of super-peer topologies have emerged. An early user of super-peer structures was the FASTTRACK P2P system [146, 152]. In FastTrack, super-peers assume server-like roles to aid in search query processing. The super-peers are interconnected by a proprietary topology [93]. [146] empirically established that each of the approximately $30,000$ probed super-peers using KAZAA, FastTrack's most common client software, had 40 to 60 connections to other super-peers while serving 60 to 150 common peers, that a distributed gossip-based algorithm maintained the super-peer subgraph, and that both RTT measurements and XOR metric computations were used by common peers to find nearby super-peers. However, the creation of super-peers solely depends on the user's willingness to let its computer act as a super-peer, indicated by checking a box in KaZaA.

The design goal for the proposed Desktop Grid is to attain a topology in which some peers will act as super-peers while the remaining peers, henceforth called *edge peers*, are assigned to exactly one of the super-peers each, respectively [212]. The design space for super-peer topology optimization contains a number of feasible objectives, such as minimizing the load a super-peer bears, minimizing the average path length, and minimizing the average (or maximum) end-to-end message delay. In the topology construction processes explored by this work, the first and the third criterion are pursued. The first criterion attempts to minimize a super-peer's load to permit as many peers as possible to act as super-peers, while the third criterion (for the average delay case) affects both the reactiveness of the topology reorganization process and the actual delay perceived by applications. In contrast, minimizing the path length is useful only if there were a significant processing delay at every forwarding peer. Hence, the topology should be created in a proximity-aware way, optimized for low end-to-end message delay in order to ensure smooth communication and swift reactions to changes in the overlay composition, and with a procedure that reduces the load super-peers need to bear to the lowest feasible level. Additionally, the number of edge peers should depend on the overlay size, and not exceed 100 edge peers per super-peer for load reasons [74].

In the remainder of this chapter, super-peers may interact directly with their edge peers and with the super-peers they are connected to, while edge peers route all communication via their respective super-peer. The problem of selecting a clique of super-peers and assigning edge peers to them to the end of optimizing a delay-focused objective function is the SUPER-PEER SELECTION PROBLEM (SPSP) which the upcoming section will address.

4.4.1 A fully meshed super-peer topology

A super-peer topology can be constructed in a way in which the super-peer subgraph is complete. Thus, the super-peers form a clique. Due to the full mesh among the super-peers, this approach yields an overlay diameter of 3 hops independent of the overlay size. Also, when super-peers keep up connections to all other super-peers, a crashed or departed super-peer is immediately detected by all remaining super-peers due to the notification of a broken connection issued by the transport layer.

An example for a topology of this kind is shown in Figure 4.3. In the example, there are 5 super-peers, s_1 to s_5. A message sent by edge peer e_{13} is routed to its destination, edge peer e_4. After the first hop, the message reaches e_{13}'s super-peer s_4. From there, it travels across the super-peer subgraph on the link to s_1. Finally, s_1 delivers the message to its edge peer e_4.

There is an analogy between a family of problems from discrete facility location and the fully meshed super-peer topology construction problem. The next section examines this analogy for the purpose of super-peer topology creation. Subsequently, a distributed algorithm that creates and maintains a fully meshed super-peer topology in a self-organized fashion is presented.

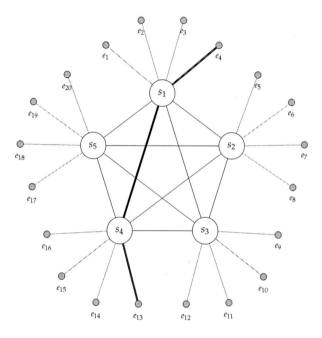

Figure 4.3: Example of a super-peer topology with fully meshed super-peers. In this example, a message is routed from edge peer e_{13} to edge peer e_4. The thickened lines indicate the path the message takes.

4.4.1.1 The Hub Location model

The construction of a fully meshed minimum-delay super-peer topology constitutes an optimization problem. When the number of desired super-peers, p, is known and a global view of the system is available, it may be cast as a special case of a HUB LOCATION problem [38, 183, 231]. Hub Location problems are NP-hard combinatorial optimization problems. All Hub Location problems have in common that a number of nodes, the so-called *hubs*, assume hierarchical superiority over common nodes, a property equivalent to the super-peer concept. A Hub Location model's solution determines what nodes become hubs and what hubs the remaining nodes are attached to, respectively, with the goal of minimizing total or average end-to-end transport costs in a HUB-AND-SPOKE network. [23]

Hub Location models differ in their objectives. For the purpose considered here, the P-HUB MEDIAN PROBLEM is closest to the super-peer topology construction problem. Like other Hub Location models, it is based on the notion of *flows* passing from origins via hubs to their destinations. There are various flavors of this model. The variant introduced here uses single allocation (every non-hub node is assigned to exactly one hub) and is uncapacitated (every hub can serve an unlimited number of nodes). The addition of capacity constraints will be discussed below after the presentation of the uncapacitated case.

A flow W_{ij} represents the total volume of items to be transported between its endpoints, origin i and destination j. The distance between any two adjacent nodes in V is expressed as d_{ij}. The topology is represented through a graph $G = (V, E)$ with $|V| = n$ vertices (nodes) $V = \{1, \ldots, n\}$. While both origins and destinations may be hubs themselves, the general assumption underlying the model is that flows travel in three hops: first from an origin at the edge of the graph to a hub (collection phase), then over a hub-hub connection which is relatively inexpensive in terms of unit transportation cost (transfer phase), and finally from the destination hub to the destination node which is again located at the edge of the graph (distribution phase). Transport costs per unit are given as χ for the first, α for the second and δ for the third hop. Hence, the transportation of a flow from origin u via hubs v and w to destination x incurs costs of $\chi \cdot d_{uv} + \alpha \cdot d_{vw} + \delta \cdot d_{wx}$ per unit. Origins and destinations cannot interact directly if neither is a hub: in this model, all flows are hub-mediated.

For every node $i \in V$, let O_i be the total flow originating at that node and D_i the total flow headed for that node. These quantities are defined as

---

[23]The term hub-and-spoke refers to the visual appearance of hub location settings from a bird's eye view as common peers are centered around hubs in a spoke-like way.

$$O_i = \sum_{j \in V} W_{ij} \tag{4.3}$$

$$D_i = \sum_{j \in V} W_{ji} \tag{4.4}$$

Furthermore, let the binary variable X_{ik} be set to 1 iff node i is assigned to node j and node j is a hub (hubs are assigned to themselves such that $X_{kk} = 1$ iff k is a hub) Let $\chi = 1$, $\alpha \in (0, 1)$ and $\delta = 1$. With these prerequisites, the *uncapacitated single-allocation p-hub median problem* can be formulated as the following quadratic integer program [37, 183]:

$$\min Z = \sum_{i \in V} \sum_{j \in V} W_{ij} \cdot \left(\sum_{k \in V} X_{ik} \cdot d_{ik} + \sum_{m \in V} X_{jm} \cdot d_{jm} + \alpha \cdot \sum_{k \in V} \sum_{m \in V} X_{ik} \cdot X_{jm} \cdot d_{km} \right) \tag{4.5}$$

$$\text{subject to} \qquad \sum_{k \in V} X_{ik} = 1 \qquad\qquad \forall\, i \in V \tag{4.6}$$

$$\sum_{i \in V} X_{ii} = p \tag{4.7}$$

$$(n - p + 1) \cdot X_{jj} \geq \sum_{i \in V} X_{ij} \qquad \forall\, j \in V \tag{4.8}$$

$$X_{ik} \in \{0, 1\} \qquad\qquad \forall\, i, k \in V \tag{4.9}$$

The objective function (4.5) accumulates the transportation cost for all node pairs which is to be minimized. Constraints (4.6) guarantee that every node is assigned to exactly one hub. Constraint (4.7) ensures that precisely p hubs are created. Constraints (4.8) see to it that any node to which at least one other node is assigned must be a hub. (4.8) can be replaced with an equivalent but less complex formulation [38]:

$$X_{ij} \leq X_{jj} \qquad\qquad \forall\, i, j \in V \tag{4.10}$$

In its original context, the model's solution was meant to minimize overall end-to-end transport costs in a hub-and-spoke network. In a P2P setting, when cost is equivalent to delay, this cost can be thought of as the cumulative end-to-end network delay between any two peers. Interpreting hubs as super-peers and common nodes as edge peers, the model discriminates super-peers from edge peers and determines the links between super-peers and edge peers, while the super-peers make up a complete subgraph. [24] Thus, the p-hub median model can provide both an exact solution and lower bounds to the super-peer topology construction problem. Due to the problem's NP-hardness

---

[24] In [74], the term *hubs* is used to designate super-peers.

preventing the computation of exact solutions for large instances in a reasonable period of time, relaxations of the model enable the provision of lower bounds such as those described in [184].

The p-hub median model introduced above can be simplified under two assumptions:

- There are no economies of scale in super-peer topologies. In hub-and-spoke networks set up for logistics, inter-hub connections benefit from using larger transport vehicles due to the accumulated transport volume, but there is no equivalent to such a discount in super-peer topologies. Thus, the unit cost of transportation remains constant ($\chi = \alpha = \delta = 1$).

- The traffic volume between all pairs of peers is identical (cf. Section 1.6).

The simplified formulation focuses on the problem of super-peer selection which remains NP-hard [231]. Given n peers, p peers are to be selected as hubs and the remaining peers assigned to them, where p is a constant provided a priori. Let x_{ik} be a binary variable denoting that peer i is assigned to peer k iff $x_{ik} = 1$. Iff $x_{kk} = 1$, peer k is chosen as a hub. The flow volume between peers $i \neq j$ equals one unit of flow, while the transportation cost of one unit of flow between peers i and j amounts to d_{ij}. The super-peer topology construction problem can now be reformulated to yield the following quadratic integer program:

$$\min Z = \sum_{i=1}^{n} \sum_{\substack{j=1 \\ j \neq i}}^{n} \sum_{k=1}^{n} \sum_{m=1}^{n} \left(d_{ik} + d_{km} + d_{mj} \right) \cdot x_{ik} \cdot x_{jm} \qquad (4.11)$$

$$\text{subject to} \qquad x_{ij} \leq x_{jj} \qquad \forall\, i, j \in V \qquad (4.12)$$

$$\sum_{j=1}^{n} x_{ij} = 1 \qquad \forall\, i \in V \qquad (4.13)$$

$$\sum_{j=1}^{n} x_{jj} = p \qquad (4.14)$$

$$x_{ij} \in \{0, 1\} \qquad \forall\, i, j \in V \qquad (4.15)$$

(4.11) yields the total all-pairs communication cost Z. The average communication delay Z' can be computed as $Z' = Z \cdot \frac{1}{n \cdot (n-1)}$. Constraints (4.12) ensure that edge peers are assigned to super-peers only. Constraints (4.13) enforce the assignment of edge peers to exactly one super-peer each. Due to constraint (4.14), there will be exactly p super-peers.

An upper bound for the number of assigned edge peers limits a super-peer's maximum load. A lower bound helps to avoid the unnecessary establishment of underloaded super-peers. Both bounds may be modelled by adding constraints to the above formulation:

$$\text{mincap} \cdot x_{jj} \leq \sum_{i=1}^{n} x_{ij} \leq \text{maxcap} \cdot x_{jj} \qquad\qquad \forall\, j = 1, \dots, n \qquad (4.16)$$

In symmetric networks where each link is used in both directions with equal volume, the objective function (4.11) can be reshaped. Let S_k be the set of peers assigned to super-peer k, including k itself, and C the set of super-peers. The latter set makes up the *core*, while links from edge peers to their super-peers are referred to as *spokes*. Now, Z is

$$Z = 2 \cdot (n-1) \cdot \underbrace{\sum_{i=1}^{n} \sum_{k=1}^{n} d_{ik} \cdot x_{ik}}_{\text{spoke connections}} + \underbrace{\sum_{k=1}^{n} \sum_{m=1}^{n} d_{km} \cdot x_{kk} \cdot x_{mm} \cdot |S_k| \cdot |S_m|}_{\text{intra-core connections}} \qquad (4.17)$$

This formulation bears the advantage of exhibiting the link weights. Spoke weights are multiplied with $2 \cdot (n-1)$, while intra-core links are weighted by a factor of $|S_k| \cdot |S_m|$. Each link is used in both directions, accounting for the factor 2. For the intra-core connections, this factor appears implicitly in the double sum. As with (4.11), dividing Z by $n \cdot (n-1)$ yields the average pairwise end-to-end delay.

While the integer program in (4.11)–(4.15) enables an exact solution to be found for small instances, several issues remain:

- The problem continues to be NP-hard. Due to this property, the size of realistic problem instances is likely to exceed the capabilities of IP solvers.

- The problem requires a global view to be solved.

- The number of super-peers, p, must be known in advance.

- Link delays d_{ij} are assumed to be constant.

- The super-peer subgraph is complete. In a connection-based setting (e. g. with TCP), every super-peer must maintain a connection to each of the remaining $p - 1$ super-peers, eventually leading to an excessive number of connections which is on the order of $O(p^2)$ in total. Section 4.4.1.5 will elaborate on this aspect.

These issues will be addressed by two distributed algorithms presented in Section 4.4.1.2 and Section 4.4.2.1, respectively. The first algorithm approximates an optimal solution for the desired topology type to the end of solving the first three issues shown above. The fourth issue, the matter of variable link delays, is dealt with through the incorporation of network coordinates that are continuously updated as the topology evolves. The second algorithm additionally solves the final issue by replacing direct intra-core links with multi-hop routes in a structured topology that interconnects the super-peers.

4.4.1.2 The Super-Peer Selection Algorithm (SPSA)

In a distributed setting with fluctuating peer numbers and communication delays, a distributed approach which can operate without a global view is desirable. To this end, this section presents the SUPER-PEER SELECTION ALGORITHM (SPSA), a distributed algorithm that creates and maintains a fully meshed super-peer topology with the goal of approximating minimum communication cost. It depends on the peers' local views only. SPSA can deal with network dynamics, including changes to the peer set and to the communications delays between the peers.

SPSA divides the SPSP into its two subproblems:

1. *Super-Peer Selection*: from the set of all peers, determine the subset of peers that makes up the set of super-peers [150].

2. *Edge Peer Association*: for every edge peer, determine the super-peer the particular edge peer should connect to.

SPSA is both delay- and capacity-oriented, basing its decisions upon super-peer load and peers' communication delays to other peers. In principle, the first subproblem is solved by having existing super-peers promote one of their edge peers to super-peer level when the need arises, and super-peers downgrading to edge peer level when they are underloaded. To solve the second subproblem, edge peers attach themselves to the super-peer which is considered closest in terms of network delay. With an extension to the selection metrics, SPSA can also include properties such as CPU load and peer capabilities.

To select super-peers, SPSA first needs to determine the optimal number of super-peers. This number depends on the preferred optimization criterion. There is a sizable number of criteria such as super-peer dispersion, fluctuation, load balance, and delay minimization. SPSA optimizes the number of connections (e. g. TCP) held by a super-peer and the average end-to-end communications delay. $|C| = \sqrt{n}$, where n is the number of peers, minimizes the number of connections a super-peer needs to keep up to other super-peers. This can be derived as follows. Let p be the number of peers that should be selected as super-peers. The edge peers are assumed to be distributed equally among the available super-peers. In the fully meshed case, every super-peer maintains one link to each of its edge peers and one link per remaining super-peer. Thus, a function $f(p)$ that returns the number of connections a super-peer needs to keep up can be defined as

$$f(p) = p - 1 + \frac{n-p}{p} \tag{4.18}$$

To the end of minimizing (4.18), the first-order condition $f'(p) = 0$ yields a minimum for $f(p)$ at $p = \sqrt{n}$. Every value for $|C|$ other than $\sqrt{n}$ will increase the number of links for the super-peer beyond $f(\sqrt{n}) = 2 \cdot (\sqrt{n} - 1)$: for smaller values the number of spokes increases, and for larger values the number of intra-core connections increases, in both cases outweighing the respective savings. When the edge peers are uniformly distributed among the super-peers, each of the $\sqrt{n}$ super-peers serves $\frac{n-\sqrt{n}}{\sqrt{n}} = \sqrt{n} - 1$ edge peers. Thus, every super-peer k is at the heart of a cluster consisting of $|S_k| = \sqrt{n}$ peers (including itself) and maintains links to the remaining $\sqrt{n} - 1$ super-peers, while edge peers maintain a link to their respective super-peer only. In this setting, every link in the topology will receive approximately the same weight assuming that every peer communicates with every other peer to an equal extent. In the unicast case, the spokes are used $2 \cdot (n-1)$ times each since every edge peer sends $(n-1)$ messages (one to every other peer) and receives $(n-1)$ messages (one from every other peer). The intra-core links are used $2 \cdot \sqrt{n} \cdot \sqrt{n} = 2 \cdot n$ times each as every super-peer receives $\sqrt{n} \cdot \sqrt{n}$ messages from each of the other super-peers and sends as many messages in the opposite direction: every peer in a super-peer-centered cluster consisting of $\sqrt{n}$ peers can reach $\sqrt{n}$ other peers via a single intra-core link, hence there are $\sqrt{n}^2 = n$ messages per direction.

Analysis of the broadcast case proceeds in a similar way. This case can be considered from the message complexity's or the experienced delay's point of view. In the message complexity case, a spoke's weight decreases from $2 \cdot (n-1)$ to n as a spoke is used once outbound for one broadcast message and $n-1$ times inbound for the incoming broadcast messages from other peers. The intra-core link weights drop from $2 \cdot n$ to $2 \cdot \sqrt{n}$ as a broadcast message from each of the $\sqrt{n}$ peers in a super-peer-centered cluster is sent only once via an intra-core link, i. e. there are $\sqrt{n}$ broadcast messages per direction. The weights in (4.17) can be adapted to reflect this modification. However, from a delay-focused point of view, the model can be left unchanged when (4.17) is interpreted to minimize the overall or average end-to-end delay, and bandwidth is assumed not to be a bottleneck. The expendability of model change exists because the 3-hop routing (spoke $\rightarrow$ intra-core link $\rightarrow$ spoke) works as before when the link weights are interpreted as counting the number of receivers that are addressed by messages which travel over the respective link. Thus, from a receiver's point of view, minimizing the overall or average end-to-end delay supports both the broadcast and the unicast case.

The optimal assignment of the edge peers to the super-peers remains an NP-hard problem and would require a global view to be solved exactly. Under SPSA, a heuristic approach is pursued: every edge peer attaches itself to the closest super-peer in terms of network delay. Based on this approach, the algorithm operates on a set of rules to improve the overlay's efficiency. All peers keep a list of the currently known super-peers which contains, for every super-peer, the super-peer's overlay ID, IP address, network coordinates, and a timestamp referring to the most recent message received from the particular super-peer. This *super-peer list* is maintained in a decentralized way, so the lists on two different peers can temporarily differ. Super-peers that detect a change notify their edge peers and broadcast the change to all other super-peers, which then in turn propagate the news to their attached edge peers. When an edge peer successfully connects to a super-peer, the super-peer sends the edge peer its current super-peer list. This way, the super-peer list is kept current on all peers.

To keep track of its edge peers, every super-peer also keeps a list containing references to its edge peers, its *edge peer list*. Every γ time units, edge peers connect to their closest super-peer unless they already are connected to it. With SPSA, a new peer joins the overlay as an edge peer unless it is the first peer, in which case it cannot contact any existing peer and thus appoints itself the first super-peer. The edge peer part of SPSA is shown in Algorithm 4.

Algorithm 4 SPSA, edge peer part

1	**every** γ **time units do:**
2	$\quad i = \text{closestSuperPeer}()$
3	$\quad$ **if** assignedSuperPeer $\neq i$ **then**
4	$\quad\quad$ connectTo(i)
5	$\quad\quad$ assignedSuperPeer $= i$
6	$\quad$ **end if**
7	**until**

With SPSA, the topology will automatically recover from peer outages. When a super-peer crashes or leaves the network, its edge peers will switch to the nearest remaining super-peer. When an edge peer crashes, its super-peer removes it from its list. Moreover, SPSA grants peers the choice to remain edge peers, e. g. in case they are unwilling to bear a super-peer's load or cannot be reached from the outside due to the presence of a firewall, by not responding to the offer of being promoted. Also, SPSA fosters cooperative behavior as super-peers can select the edge peer to be promoted. Thus, only edge peers considered trustworthy can become a super-peer.

Let k be an arbitrary super-peer in the overlay, and let E_k be the set of edge peers k serves, i. e. $E_k = S_k \setminus \{k\}$. k regularly checks the number of edge peers, $|E_k|$, it is serving, every $\gamma \in \mathbb{R}^+$ time units. If the number of k's edge peers is sufficiently high, k asserts that its current load exceeds its load threshold, and promotes one of its edge peers to super-peer level. Conversely, if k serves an insufficient number of edge peers, k considers its load too low, and downgrades to edge peer level. However, if the number of its edge peers remains within these bounds, k attempts to replace itself by looking for a better super-peer $j^* \in E_k$. j^* is determined using (4.20): [25]

$$G(E_k, C, j, k) = \left(\sum_{i \in C} d(p_k, p_i)\right) - \left(\sum_{i \in C} d(p_j, p_i)\right) + \left(\sum_{i \in E_k} d(p_k, p_i)\right) - \left(\sum_{i \in E_k} d(p_j, p_i)\right) \quad (4.19)$$

$$j^* = \arg\max_{i \in E_k} G(E_k, C, i, k) \quad (4.20)$$

For a super-peer k, $G(E_k, C, j, k)$ represents the gain of replacing itself with edge peer j, expressed as the total savings in cumulative communication delay. j^* is the edge peer that maximizes this gain. If such a super-peer candidate edge peer j^* is found with $G(E_k, C, j^*, k) > 0$ and it agrees to become a super-peer, j^* is promoted to super-peer level, and k downgrades to edge peer level. The remaining edge peers from E_k and k itself are now free to connect to j^* or to another super-peer.

In (4.19), all edges are equally important. As every spoke carries $2 \cdot (n-1)$ messages and every intra-core connection $2 \cdot n$ in unicast communications, this is a simplification but asymptotically correct as $\lim_{n \to \infty} \frac{2 \cdot n}{2 \cdot (n-1)} = 1$. For weights to be useful in the non-asymptotic case, n must be known exactly but this knowledge is available only with a global view of the network.

Algorithm 5 SPSA, super-peer part

---

1   **every** γ **time units do:**
2   **if** $|E_k| < \frac{1}{2} \cdot |C|$ and $|C| > 1$ **then**
3           $\text{role}_k \leftarrow$ edge peer
4   **else if** $|E_k| > 2 \cdot (|C| - 1)$ **then**
5           $j = \arg\max_{i \in E_k} G(E_k, C, i, k)$
6           $\text{role}_j \leftarrow$ super-peer
7   **else**
8           $j = \arg\max_{i \in E_k} G(E_k, C, i, k)$
9   **if** $G(E_k, C, j, k) > 0$ **then**
10   request j to become super-peer
11   if j accepts, downgrade to edge peer level
12   **end if**
13   **end if**
14 **until**

Since a number of $\sqrt{n}$ super-peers and $\sqrt{n} - 1$ edge peers per super-peer is the desired goal, SPSA needs to strive to keep this balance. Considering a super-peer k, downgrading to edge peer level if $|E_k| < \sqrt{n} - 1$ and at least one other super-peer exists ($|C| > 1$), and

---

[25]This approach assumes delays to be symmetric. As they will be estimated using network coordinates in practice, the symmetry is observed already by the estimation procedure.

promoting one of its edge peers to super-peer level if $|E_k| > \sqrt{n} - 1$ would be a natural rule to keep the number of super-peers close to $\sqrt{n}$. However, in the face of overlay dynamics, super-peers would constantly upgrade and downgrade as edge peers switch to other super-peers, perhaps for insignificant causes such as minor delay fluctuations. The situation improves when a degree of tolerance is introduced into the process. Let $\alpha \in \mathbb{R}^+$ designate the maximum tolerable deviance from the optimum number of edge peers before downgrading, while $\beta \in \mathbb{R}^+$ designates the maximum tolerable deviance before promotion. A super-peer k would downgrade only if $|E_k| < (1 - \alpha) \cdot (\sqrt{n} - 1)$, or otherwise promote (upgrade) an edge peer only if $|E_k| > (1 + \beta) \cdot (\sqrt{n} - 1)$. α and β need to be chosen carefully to leave both super-peers viable when an edge peer is promoted to super-peer level. Both the new and the existing super-peer must have sufficient numbers of edge peers not to downgrade immediately. Hence, under the assumption that edge peers will choose either super-peer with equal probability, the promotion bound must specify at least twice as many edge peers as the downgrade bound. The viability condition is therefore $\frac{1+\beta}{2} \geq 1 - \alpha$. Observing the domains of α and β, this can be transformed to $\alpha \geq \max\left(\frac{1-\beta}{2}, 0\right)$.

The overlay dynamics benefit from $\alpha < \beta$ and a minor change to the downgrade condition. With $\alpha = \frac{1}{2}$ and $\beta = 1$, splitting an overloaded super-peer's edge peer complement relieves it of $\sqrt{n} - 1$ edge peers, and the downgrade of two underloaded super-peers will yield $\sqrt{n}$ peers out of which one can become a new super-peer. This requires the downgrade condition to be modified to $|E_k| < \frac{1}{2} \cdot \sqrt{n}$ which is equivalent to $|S_k| \leq \frac{1}{2} \cdot \sqrt{n}$. The minimum number of edge peers that make a super-peer k consider promoting one of them to super-peer level is $|E_k| = 2 \cdot (\sqrt{n} - 1) + 1 = 2 \cdot \sqrt{n} - 1$, a condition which is equivalent to $|S_k| = 2 \cdot \sqrt{n}$ because in the former formulation, k needs to be added to the cluster while its presence is already incorporated in $|S_k|$. One of k's edge peers is selected for promotion to super-peer level, leaving a remainder of $2 \cdot (\sqrt{n} - 1)$ edge peers with k. Assuming uniform distribution over the super-peers, $\sqrt{n} - 1$ of these edge peers will stay with k while another $\sqrt{n} - 1$ edge peers will switch to the newly promoted super-peer. Thus, both k and the new super-peer will each serve the optimum number of edge peers, $\sqrt{n} - 1$.

On the contrary, a downgrading super-peer serves at most $\frac{1}{2} \cdot \sqrt{n} - 1$ edge peers. Once two super-peers with this number of edge peers downgrade, each will set its respective edge peers free, and both super-peers will become edge peers, hence there are $2 \cdot \frac{1}{2} \cdot \sqrt{n} = \sqrt{n}$ peers out of which one can become a new super-peer. At any time, there needs to be at least one super-peer in the overlay to which new peers and lingering edge peers can connect. As a consequence of this rule, a downgrade is possible only if there is at least one other super-peer around. This prevents a premature downgrade of a super-peer which has just founded the overlay.

Algorithm 5 shows the super-peer part of SPSA with $|C|$ as an estimate of $\sqrt{n}$. [26] Without a global view of the overlay, the explicit value of n (and thus $\sqrt{n}$) is unknown, but it can be estimated with the help of the super-peer list that every peer maintains. Provided that super-peers periodically disclose the number of edge peers they serve, this value can be stored inexpensively in a single field within the respective list entry. For a list S, let e_s be the number of edge peers served by super-peer $s \in S$ according to s's list entry. Then, $\hat{n}$, an estimate of n, can be computed by the list-keeping peer as

$$\hat{n} = \sum_{s \in S} (e_s + 1) = |S| + \sum_{s \in S} e_s \qquad (4.21)$$

Even if super-peers do not disclose the number of their associated edge peers, the overlay size can be estimated through $|C|$, the mere number of known super-peers, autonomously by every peer, where C is tracked by the super-peer list. [27] The key idea is that super-peers will, in a self-organized way, increase or reduce $|C|$ as necessary to provide a good estimate of $\sqrt{n}$, or equivalently, of $|C|^2$ to estimate n. It is based on the assumption that edge peers are evenly distributed over the super-peers, and super-peers communicate the appearance or loss of super-peers to the remainder of the overlay such that every peer is able to update its copy of the super-peer list. Let the estimation error $|n - \hat{n}|$ denote the difference between the actual number of peers in the overlay, n, and the current estimate, $\hat{n} = |C|^2$. If C is accurate, i.e. $|C| = \sqrt{n}$, nothing happens. The estimation error is zero as $n - |C|^2 = 0$. In that case, every super-peer will serve $\frac{n-\sqrt{n}}{\sqrt{n}} = \sqrt{n} - 1$ edge peers. The upcoming analysis will show that if $|C| \neq \sqrt{n}$, SPSA can rectify C in a way that lets $|n - \hat{n}|$ move towards zero. A positive difference $(n - \hat{n} > 0)$ will decrease and a negative difference $(n - \hat{n} < 0)$ will increase without manual intervention. For this analysis, the set C is assumed to be fixed and non-empty, but otherwise arbitrarily composed.

If C is too small $(|C| < \sqrt{n})$, there are $n - |C|$ edge peers in the overlay, leading to $\frac{n-|C|}{|C|} > \sqrt{n} - 1$ edge peers per super-peer. A super-peer x will promote one of its edge peers to super-peer status if $|E_x| > 2 \cdot (|C| - 1)$. Under the equal distribution assumption, $|E_x| = \frac{n-|C|}{|C|}$, so the promotion condition can be transformed:

$$|E_x| > 2 \cdot (|C| - 1) \Leftrightarrow \frac{n - |C|}{|C|} > 2 \cdot |C| - 2 \Leftrightarrow n - |C| > 2 \cdot |C|^2 - 2 \cdot |C| \Leftrightarrow n > 2 \cdot |C|^2 - |C|$$

$$(4.22)$$

The critical situation to consider is $n = 2 \cdot |C|^2 - |C|$, i.e. all super-peers are maximally loaded for the given $|C|$. This reflects the worst case: there is one peer short of triggering the promotion process. At this stage, the number of peers in the overlay is estimated as

---

[26] After every modification to the local super-peer list, the updating super-peer forwards the change to its edge peers and the remaining super-peers. This part is omitted in the listing.

[27] Moreover, super-peers can compute $|C|$ through the number of connections they maintain to other super-peers.

$\hat{n} = |C|^2$, hence the worst-case estimation error equals $|n - \hat{n}| = |C|^2 - |C|$. [28] Eventually, a new peer joins the overlay as an edge peer by connecting to super-peer x. Because of this, x's load exceeds its upper bound. Controlled by SPSA, x reacts to the situation by promoting one of its edge peers to super-peer level. Then, $|E_x|$ will decrease by one and $|C|$ will increase by one. Once the new edge peer joins x, the estimation error decreases when x promotes one of its edge peers to super-peer level: there will be $|C| + 1$ super-peers after the promotion, hence the estimate $\hat{n}$ increases to $\hat{n} = (|C| + 1)^2$. This leads to a diminished estimation error of $(2 \cdot |C|^2 - |C| + 1) - (|C| + 1)^2 = |C|^2 - 3 \cdot |C| < |C|^2 - |C|$. Thus, due to the adaptation of C, the estimation error for n decreases by $2 \cdot |C|$.

If C is too large ($|C| > \sqrt{n}$), there are $n - |C| < n - \sqrt{n}$ edge peers in the overlay, and a super-peer x eventually notices low load. Provided that $|C| > 1$, a super-peer x downgrades to edge peer level if $|E_x| < \frac{1}{2} \cdot |C|$. This condition can be transformed to

$$|E_x| < \frac{1}{2} \cdot |C| \Leftrightarrow \frac{n - |C|}{|C|} < \frac{1}{2} \cdot |C| \Leftrightarrow n < \frac{1}{2} \cdot |C|^2 + |C| \qquad (4.23)$$

The critical situation to consider now is $n = \frac{1}{2} \cdot |C|^2 + |C|$. x is at its minimum load threshold, and the overlay size is estimated as $\hat{n} = |C|^2$. Here, the estimation error reaches its worst-case level at $|n - \hat{n}| = \frac{1}{2} \cdot |C|^2 - |C|$. When one of x's edge peers leaves the overlay, x downgrades, eventually removing itself from C. Thus, $\hat{n}$ now amounts to $(|C| - 1)^2$ which lets the estimation error decrease as $\left|(\frac{1}{2} \cdot |C|^2 + |C| - 1) - (|C| - 1)^2\right| = \frac{1}{2} \cdot |C|^2 - 3 \cdot |C| + 2 < \frac{1}{2} \cdot |C|^2 - |C|$, which is true for $|C| > 1$. Hence, the estimation error drops by $\frac{1}{2} \cdot |C|^2 - |C| - \left(\frac{1}{2} \cdot |C|^2 - 3 \cdot |C| + 2\right) = 2 \cdot |C| - 2$. Since $|C| > 1$ holds in all cases of downgrades, the estimation error diminishes by a strictly positive margin.

The adaptation process could suffer from edge peers that are unevenly distributed over the super-peers, and there can be concurrent promotions of edge peers. Moreover, the tolerance induced by $\alpha = \frac{1}{2}$ and $\beta = 1$ may cause SPSA not to adapt C immediately. For a given overlay size $n \geq 1$, the number of super-peers $|C|$ that handles this size is therefore not unique: for every value of n, there is a range of adequate super-peer numbers. Only if the number of super-peers is outside the range will an individual super-peer consider promotion or downgrade, respectively. The minimum acceptable number of super-peers, h_{min}, is determined by means of the assumption that all super-peers serve the maximum possible load ($2 \cdot (\sqrt{n} - 1)$ edge peers per super-peer) which causes no super-peer to consider promoting one of its respective edge peers. Conversely, the maximum acceptable number of super-peers, h_{max}, is determined on the assumption that all super-peers serve the minimum possible number of edge peers ($\frac{1}{2} \cdot \sqrt{n}$) which causes no super-peer to consider a downgrade. When all variables are continuous and h_{min} is sought, the composition of the overlay is expressed through the equation

---

[28]The absolute value bars can be omitted since $|C| \geq 1 \rightarrow |C|^2 > |C| \vee |C|$.

$$h_{\min} + h_{\min} \cdot 2 \cdot (\sqrt{n} - 1) = n \tag{4.24}$$

which can then be solved for $h_{\min}$ as

$$h_{\min} = \frac{n}{2 \cdot \sqrt{n} - 1} \tag{4.25}$$

Similarly, for $h_{\max}$, the overlay composition is determined by the equation

$$h_{\max} + h_{\max} \cdot \frac{1}{2} \cdot \sqrt{n} = n \tag{4.26}$$

which is solved for $h_{\max}$ as

$$h_{\max} = \frac{n}{\frac{1}{2} \cdot \sqrt{n} + 1} \tag{4.27}$$

Equations (4.24)–(4.27) assume that $\sqrt{n}$ is continuous, hence fractions of single peers could be assigned to super-peers. Also, the fractions in (4.25) and (4.27) possibly yield continuous results. When these quantities are considered integer, (4.25) becomes

$$h_{\min}^{\text{integer}} = \left\lceil \frac{n}{2 \cdot \lfloor \sqrt{n} \rfloor - 1} \right\rceil \tag{4.28}$$

while (4.27) becomes

$$h_{\max}^{\text{integer}} = \left\lceil \frac{n}{1 + \lceil \frac{1}{2} \cdot \sqrt{n} \rceil} \right\rceil \tag{4.29}$$

SPSA's adaptation process relies on the presence of dynamics. If no new peer joins the system, changes its super-peer, replaces itself with another peer, or departs, the overlay remains unchanged. These dynamics, composed of individual peer actions and fluctuating link delays, can be interpreted as noise. Thus, the adaptation component of SPSA fulfills criteria of self-organizing systems as defined in Section 1.2 such as self-organized criticality and susceptibility to noise.

Evaluating $G(E_k, C, j, k)$ in (4.19) means measuring the communication cost of all links from j and k to all super-peers C and all edge peers E_k. Generally, this measurement may be achieved by sending a ping message across a link. Under the equal edge peer distribution assumption, each of the $O(\sqrt{n})$ super-peers serves $O(\sqrt{n})$ edge peers, and each of these super-peers needs to determine its delay to each of the remaining $O(\sqrt{n})$ super-peers, creating $O(\sqrt{n^3})$ messages in total. Furthermore, every super-peer needs to quantify the delay of each of its $O(\sqrt{n})$ links, resulting in $O(n)$ messages. In total, the message complexity is therefore on the order of $O(\sqrt{n^3}) = O(n^{1.5})$ ping messages per round. Due to the large number of messages, SPSA was hardly able to scale well if it had not been for network coordinates. The addition of network coordinates decreases the amount of delay estimation messages considerably, allowing SPSA to scale well until the maximum number of connections a super-peer is able to handle is reached. A discussion of this limit and its practical implications for SPSA is provided in Section 4.4.1.5.

SPSA uses a set of messages for its operation. The remainder of this section discusses the messages sent to accomplish the operations shown in Algorithm 4 and Algorithm 5. In the bootstrapping phase, a node x that wants to join the overlay as a peer first contacts an arbitrary peer y known to already participate in the overlay, and sends a QUERYSUPERPEER message to y. y responds with a list of all super-peers it knows, encapsulated in a SUPERPEERLIST message. x picks the closest super-peer z from the list and asks z for being accepted as one of its edge peers, sending a CONNECT message to z. y and z may be identical. Depending on its local state, z replies with either ACCEPT or REJECT. In the case of ACCEPT, x is now linked to z as one of its edge peers, and as such, x has been accepted as a participant in the overlay, while in the case of REJECT, x will locally mark z as unavailable, pick another super-peer from its list, and try again. When x later wants to disconnect from z, x sends a DISCONNECT message to z which requires no reply. Alternatively, if a connection between x and z exists (e. g. TCP), x may simply close the connection. z is notified of the closed connection and removes x from its edge peer list. An edge peer's life cycle is depicted in Figure 4.4.

A super-peer k may pick one of its edge peers, l, and promote it to super-peer level. In this case, it evaluates (4.20) to pick the most suitable of its edge peers, l, and appoints it super-peer by sending a NEWSUPERPEER message to l. [29] If l accepts the appointment, it replies with an ACCEPTSUPERPEER message. This procedure is depicted in Figure 4.5. Eventually, l broadcasts its presence by sending INSERTSUPERPEER messages to all super-peers.

Conversely, an underloaded super-peer k may find itself wishing to downgrade to edge peer level and distribute its currently supported set of edge peers to other super-peers. This situation is depicted in Figure 4.6. A similar situation may arise if k determines one of its edge peers, l, to be a better super-peer than itself. In the latter case, k sends a RECONNECT message to all of its edge peers excluding l, asking them to switch to l voluntarily, and waits a pre-defined time span, designated the *Pre-Reject Phase*, while in the former case, a similar message is sent without containing a redirection to a particular super-peer. Both cases converge at this point. k now sends REJECT messages to each of its remaining edge peers, disconnecting them. k also sends REMOVESUPERPEER messages to all super-peers which in turn may forward this information to their respective edge

---

[29](4.20) serves a dual purpose as it can be used for both replacement and promotion. In both cases, (4.20) is computed to find the particular edge peer that maximizes the gain. The difference lies in the fact that replacement occurs only if the gain is positive, while a promotion occurs in any case. With promotion, the first and third summand in (4.19) are expendable as they represent constants if the reference super-peer is fixed, and only a rank ordering of the edge peers according to the gain is required to determine the edge peer most suitable for being promoted.

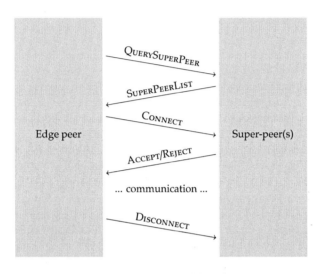

Figure 4.4: Edge peer life cycle

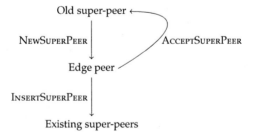

Figure 4.5: Super-peer reorganization phase: new super-peer

peers.

A peer changes its super-peer by sending a CONNECT message to the new super-peer and, in case it is accepted, a DISCONNECT message to the old super-peer. Super-peers keep track of super-peer memberships and provide common peers with lists of super-peers, particularly when they issue a REJECT message to a prospective edge peer. The predominant amount of messages is expected to be generated by the insertion and degradation of super-peers since this information needs to be forwarded to all peers, while all other messages are exchanged between one edge peer and its super-peer only.

In addition to keepalive mechanisms maintained by transport layer protocols, an edge peer may periodically want to send *heartbeat* messages to its super-peer to signal its presence [240]. A super-peer then sets up a timer for the edge peer. The timer is reset upon reception of a heartbeat message from the edge peer, and its timeout interval depends on the delay to the edge peer which can be estimated inexpensively using network coordinates. Edge peers for which the heartbeat timeout is triggered are considered dead and will be removed from the edge peer set. A heartbeat message may carry edge peer state information such as its current network coordinates or a flag indicating the willingness to act as a super-peer.

4.4.1.3 Evaluation

Event-oriented simulations based on the delay between hosts as the communication cost for the edges in the overlay were performed using NetSim. Each simulation run lasted for $2,500,000$ time units, where 1 time unit corresponded to 1 ms of simulated time.

The simulation covered major aspects of self-organizing behavior as edge peer connections to super-peers were established, rejected, and dissolved. Peers were restricted to their local view of the overlay and equipped with a possibly outdated super-peer list. The actual network coordinates exchange was streamlined in the sense that edge peers received super-peers' coordinates via their assigned super-peer, while super-peers knew all remaining super-peers' coordinates. Additionally, super-peers knew their attached edge peers' coordinates. In practice, this may be achieved by having every peer piggyback its coordinates on outbound messages.

All peers joined the network at the same time. One peer was randomly chosen as the first super-peer. Each peer had a reorganization cycle every $\gamma = 4,000 \pm 20$ time units. The small variation was introduced to prevent all peers from performing their reorganization cycles concurrently. In the reorganization cycle, an edge peer would change its super-peer when appropriate, while super-peers would either stay put or perform one of SPSA's reorganization steps specified in Section 4.4.1.2. With Vivaldi, peers sent requests for distance estimation to other peers every $2,000$ time units, routed to random peers via the super-peers, which then established their pairwise force using a three-way handshake. When routing involved an intermediate hop between two super-peers, this hop would enable the transmitting super-peer to communicate its coordinates to the receiving super-peer, ensuring the dissemination of super-peer coordinates. With GNP*, static coordinates were computed at the experiment's start and spread to other peers using a piggybacking strategy. In all contexts in which randomness was involved, values shown are averages over 30 runs.

Simulation results were expected to be influenced by two error sources in particular. The first source is the error introduced by network coordinates which splits itself again into an embedding error stemming primarily from violations of the triangle inequality [153, 244] and a gap between the optimum and the achieved solution for heuristical approaches to computing such coordinates. The second error source, introduced by SPSA, is the gap between the optimum and the proposed super-peer selection.

While the experiments focused on SPSA's effects in a static environment, churn was taken into account implicitly: the dynamics present with SPSA also cover churn-like behavior. When the connection to an edge peer is lost, a super-peer removes it from its edge peer list. Unless the edge peer connects to a different super-peer, the edge peer is considered gone or lost. Likewise, when a super-peer downgrades or an edge peer is promoted, the respective peer dissolves its connections to other peers in the overlay for a brief period of time to perform the role change. In this period, the peer is considered gone, and the topology adapts to the loss. Later, when such a peer returns, the topology incorporates the peer in a different role and/or at a different position. This way, the frequent dynamics of edge peers switching super-peers, downgrades and promotions cover the churn phenomenon; peers that have truly crashed are considered gone, and since the mechanism is stateless in this respect, no record is kept of the gone peer. For these reasons, ordinary overlay dynamics match churn with SPSA.

4.4.1.3.1 Lower bounds

Table 4.2 contains lower bounds for the Hub Location problem. The *All-Pairs Shortest Path* (APSP) lower bound gives the average delay between peer pairs when routing over shortest paths only. Column *LB1* holds the lower bound defined in [184], except for Meridian which proved too large to handle. The numbers in Table 4.2 reflect the average end-to-end message delay (cost).

In the columns *Best* and *Excess* in Table 4.2, the best solution found by a global view heuristic [232] is compared to these bounds. Its global view enables the heuristic to

Network	Size	APSP	LB1	Direct	Best	Excess	Random
01-2005	127	153 ms	156 ms	251 ms	182 ms	18.9 %	56.0 %
02-2005	321	154 ms	158 ms	204 ms	181 ms	17.3 %	28.0 %
03-2005	324	164 ms	168 ms	222 ms	198 ms	20.5 %	29.5 %
04-2005	70	137 ms	143 ms	165 ms	153 ms	11.6 %	22.9 %
05-2005	374	124 ms	128 ms	209 ms	184 ms	48.3 %	30.7 %
06-2005	365	137 ms	141 ms	225 ms	166 ms	21.0 %	33.8 %
07-2005	380	173 ms	176 ms	270 ms	215 ms	24.6 %	30.7 %
08-2005	402	171 ms	175 ms	247 ms	192 ms	12.0 %	31.2 %
09-2005	419	132 ms	135 ms	238 ms	188 ms	42.1 %	29.0 %
10-2005	414	166 ms	169 ms	271 ms	192 ms	16.1 %	37.7 %
11-2005	407	143 ms	146 ms	211 ms	169 ms	17.6 %	33.0 %
12-2005	414	119 ms	122 ms	388 ms	167 ms	39.9 %	47.7 %
King	1,740	99 ms	104 ms	184 ms	176 ms	77.4 %	29.0 %
Meridian	2,500	13 ms	n/a	80 ms	47 ms	246.7 %	87.5 %

Table 4.2: Lower bounds for the considered networks. From left to right: Network name, size in number of nodes, All-Pairs-Shortest-Path lower bound, lower bound LB1, direct connection, best known solution found by a global view heuristic, its excess above the APSP lower bound, and the excess of unoptimized random configurations over the best known solution

address the problem of optimally assigning the edge peers to the selected super-peers. Its performance was evaluated on a large number of networks, and it has found near-optimum solutions in cases where the optimum was known. It is for this reason that these best known solutions are likely to be very close to the optima of the networks considered here.

A comparison of the best known solutions to a direct connection topology (column *Direct* in Table 4.2) yields a noteworthy result. In such a topology, all peers are directly connected to every other peer, producing a complete graph. For all considered networks, a somewhat counterintuitive finding was that this topology proved inferior to the best known super-peer topology. This effect occurs because of the high amount of triangle inequality violations observable in the networks.

The comparison of the best known solutions to unoptimized networks quantifies the benefit of optimization. The column *Random* in Table 4.2 gives the excess of an average random configuration's cost over the best known solution's cost. In unoptimized networks, super-peers were picked randomly but edge peers had been assigned to their closest super-peer, respectively.

4.4.1.3.2 Outcome

First, a flawless embedding was assumed, i. e. each peer knew its delay to every other peer without any embedding error. This assumption removed the error introduced by network coordinates, leaving the heuristic's error as the total error. In practice, this means measuring the weights of all $O(n^2)$ edges for a complete snapshot of the pairwise network delay, or sending $O(\sqrt{n^3})$ messages in each round in the super-peer overlay. Thus, results obtained using flawless embedding are not representative of a real-world application. Rather, they convey information on the quality of SPSA's work compared to the best known solution given impeccable knowledge. In Table 4.3, the column *Flawless* contains the obtained results while the column *Direct* shows the excess of the direct connection topology over SPSA's solution. With flawless embeddings, SPSA proved superior to direct-connection and random topologies for all networks.

As with the lower bounds discussed in Section 4.4.1.3.1 and shown in Table 4.2, the super-peer topology may provide shorter paths on average than a direct-connection topology, although this is not always the case. With respect to the effectiveness of network co-ordinates, the gap between a flawless embedding's performance (i. e. network coordi-nates mechanisms generate no error) and the outcome delivered by the estimation-based mechanisms suggest the impact of triangle inequality violations hampering the network coordinates-based distance estimation. However, a flawless embedding represents a theoretical possibility only as a prohibitively costly full probing of the network would be required. On the other hand, since the topology created by SPSA is able to forward messages along different paths than the network layer routing policy specifies, triangle inequality violations can be circumvented through overlay routing. This is why the direct connection topology fares worse than the overlay maintained by SPSA. In the super-peer topology, heightened pairwise delay present due to triangle inequality violations is al-leviated by selecting different paths connecting the ends in the overlay. Additionally, Table 4.3 conveys SPSA's performance results using Vivaldi and GNP*.[30] SPSA using GNP* required little time to find suitable topologies. After 40 s to 60 s, equivalent to ap-proximately 10 to 15 reorganization cycles of SPSA, the total communication cost arrived at the values shown. In essence, SPSA with GNP* quickly reached its optimization goal, creating topologies that are substantially better than unoptimized networks.

Using Vivaldi, peers updated their coordinates and estimated distances to remote peers while SPSA was working. The Vivaldi implementation regularly initiated Vivaldi cycles to update the peers' coordinates. For the sake of comparability, only values from a point in time where Vivaldi and SPSA had already converged were used. The time to topology convergence is not directly comparable to GNP* since Vivaldi needs a certain number of

---

[30] A presentation of these network coordinates-related results is also contained in a different format in Table 4.4.

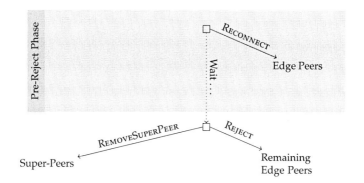

Figure 4.6: Super-peer reorganization phase: downgrade

Network	Size	Flawless Excess	Flawless Random	Flawless Direct	GNP* Excess	GNP* Random	Vivaldi Excess	Vivaldi Random
01-2005	127	9.6 %	42.3 %	26.1 %	55.6 %	10.4 %	50.5 %	26.3 %
02-2005	321	5.4 %	21.4 %	7.0 %	48.9 %	7.6 %	31.5 %	39.0 %
03-2005	324	6.4 %	20.8 %	5.3 %	52.7 %	6.8 %	29.2 %	41.4 %
04-2005	70	4.5 %	16.6 %	3.2 %	34.8 %	3.7 %	20.3 %	30.1 %
05-2005	374	8.5 %	19.5 %	4.3 %	47.8 %	19.0 %	31.0 %	48.5 %
06-2005	365	7.8 %	23.3 %	25.5 %	70.3 %	13.4 %	48.9 %	59.1 %
07-2005	380	11.6 %	16.2 %	12.4 %	42.0 %	20.9 %	45.5 %	32.2 %
08-2005	402	5.9 %	23.9 %	21.5 %	44.4 %	23.6 %	46.2 %	51.7 %
09-2005	419	5.9 %	21.8 %	19.3 %	49.7 %	16.0 %	49.1 %	48.7 %
10-2005	414	8.4 %	26.1 %	29.6 %	69.0 %	13.1 %	64.0 %	55.2 %
11-2005	407	5.7 %	25.8 %	18.4 %	60.6 %	14.3 %	45.6 %	61.6 %
12-2005	414	16.5 %	25.9 %	100.1 %	158.8 %	9.9 %	136.6 %	53.7 %
King	1,740	3.6 %	24.5 %	0.8 %	38.1 %	21.4 %	37.9 %	54.6 %
Meridian	2,500	4.6 %	79.3 %	64.6 %	174.1 %	22.4 %	137.4 %	54.5 %

Table 4.3: Excess of SPSA's solution over the best known solution and excess of random configurations and direct connection topologies over SPSA's solutions

cycles to converge. Once stable coordinates are reached, SPSA also converged. While GNP* or flawless embeddings led SPSA to optimization times of less than a minute, SPSA with Vivaldi took approximately 5 minutes of simulated time to converge.

4.4.1.4 Geographic coordinates

To quantify the loss of embedding accuracy and the associated impact on topology quality when only geographic distances are used to establish a proximity-sorted order of peers, experiments were conducted to compare GNP*, Vivaldi, geographic coordinates, and randomly assigned coordinates by means of simulation using NetSim. NetSim has successfully handled the largest networks for which delay information was publicly available including the 2,500-node Meridian network, but IP addresses and therefore geographical coordinates were unavailable for those networks' nodes. Hence, this investigation was conducted exclusively with PlanetLab network data.

To deploy geographical coordinates, a source for them is required. There are three options. A first way to deal with the issue is to require every peer to know its coordinates, be able to look them up on its own, or acquire them by technical equipment. A second option is to dynamically extract geographical information from IP addresses. A third alternative is to consult a third-party service that maps the IP address space to the space of geographical coordinates.

Three approaches that implement the second option are introduced in [186] under the package name IP2Geo. The first technique, GeoTrack, attempts to retrieve location information from symbolic (DNS) names of routers, while GeoPing performs network delay measurements to infer geographic locations. GeoCluster links known IP-to-location mappings with Border Gateway Protocol (BGP) prefix information to improve the mappings. As documented in [186], GeoTrack has a high median error, while GeoPing is useful for coarse estimates only. GeoCluster requires access to an IP-to-location mapping and is therefore not operating in an autonomous way, effectively linking its utility to the quality of the consulted mapping.

For the experiments related to the estimation quality of geographical coordinates, the third option was chosen due to the large error of IP2Geo's methods and the exceedingly strong assumption of peers knowing their own geographical coordinates. Several deployed IP-to-geocoordinates mapping services exist. The NetGeo project to which [179] had resorted was not taken into consideration as a source because active maintenance of its data ceased years ago. Apart from being up-to-date, the database was required to be a stable release (no beta status) which was freely available to the general public with no restrictions on the maximum number of queries. Additional requirements included the coverage of the full IP address space, a known maintainer who supervised the quality

Network	Size	Geography	Vivaldi	GNP*	Random
01-2005	127	1.61	1.37	1.42	3.40
02-2005	321	1.50	1.25	1.41	2.94
03-2005	324	1.61	1.21	1.44	3.13
04-2005	70	2.05	1.15	1.29	2.55
05-2005	374	1.50	1.21	1.36	2.83
06-2005	365	1.89	1.38	1.58	3.08
07-2005	380	1.41	1.30	1.27	3.03
08-2005	402	1.64	1.38	1.36	3.29
09-2005	419	1.65	1.41	1.41	3.09
10-2005	414	2.66	1.51	1.56	3.88
11-2005	407	1.81	1.38	1.52	3.09
12-2005	414	2.67	2.03	2.22	6.23

Table 4.4: Objective function values for all 12 tested networks, normalized to the flawless outcome

of coordinates information, and no need for extra infrastructure to be deployed. All requirements were fulfilled only by GeoLite City from MaxMind LLC [159]. Using GeoLite City, longitude and latitude information were assigned to known PlanetLab node IP addresses, allowing geographical coordinates to provide a distance measure.

As the large King and Meridian matrices were not involved this time, it was sufficient to limit each simulation run to $900,000$ time units where one time unit again corresponded to one millisecond of simulated real time. Apart from this modification, the same values as in Section 4.4.1.3 were chosen for the simulation parameters.

Table 4.4 contains the terminal objective function values representing total all-pairs communication cost for all 12 tested PlanetLab networks, normalized to the outcome attained with a flawless embedding. The table compares, for every network, the performance of SPSA using various kinds of coordinates mechanisms. It also provides the objective function value for a random assignment of super-peers as a benchmark.

With all tested mechanisms, convergence set in before the simulated period of time had elapsed. In line with the findings captured by Table 4.3, Vivaldi fares best in most experiments but needs some time to establish reasonably accurate coordinates. GNP* quickly creates stable coordinates and performs only marginally worse than Vivaldi in these experiments.

In contrast, geographical coordinates led to the creation of substantially worse topologies. The reason is twofold. First, individual link capacity, technology and utilization are not incorporated into distance estimation [179]. Moreover, an estimate's quality also depends on the underlying database. In the case of GeoLite City, Chinese PlanetLab nodes were all mapped to a single location in Beijing, China. This lack of resolution distorts distance estimates.

The results show that delay estimation using geographical coordinates is inferior to embedding approaches such as Vivaldi and GNP*. Moreover, one needs to acquire geographical coordinates which is a nontrivial issue.

4.4.1.5 Discussion

SPSA has successfully reduced the communication cost in comparison to unoptimized topologies. The participating peers benefitted from this as their average communication delays to other peers declined. With a flawless embedding, the gap to the best known solution remained small. While network coordinates introduce an additional error, increasing the excess over the best known solution, they are indispensable in realistic large-scale scenarios. On average, topologies created using Vivaldi had slightly lower delays than those created using GNP*.

A comparison of the super-peer topologies created by SPSA to other topologies exhibits the advantages of the proposed approach. Using the shortest paths for every peer pair gives the best communication cost (the APSP column in Table 4.2), but also brings the necessity of determining all these routes and storing the next respective hop for every destination at every peer. The excessive number of maintained links and the increased communication cost caused by triangle inequality violations are serious downsides of a direct connection topology.

In the NetSim environment, SPSA has shown to converge quickly while setting up topologies substantially better than random solutions. With GNP*, SPSA arrived at a stable state in less than a minute, with Vivaldi in less than 5 minutes of simulated time. Moreover, SPSA can automatically fix overlay partitions and adapt the number of super-peers to the overlay size. However, there is a scalability issue. In a super-peer topology with a fully meshed super-peer core and n peers in total, every super-peer maintains one link per remaining super-peer and one link to each of its edge peers. Assuming an even distribution of the edge peers over the super-peers, the optimal number of super-peers equals $\sqrt{n}$, yielding $2 \cdot (\sqrt{n} - 1) \in O(\sqrt{n})$ connections per super-peer. While such a network bears significant advantages including a small diameter of only 3 hops, the load super-peers need to handle in this setting may become prohibitively high in large networks. When the maximum number of connections a super-peer is able to handle is d, solving $2 \cdot (\sqrt{n} - 1) = d$ for n yields $(\frac{d}{2} + 1)^2$, i.e. the function $f(d) = (\frac{d}{2} + 1)^2 \in O(d^2)$ gives the maximum total number of peers in the overlay under the constraint that super-peers cannot handle more than d connections each. For

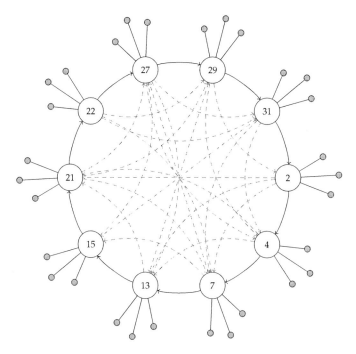

Figure 4.7: Example super-peer topology with the super-peers interconnected by a Chord ring

instance, if $d = 300$, $f(d) = 22,801$, i.e. a super-peer's capacity needs to be extended considerably beyond $d = 300$ in order to enable networks with millions of peers. In the case of half a million peers ($n = 5 \cdot 10^5$), a super-peer would need to be able to keep up $2 \cdot (\sqrt{5 \cdot 10^5} - 1) = 1,412.2$ connections, a requirement beyond the capabilities of today's desktop computers. This is a scalability issue. To solve it, the super-peer clique can be replaced with a Chord ring that interconnects the super-peers, and the maximum number of edge peers per super-peer can then be linked logarithmically to the ring size. The next section introduces this approach.

4.4.2 A Chord-based super-peer topology

As an improvement in terms of scalability over the fully meshed super-peer topology, a topology in which the super-peers are interconnected with a Chord ring replaces the direct intra-core connections with multi-hop routes passing through the ring. Figure 4.7 depicts an example of this topology type. All members of the Chord ring are super-peers and vice versa. When a super-peer downgrades, it immediately leaves the Chord ring. Conversely, when an edge peer is promoted to super-peer level, it joins the Chord ring. As with SPSA, a super-peer list is maintained by all peers, and edge peers connect to their closest super-peers. In contrast to the fully meshed super-peer subgraph established by SPSA, the use of a Chord ring vastly reduces the number of links to other super-peers from $O(\sqrt{n})$ to $O(\log n)$ per super-peer. The average path length, given an intact Chord ring, rises from $O(1)$ to $O(\log n)$ hops in the average case. The network diameter is no longer constant but grows to $\log_2 n$ in an intact ring, and to $n-1$ if only the successor ring is available. Also, Chord in its original form has no sense of locality. There is no proximity awareness in overlay construction or routing [43]. The situation can be improved by replacing a super-peer topology's fully meshed core with a Chord ring, linking the benefits of super-peers with the advantages of Chord. A distributed mechanism can manage an overlay of this type and provide both proximity awareness and self-stabilization.

Unlike the fully meshed super-peer topology, super-peers no longer maintain direct links to all other super-peers. This creates a necessity for periodic or event-driven updates. Two mechanisms to solve this problem are presented in Section 4.4.2.2. With these mechanisms, updates are propagated both among the super-peers and by the super-peers to their edge peers. Such updates may include the most recent edition of information that changes over time, such as a super-peer's network coordinates. While updated local network coordinates are also disseminated with dynamic network coordinates mechanisms such as Vivaldi, the propagation of updates to peers currently not involved in Vivaldi cycles creates a more accurate representation of all super-peers' current network coordinates.

While Chord itself is known to scale adequately with rising numbers of peers and recovers well from individual peer outages, it has the drawback that every ring member needs to be reachable from the outside to accept incoming messages from fingers pointing to it, and from new peers joining the ring. This issue is solved by the introduction of super-peers. Only super-peers need to be reachable from the outside for the overlay to work. Since edge peers initiate connections to their respective super-peers, firewalls are circumvented. Super-peers can fulfill a proxy function for their edge peers in relaying messages to them. As in the Hub Location model, edge peers still connect to one super-peer each, creating a star-shaped topology within each cluster of edge peers managed by a super-peer. It can be shown that this setup generates less traffic than interconnecting the edge peers with structured topologies or full meshes [248].

Beyond addressing the firewall issue, the proposed topology type offers the following benefits to P2P Desktop Grids with n peers: [31]

- There is an efficient way to implement a broadcast mechanism in Chord [76, 163] and a modification that adapts this mechanism to the two-tier structure imposed by the presence of super-peers. With both mechanisms, for every broadcast instance, super-peers forward only $O(\log n)$ messages to other super-peers instead of $O(\sqrt{n})$ as in the fully meshed case.

- A variant of the broadcast mechanism enables a constrained broadcast that is intended to reach a portion of the peers only. This is particularly useful for job initiators that do not wish to receive a wave of replies from an overwhelmingly large number of peers after having broadcast a request for workers.

- In addition to broadcast, there is also an efficient way to perform multicast. Using original Chord message forwarding, all multicast destinations reached via the same finger will result in only one message sent over this finger, limiting the number of messages sent per super-peer to a maximum of $O(\log n)$ for a multicast message.

- Super-peers need to keep up only $O(\log n)$ connections to other super-peers compared to $O(\sqrt{n})$ in the case of a super-peer clique.

- There is locality: edge peers can connect to the closest super-peer in terms of network delay, enabling topology awareness. Thus, fewer messages are transmitted over long-haul connections [93].

- Super-peers may multiplex messages sent from several of their edge peers to the same destination within a short time window, reducing network load by removing overhead. This is particularly useful when edge peers reply to a remote peer's request for workers.

- On average, churn triggers less reorganization effort in a super-peer topology than in a flat structured topology [32]. If an edge peer leaves the overlay, its super-peer simply needs to close the connection while in pure Chord, all peers with fingers pointing to a departed peer need to update their finger tables.

- Moving peers from the Chord ring to edge peer positions outside the ring can reduce the average path length compared to original Chord [93, 170].

- Since overlay routing is accomplished by forwarding messages through the Chord ring, all improvements to Chord routing also apply to the Chord core of this super-peer topology type.

- Chord may be replaced by any other structured topology with $O(\log n)$ connections per peer and $O(\log n)$ average path length, such as Pastry, without endangering

---

[31]This list includes general benefits stemming from the inclusion of super-peer structures and the Chord ring.

the key properties presented for the super-peer topology.

- With efficient broadcast available, a super-peer list can be kept current on every peer. This list enables various advantages such as being able to estimate the Chord ring size at virtually zero cost using the list's length. Additional advantages are discussed in Section 4.4.2.3.

The following section elaborates on an algorithm which builds a topology of the desired type.

4.4.2.1 Super-peer selection with Chord: The ChordSPSA algorithm

This section describes an extension to SPSA that handles a dynamic Chord core. This extended variant is denoted CHORDSPSA. Like SPSA, ChordSPSA relieves overloaded super-peers by promoting edge peers to super-peer level, assigns edge peers to their closest super-peers in terms of network delay, and downgrades underloaded super-peers to edge peer level.

With ChordSPSA, super-peers become part of the Chord ring, while super-peers falling back to edge peer level instantly leave the Chord ring. Hence, the set of super-peers matches the set of Chord ring members. Messages sent by an edge peer for another edge peer enter the Chord ring at the sender's super-peer, are routed through the ring, and exit it at the receiver's super-peer. ChordSPSA uses a subset of SPSA's messages plus messages to transport the Chord overlay maintenance signals described in [219]. As with SPSA, every peer periodically enters a reorganization phase. During this phase, a peer decides whether to change its state depending on its role (edge peer or super-peer). Besides the structural difference, another distinction to SPSA lies in the way the optimum number of super-peers is found.

With a Chord ring interconnecting the super-peers, an analytical approach to minimizing the number of a super-peer's connections, as performed on the basis of the fully meshed model with SPSA before, does not produce useful results. This can be shown as follows. Let

$$f(p) = \log_2 p + \frac{n-p}{p} \tag{4.30}$$

be the function that gives the number of connections a super-peer needs to keep up, given $n > 0$ the total number of peers in the overlay and $p > 0$ the sought optimum number of super-peers that minimizes an individual super-peer's connection count. As with SPSA, edge peers are assumed to distribute themselves evenly over the super-peers.

From (4.30), one computes the derivative,

$$f'(p) = \frac{1}{\ln 2} \cdot \frac{1}{p} - \frac{n}{p^2} \tag{4.31}$$

With (4.31), the first-order condition is

$$f'(p) = 0$$

$$\Leftrightarrow \qquad p^2 - n \cdot p \cdot \ln 2 = 0$$

$$\Leftrightarrow \qquad p_{1,2} = \frac{n \cdot \ln 2}{2} \pm \sqrt{\left(\frac{-n \cdot \ln 2}{2}\right)^2} \tag{4.32}$$

The first outcome, $p_1 = 0$, does not constitute a valid solution as (4.30) is undefined for $p = 0$. Besides, this outcome would imply no super-peers to be present. The second result, $p_2 = n \cdot \ln 2$, is valid but of little use as it would involve $O(n)$ super-peers. In this case, for any $n > 0$, approximately 69.3 % of all peers in the overlay became super-peers, more than twice the number of edge peers. An exemplary scenario with $n = 5,000$ peers in the overlay illustrates the problem. There, (4.32) yields $p = n \cdot \ln 2 = 3,465.7 \approx 3,466$ super-peers and $n - p \approx 1,534$ edge peers. Thus, the mechanism that estimates the optimum number of super-peers based on minimizing the number of connections as derived in Section 4.4.1.2 is not applicable to the Chord-backed super-peer topology.

To remedy this issue, a different solution to the super-peer selection problem with Chord-connected super-peers is proposed. The proposal is still based on super-peer capacities but no longer related to a Hub Location model. Let n be the total number of peers in the topology and p the optimal number of super-peers to populate the Chord ring. ChordSPSA operates on the basis of super-peers having $f = \log_2 p$ distinct finger connections to other super-peers. The number of edge peers a super-peer can handle depends logarithmically on the size of the super-peer core, no longer polynomially as with SPSA. Hence, a super-peer has $O(\log p)$ connections with ChordSPSA, in contrast to $O(\sqrt{n})$ as with SPSA.

Given a maximum number $m > 0, m \in \mathbb{R}$ of edge peers a super-peer is supposed to handle per distinct finger, (4.33) exhibits the composition of the overlay:

$$p \cdot f \cdot m + p = n \tag{4.33}$$

ChordSPSA numerically solves (4.33) for p in a distributed way. Let g be the number of edge peers currently managed by a particular super-peer. That super-peer is able to handle as many edge peers as its limit, $f \cdot m$, permits. If the super-peer in its reorganization phase finds that $g > f \cdot m$ holds, it promotes one of its edge peers to super-peer level such that a portion of its edge peers will relocate to the new super-peer. That way, the number of super-peers grows as long as unserved edge peers require more super-peers. The growth stops once every edge peer is under management by a super-peer, i. e. the minimum stable number of super-peers is reached when every super-peer serves the maximum number of edge peers. This reflects the optimal situation as described by (4.33). A super-peer's edge peer set grows merely logarithmically with the ring size p as $f \cdot m \in O(\log p)$ compared to $O(\sqrt{n})$ in the fully meshed case. This is seen better when (4.33) is transformed to

$$\frac{n-p}{p} = m \cdot \log_2 p \qquad (4.34)$$

where $\frac{n-p}{p}$ represents the number of edge peers a super-peer serves under the uniform distribution assumption. The right side of (4.34) grows logarithmically with p. The logarithmic growth is slow enough to support all practically relevant overlay sizes with reasonable numbers of edge peers per super-peer. Conversely, $\frac{p}{n}$, the fraction of super-peers per peer, is found with (4.33) to be

$$\frac{p}{n} = \frac{1}{1 + m \cdot \log_2 p} \qquad (4.35)$$

Asymptotically, (4.35) converges to zero for $p \rightarrow \infty$.

Table 4.5 contains the values of p according to (4.33) for selected combinations of m and n, approximated with the Newton-Raphson algorithm and rounded to the closest integer value. [32] The table shows the graceful growth of the super-peer set in relation to the overlay size. For instance, in a 100-peer overlay and $m = 1$, 19 % of the peers are super-peers, while in a 10,000,000-peer overlay, the super-peer fraction declines to approximately 5 %. Moreover, the table shows the impact of m on the number of super-peers which influences both a super-peer's load and the average path length. In the case of a 1,000,000-peer overlay, $m = 1$ leads to the creation of 59,325 super-peers, implying 15.856 edge peers per super-peer and an average path length of 7.93, while the choice of $m = 6$ creates only 12,136 super-peers, reducing the average path length to 6.78 hops but increasing the number of edge peers per super-peer to 81.4.

Figure 4.8 depicts the dispersal of super-peers, showing 1,000 times the value of (4.35) for $m \in \{1, \dots, 5\}$. In line with (4.35), this figure indicates that the number of super-peers as a fraction of 1,000 peers steadily recedes. Conversely, in compliance with (4.34) and the fact that p grows with n, this figure implies that the number of edge peers per super-peer grows with the overlay size. This finding is consistent with Figure 4.9 that shows the

---

[32] Table 4.5 is limited to approximations for the following reasons. Peer numbers and finger counts are integers, but the table's elements were computed iteratively with floating-point precision by the Newton-Raphson algorithm. The resulting value was rounded to account for the fact that the number of super-peers is always integral. Moreover, the numbers in Table 4.5 assume all super-peers to serve the same number of edge peers. There is no tolerance window for the number of edge peers a super-peer serves.

Size (n)	Edge peers per distinct finger (m)								
	1	2	3	4	5	6	7	8	9
100	19	12	9	8	7	6	5	5	5
200	33	21	16	13	11	10	9	8	7
500	70	42	31	25	22	19	17	15	14
1,000	125	74	55	44	37	32	29	26	24
2,000	227	132	96	77	64	56	49	45	41
5,000	501	288	208	164	137	118	104	94	85
10,000	922	524	375	296	246	211	186	167	151
20,000	1,704	961	684	537	445	381	335	299	271
50,000	3,870	2,160	1,528	1,194	986	843	739	659	596
100,000	7,235	4,010	2,825	2,202	1,814	1,548	1,355	1,206	1,089
200,000	13,579	7,480	5,253	4,083	3,358	2,861	2,500	2,223	2,005
500,000	31,373	17,162	12,004	9,305	7,635	6,494	5,664	5,031	4,532
1,000,000	59,325	32,301	22,533	17,434	14,284	12,136	10,573	9,384	8,446
2,000,000	112,490	60,989	42,445	32,785	26,825	22,767	19,817	17,573	15,806
5,000,000	263,086	141,926	98,496	75,931	62,032	52,580	45,719	40,504	36,399
10,000,000	501,601	269,675	186,799	143,812	117,366	99,398	86,365	76,464	68,678

Table 4.5: Approximated solutions for p in (4.33), rounded to integer values

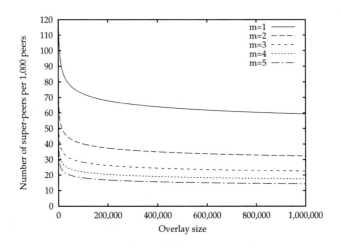

Figure 4.8: Number of super-peers per $1,000$ peers

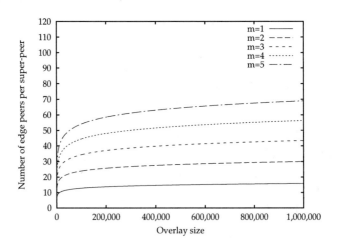

Figure 4.9: Number of edge peers per super-peer

number of edge peers per super-peer for the same values of m as the previous figure. As desired, this number grows logarithmically.

Since the super-peer structure adds two additional hops to message paths when two edge peers communicate, the choice of m determines the average path length. If m is sufficiently large to allow an p small enough, the average path length will diminish compared to pure Chord. The super-peer overlay's average path length h_{avg} equals $2 + \frac{1}{2} \cdot \log_2 p$ when two edge peers communicate. [33] The average path length in the overlay is less than with pure Chord if

$$\frac{1}{2} \cdot \log_2 n > 2 + \frac{1}{2} \cdot \log_2 p \qquad (4.36)$$

(4.36) can be reshaped to

$$\log_2 \frac{n}{p} > 4 \qquad (4.37)$$

Solving (4.33) for $\frac{n}{p}$ and putting the result into (4.37) yields

$$\log_2(f \cdot m + 1) > 4 \Leftrightarrow f \cdot m > 15 \qquad (4.38)$$

In effect, this means that already a small value of m suffices to lower the average path length. For instance, in an overlay with 272 peers, a Chord ring core with 16 super-peers expects $f = 4$ distinct fingers per super-peer under the assumption of uniform Chord ID distribution and uniform edge peer distribution. At $m = 4$, every super-peer would accommodate $f \cdot m = 16$ edge peers while lowering the average path length from $\frac{1}{2} \cdot \log_2 272 = 4.0437$ to $2 + \frac{1}{2} \cdot \log_2 16 = 4$ hops.

This effect can also be investigated by considering overlay sizes as functions of the average path length in the context of transforming a pure Chord ring into a super-peer topology with a Chord core. In a Chord ring with n peers, the average path length h_{avg} amounts to $h_{avg} = \frac{1}{2} \cdot \log_2 n$ hops. Solving for n, one attains $n = 4^{h_{avg}}$. This can be written as a function of h_{avg}: $f(h_{avg}) = 4^{h_{avg}}$. In a super-peer topology, the average path grows by 2 spoke hops to attain a length of $h_{avg} + 2$. $f(h_{avg} + 2) = 16 \cdot 4^{h_{avg}}$, i. e. the pure Chord ring that has the same average path length as the super-peer topology can accommodate 16 times the number of peers than the Chord ring that backs the super-peer topology. If the super-peer Chord ring has less than $\frac{1}{16}$ the size of the Chord ring that is equivalent to the super-peer topology in terms of average path length, the topology's average number of hops is less than in the original Chord ring. Hence, more than $\frac{15}{16} = 93.75\%$ of peers need to be drawn from the original Chord ring into edge peer positions for a lower average path length than with the original Chord ring. Alternatively, out of every 16 peers in

---

[33]h_{avg} is less when one or both communication endpoints are super-peers, but the given h_{avg} is considered the average path length for the worst-case situation that both endpoints are edge peers.

the original ring, 15 become edge peers and the remaining one becomes a super-peer in equilibrium. If the average path length is to diminish in the super-peer topology, $k - 1$ edge peers and a single super-peer emerge from any set of $k > 16$ peers present in the original Chord ring.

Besides a reduced average path length, shrinking the Chord ring also means that fewer super-peers need to announce their existence to enable others to connect to them as edge peers, and the super-peer list maintained by individual peers remains short. Keeping the Chord ring reasonably small holds the network traffic caused by super-peer announcements on a low level, improving scalability. Hence, it is reasonable to concentrate the major portion of overlay growth at the overlay's edges.

When edge peers leave the overlay, some super-peers may find themselves underloaded. In their reorganization phase, super-peers downgrade to edge peer level if they find that $g < \frac{f \cdot m}{k}$ holds. $k = 2$ represents a lower bound considering the requirement of viable edge peer sets after splitting: when a super-peer finds its load too high (i. e. $g = f \cdot m + 1$), it promotes one of its edge peers to super-peer level and splits the remaining $f \cdot m$ edge peers evenly among itself and the new super-peer such that neither super-peer downgrades due to low load. As with SPSA, the split occurs under the assumption of uniform edge peer distribution over the super-peers such that in equilibrium, all super-peers serve the same number of edge peers. An even split maintains $\frac{1}{2} \cdot f \cdot m$ edge peers with the old super-peer and relocates another $\frac{1}{2} \cdot f \cdot m$ edge peers to the new super-peer. If k were lower than 2, both super-peers would consider themselves underloaded after the split, and decide to downgrade. Also, the given bound requires an even split. Otherwise, assuming a non-even split, one super-peer would receive more than $\frac{1}{2} \cdot f \cdot m$ edge peers while the other one would receive less, causing the latter super-peer to downgrade, nullifying the benefit. In practice, a larger value for k may be chosen to dampen the Chord ring's dynamics and reduce the dependence on the assumption of uniform edge peer distribution.

The parameters k and m regulate the downgrade and promotion bounds similar to α and β with SPSA. Like SPSA, ChordSPSA adapts the number of super-peers to the overlay size in a self-organized way. The larger the difference between $\frac{1}{k}$ and m, the more cumbersome the super-peers will be with initiating promotions and downgrades. A super-peer x downgrades if $|E_x| < \frac{f \cdot m}{k}$. With a low value of $\frac{1}{k}$, many super-peers are likely to be created; each will serve only few edge peers, but the Chord ring becomes large (hence, f grows) such that the downgrade bound $\frac{f \cdot m}{k}$ grows. Eventually, in the face of a growing Chord ring and no new edge peers, a super-peer will consider itself underloaded which causes it to downgrade and its edge peers to switch to other super-peers, slowing down the Chord ring's growth. Conversely, a super-peer x creates a new super-peer by promoting one of its edge peers whenever $|E_x| > f \cdot m$. This self-organizing process adapts the number of super-peers to the current overlay size.

The selection that an overloaded super-peer x performs to promote an edge peer to super-peer level assumes that since x is overloaded, $|E_x| > 0$. Based on the notion of edge peers connecting to their closest super-peers, x filters E_x to attain the set E'_x containing all edge peers of x which, if selected as a super-peer, would cause the post-promotion edge peer numbers of both itself and x to reach or exceed the lower bound. This prevents instant downgrades. x can accomplish this on its own by using its edge peers' network coordinates to attain inter-peer delays. Out of all $e \in E'_x$, x picks e' for which the optimal Chord ID choice yields minimal total finger delay. [34] e' is asked to become a new super-peer. If e' declines or fails to respond, x will retry in its next reorganization phase and may exclude e' that time. Since some edge peers can be unwilling to act as super-peers, announcing this to their super-peers at connect time may spare them from being asked for promotion.

Compared to pure Chord, the average reorganization effort required to be undertaken when a new peer enters the overlay or leaves it is smaller with the proposed super-peer topology [32]. In Chord, when a new peer joins the ring, it needs to populate its finger table, and other peers will set up finger connections to the new peer. Also, when a peer leaves the ring – due to a crash or voluntary departure –, all peers having fingers pointing to the departing peer will need to update their finger tables. In the super-peer case, a departing edge peer incurs no reorganization cost except for the inexpensive state update at the departing edge peer's super-peer. Conversely, a newly joining peer will be an edge peer unless it is the first peer in the overlay, hence only the associated super-peer's state is affected but the Chord ring remains untainted. [35] The analysis focuses on the departure/leave case. Let time be discrete, divided into rounds, and let p be the probability that an arbitrary peer leaves the overlay in a round. In a Chord ring with n peers, the probability that at least one peer departs in a round is $1 - (1 - p)^n$. For instance, a configuration of $p = 0.001$ and $n = 2,000$ yields a probability of 86.4 % that at least one peer departs the overlay in a given round, causing the need for ring reorganization. In contrast, a super-peer overlay has only $n' \ll n$ Chord peers, lowering the probability for at least one failure in a round to $1 - (1 - p)^{n'}$. To continue the example, if $\frac{15}{16}$ of the Chord ring peers move into edge peer positions, $n' = 125$ super-peers remain in the Chord ring. The probability that in this configuration at least one failure occurs in a round is 11.8 %, approximately $\frac{1}{8}$ of the original failure probability with pure Chord. The analysis of the join case proceeds in an analogous way.

In a topology of this kind, a broadcast can be efficiently performed. The approach

---

[34] The associated proximity-aware identifier picking scheme will be discussed in detail in Section 4.4.2.3.2.

[35] There are two exceptions. When a departing edge peer causes its super-peer to downgrade or a newly joining edge peer causes the super-peer to promote a new edge peer, the ring composition will change. For the analysis, these special cases are neglected.

corresponds to efficient broadcast in a Chord ring as discussed in Section 4.2.1 with the extension that an additional hop is taken to deliver the broadcast message to a super-peer's edge peers. If an edge peer wants to broadcast a message, the message is forwarded to the edge peer's super-peer first.

4.4.2.2 Updating the super-peer list

Similar to SPSA, a super-peer list containing all Chord ring members enables edge peers to connect to their closest super-peers. The super-peer list contains, for every super-peer, its respective Chord ID, IP address, network coordinates, a timestamp referring to the last perceived sign of activity, and possibly the number of served edge peers. [36] If a super-peer fails, its edge peers may connect to other super-peers picked from the super-peer list. Furthermore, the super-peer list enables peers to compute the Chord ring size and deploy delay-optimized Chord ID selection as will be set forth in Section 4.4.2.3.

One way to keep the super-peer list current is to let every super-peer periodically broadcast a beacon message that signals its presence. This does not distribute an explicit list: it exclusively notifies other super-peers of the beacon-transmitting super-peer's existence. Also, a super-peer immediately broadcasts a signal message when the connection to a neighboring super-peer was lost. Super-peers forward such information to their edge peers. All peers refresh their super-peer lists upon reception of such a message. On the contrary, every super-peer list entry can be marked with a TTL field which is decremented in every reorganization phase. Eventually, entries will time out if they are not refreshed. This approach requires an efficient broadcast mechanism to remain scalable, a requirement that can be satisfied in a Chord ring as discussed in Section 4.2.1. When every super-peer broadcasts a beacon message every κ time units, the trade-off between network load and timely dissemination of changes in the network can be adjusted by modifying κ. The larger κ, the lower the load, the higher the probability of outdated information in individual peers' super-peer lists.

Another way to maintain a super-peer list is *deterministic gossip*. Deterministic gossip intends to capture perceived changes and to notify other ring members about them. It is a method to perform anti-entropy super-peer list synchronization [64]. The list is loosely consistent: gossip provides a best-effort approach to continuously keeping the list's contents current. In contrast to beacon broadcasts, deterministic gossip concerns the distribution of list updates that may concern remote super-peers, and in contrast to conventional gossip, the peer targeted for exchanging gossip information is not selected randomly but according to a deterministic scheme.

---

[36]The timestamp can be replaced with a sequence number as will be shown shortly.

With deterministic gossip, all peers log recorded ring changes to a locally stored *update set* whose elements are *updates*. Each update contains the affected remote peer's Chord ID, its IP address, its most recently propagated network coordinates, a propagation count, and a sequence number allocated by a scheme presented in [187]. An entry with a higher sequence number overrides an entry with a lower sequence number, provided that the same peer is concerned. An odd sequence number marks a peer as not belonging to the Chord ring, while an even sequence number marks it as an alive Chord peer. Every peer starts with a sequence number of 1 and increments it upon joining the ring, turning it even. Once a Chord peer notices the failure of one of its finger peers, it increments that peer's sequence number, making it odd, and propagates the information using gossiping. Should the failing peer be revived, it adds 2 to its locally stored pre-outage sequence number, overriding the outdated failure mark, and disseminates that information in the overlay via deterministic gossip.

Information is propagated by every super-peer. A Chord peer periodically transmits super-peer list updates to one of its finger peers, iterating through its finger set in a round-robin way, and requests the target peer to reply with its own set of recent updates. The propagation count contained within each entry in the update set is initialized with the number of distinct fingers and decremented every time the message is sent to a finger peer. When the counter reaches zero, the entry is discarded and set taboo: if this entry arrives again, it will not be included in the update set any more. Taboo list entries are timestamped and decay after a customizable period of time. Additionally, a super-peer instantly forwards received updates to its edge peers.

To deal with churn, the deterministic gossip scheme deploys redundancy by transmitting every update to all finger targets before the update is discarded. With p peers in an intact Chord ring, every update is transmitted consecutively over $\log_2 p$ fingers, one finger per gossip round. The updates sent over a finger may be combined in a single message, resulting in a total of p messages sent per round. This is more efficient than broadcast which has a message complexity of $O(p)$ per broadcast initiator. If all super-peers emit a broadcast message per round, there are $O(p^2)$ messages per round with the broadcast scheme. In deterministic gossip, a Chord peer uses one finger per round to send a message, while broadcast uses all fingers. Additionally, the departure of a single peer may severely hamper the propagation effort if broadcast is used. If, for instance, the farthest finger peer crashes, the broadcast will fail to reach $\frac{p}{2}$ peers. On the other hand, deterministic gossip may propagate outdated information, and the messages' contents are voluminous compared to the broadcast case since they contain a full list of $O(p)$ super-peers' metadata.

4.4.2.3 Delay minimization

Originally, Chord considers the average path length, quantified by the average number of hops a routed message takes, to be its main optimization goal [219]. While the Chord-enhanced super-peer topology can further reduce the average path length by shrinking the Chord ring, it is worthwhile to concentrate on end-to-end delay (i. e. message latency) [103] as the major objective to optimize the performance experienced by applications and to accelerate the reorganization processes in the overlay necessitated by churn. With optimization geared towards minimizing the end-to-end delay instead of the average path length, messages may travel more hops on average but arrive earlier. There is a tradeoff between reducing the average path length and reducing the average end-to-end latency [103]. In a Desktop Grid context, latency is more important. Besides the benefit for Desktop Grids, a low delay will also improve Chord's self-stabilization properties since updates about ring composition changes are propagated faster. This section explores ways to modify Chord's routing and forwarding procedures to the end of reducing the average end-to-end message delay in the context of a super-peer topology in which the super-peers are interconnected with a Chord ring, and every peer maintains a super-peer list.

As edge peers connect to the closest known super-peer, ChordSPSA provides locality by clustering edge peers around their closest super-peers. In addition, a notion of locality can also be introduced to those operations that involve super-peers. In [103], the generic schemes of PROXIMITY ROUTE SELECTION (PRS) and PROXIMITY IDENTIFIER SELECTION (PIS) have been introduced to provide general guidelines for delay-based optimization in structured P2P topologies; similar schemes are discussed in [43]. In line with these generic schemes, this section proposes tangible designs for PRS and PIS mechanisms to reduce Chord's average end-to-end message delay. Two out of the three proposed methods need a list of all Chord peers which may become exceedingly large in pure Chord but reasonably small when only a negligible number of super-peers populate the Chord ring. All proposed methods can be implemented to run in polynomial time, require no extra messages, and work in a distributed setting.

There is a third kind of proximity-aware improvement: PROXIMITY NEIGHBOR SELECTION (PNS) selects neighbors in the overlay according to the link delay [103]. With PNS, a Chord finger table is populated with fingers that may point to peers beyond the successor of the ideal finger location in the identifier space. PNS is not discussed here for two reasons. First, it was studied before in the same setting that is considered here (Chord and Vivaldi) [61]. Second, the use of PNS forestalls the deployment of a sophisticated lookahead forwarding scheme (to be introduced shortly) that relies on Chord peers to populate their finger tables in the conventional way.

The remainder of this section first focuses on improving the use of fingers in routing (PRS), then addresses proximity-aware identifier selection (PIS).

4.4.2.3.1 Finger use in routing

When determining the distance between two peers, Chord relies on their clockwise distance in the identifier space which can translate to arbitrary end-to-end delays in the underlying network. In plain Chord, a peer x forwards a message onward by picking the finger peer which covers the largest portion of the identifier space but targets a location which is not beyond the destination in the clockwise direction. This makes for a greedy finger selection process based on hop count minimization only. A proximity-aware refinement for this process is as follows. Out of all suitable fingers, the one with lowest delay per covered identifier space unit is preferred for forwarding the respective message. Since the super-peer list contains all finger peers' network coordinates, the finger can be chosen instantly without the need to measure the delay first. With F_x as x's finger set, all fingers whose IDs occur on or before the message destination's ID on the ring in clockwise direction are considered. The filtered finger table that contains only those fingers is designated F'_x. Subsequently, one picks x's finger peer y which satisfies

$$y = \underset{y' \in F'_x}{\arg \min} \frac{d_{Link}(x, y')}{d_{ID}(x, y')} \tag{4.39}$$

as the next message hop. This plan corresponds to a PRS approach. While it may incur additional hops, it aims to reduce the average end-to-end message delay. Chord's convergence invariant is not affected as only finger locations that are on or before the message's destination on the ring are considered.

The proposed PRS mechanism is greedy. It picks the best out of all fingers for the next hop. All subsequent hops are also picked in this way. However, the overall delay might fail to reach the global minimum as a peer makes its decisions based on its local knowledge only. The subsequent hop's delay could alleviate the gains made in the current hop. With p super-peers, PRS has a runtime complexity of $O(\log p)$ per forwarded message as every finger is considered.

An example for the greedy PRS procedure is depicted in Figure 4.10. In this example, peer 7 wants to transmit a message to peer 27. It is temporarily assumed for the scope of this example that a link's delay is constant and known to the adjacent peers. The dashed arrows in Figure 4.10(b) mark all unused finger connections that point to finger targets not beyond peer 27, i. e. those fingers that could be chosen for forwarding the message but are not used here. The thick arrows mark those fingers actually used by PRS in this

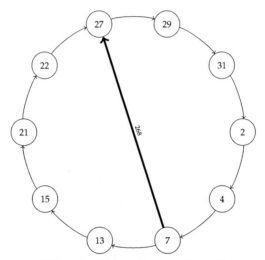

(a) Conventional Chord routing from peer 7 to peer 27

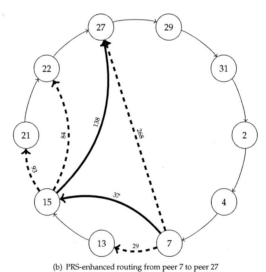

(b) PRS-enhanced routing from peer 7 to peer 27

Figure 4.10: Conventional Chord routing in contrast to PRS

example. Numbers next to the arrows give the delay of the respective link, specified
in milliseconds (ms). With conventional Chord, since there is a finger pointing to the
destination, in the example affected by a delay of 268 ms, peer 7 directly forwards the
message to peer 27 as shown in Figure 4.10(a)

In contrast, with PRS, peer 7 first checks all of its fingers that point to IDs on or before 27
in clockwise direction. There are three fingers that fulfill this criterion: those pointing to
peers 13, 15, and 27 itself, with delays of 29, 37, and 268 ms, respectively. The respective
delays per covered unit of identifier space amount to $\frac{29}{13-7} \approx 4.833$ ms, $\frac{37}{15-7} = 4.625$ ms
and $\frac{268}{27-7} = 13.4$ ms. In accordance with (4.39), peer 7 forwards the message to peer 15 in
the face of a direct connection to the destination peer 27.

After the propagation delay of 37 ms and the transmission delay have elapsed, the
message is with peer 15. Peer 15 proceeds in an analogous way as peer 7 did. It has
three fingers pointing to peers that are on or before the destination: these are peers
21, 22, and 27. The delays per covered unit of identifier space are $\frac{93}{21-15} = 15.5$ ms,
$\frac{84}{22-15} = 12$ ms, and $\frac{138}{27-15} = 11.5$ ms, respectively. Thus, peer 15 forwards the message to
its destination, peer 27. Compared to conventional routing, PRS has accelerated message
delivery by $268 - (37 + 138) = 93$ ms (34.7 %) in this example. PRS benefits from network
coordinates in that reasonably accurate estimates of link delays are instantly available
without explicitly measuring a link's delay first.

In PRS, the peer making a forwarding decision knows about its local state only. Peer
7, therefore, has no idea of peer 15's subsequent forwarding decision. This drawback is
removed with the help of the super-peer list. The presence of a super-peer list containing network coordinates enables the deployment of a more sophisticated PRS scheme
which implements an approximated lookahead over future message forwarding decisions. Given a locally maintained list of super-peers that contains the super-peers' Chord
IDs and network coordinates, and assuming that the Chord ring is intact with all finger
tables properly populated, a super-peer can construct the finger table of every other
super-peer merely from the set of Chord IDs provided by the super-peer list. The finger
table construction procedure for each remote super-peer is executed as if the constructing super-peer had the remote super-peer's Chord ID, yielding the finger targets for the
remote super-peer. The result is a directed graph that represents all finger connections
between the super-peers. As network coordinates can be used to estimate delays between
any two peers, the graph's edge weights can be inexpensively computed using network
coordinates. In the final step, the resulting weighted graph is used as input for DIJK-
STRA's single-source shortest-path algorithm [54, 66]. Thus, for any message to be sent,
network coordinates and remote finger table construction jointly provide an estimate of
a lookahead over all future forwarding decisions. The graph changes if the super-peer
list changes, the graph owner's finger table changes, or new network coordinates are

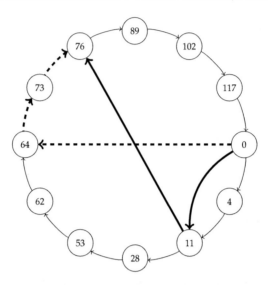

Figure 4.11: Due to its lack of greed, LPRS can reduce the path length in a partially populated Chord ring. In this example, a message from peer 0 is to be routed to peer 76. The dashed lines show the finger choices made by ordinary Chord, while the solid lines indicate the finger choices made by LPRS.

obtained. Eventually, Dijkstra's algorithm needs to be re-executed on the updated graph, but as the graph remains stable between those three change-inducing events, it need not be recomputed for every single message forwarding decision.

With p super-peers, it is sufficient for a super-peer to store the next hop for each of the $p-1$ remaining super-peers. This storage occupies memory on the order of $O(p)$ and enables forwarding decisions to be made in $O(1)$ time. Should the destination not be in the super-peer list and hence not in the computed graph (for instance, because the destination peer has only recently been upgraded), the forwarding algorithm can forward the message to the receiver's precedessor according to the current super-peer list. Alternatively, it is free to temporarily fall back to greedy PRS. To distinguish this lookahead-approximating approach from greedy PRS as introduced above, it will be referred to as Lookahead PRS (LPRS). Like PRS, LPRS works in a fully distributed way and requires no additional messages.

In contrast to original Chord forwarding and PRS, however, LPRS is not greedy. With LPRS, it may become advantageous to choose a short hop in the identifier space first and a long one subsequently. This can reduce the average number of taken hops. An example for this phenomenon is shown in Figure 4.11. In this example, the forwarding decisions lead to 3 hops with ordinary Chord but only 2 hops with LPRS. Chord's desire to greedily pick the finger which maximizes the covered portion of identifier space at every forwarding peer is counterproductive in this situation. LPRS also circumvents the effect that in greedy latency-sensitive forwarding, "the last few hops of a lookup dominate the total latency" [61]. Since LPRS has the benefit of an approximated lookahead, it can decide to take more expensive hops in the beginning but be rewarded for this non-greedy behavior when inexpensive hops become available in the end.

In a Chord ring consisting of p super-peers, $p-1$ other super-peers' finger tables need to be computed by the LPRS-performing super-peer. For this purpose, for each other super-peer, p super-peers' Chord IDs must be examined to see if they are the best fit for each of the remote super-peer's $\log_2 p$ fingers. Thus, the remote finger table construction effort can be performed in $O(p^2 \cdot \log p)$ time. A straightforward implementation of Dijkstra's algorithm runs in $O(p^2)$ time which is dominated by the finger table construction effort. [37] Thus, the runtime complexity of building the LPRS graph is $O(p^2 \cdot \log p)$ per peer, and $O(p \cdot \log p)$ edges need to be stored in memory.

PRS and LPRS are particularly useful for accelerating the delivery of unicast messages that are routed through the Chord ring. For instance, the Chord stabilization procedure which is periodically executed by every Chord peer transmits unicast messages to ideal finger targets. PRS and LPRS can speed up the stabilization process such that outdated entries in Chord finger tables are fixed earlier, leading to more accurate finger tables. While LPRS can route messages to known super-peers only, it is free to send messages to the known predecessors of ideal targets which then can use PRS to forward the message as close to the actual destination as possible.

4.4.2.3.2 Proximity-aware identifier selection

A Chord peer picks a random ID from a large identifier space whose definition is publicly known. The odds of assigning the same ID twice are negligible due to the sheer size of that space and the uniform probability with which each ID is drawn. However, this approach does not account for proximity. Since a peer's ID choice determines the placement of its fingers, it is desirable to assign IDs that lead to low-delay finger connections. With a super-peer list, a new Chord peer may pick an ID such that the sum of delays of its finger connections is minimized. Since the list contains network coordinates, the new peer can select its optimal position without sending any messages. Apart from the ID choice, ring joining is performed as in original Chord.

---

[37] A more efficient implementation of Dijkstra's algorithm resorts to a binary heap [19]. Given a graph $G = (V, E)$, it runs in $O(|E| + |V| \cdot \log |V|)$ time.

In principle, every non-occupied element of the identifier space needs to be checked because every ID leads to different fingers. To limit this effort, a heuristic approach is proposed. The first peer picks an arbitrary ID. The second peer picks its ID such that it places itself at maximum distance in the identifier space from the first peer. All peers joining subsequently perform a *gap check*: in a Chord ring with r peers, there are at most r gaps between peers. Peers evaluate the positions marked by the middle ID of each gap, and choose the ID for which their total finger delay is minimized. Since the gaps' middle positions are powers of 2 away from the adjacent peers, a finger is likely to point to its ideal position (a power of 2 away from the finger-setting peer) provided that all peers perform PIS.

For the third and all subsequent peers, this scheme relies on the super-peer list to specify the r super-peers with their Chord IDs and network coordinates. These IDs are extracted to a separate list L which is then sorted. Since gaps cannot exist between two Chord peers whose IDs are adjacent in the identifier space, the higher ID is removed from the list of IDs. Let the $s \leq r$ remaining IDs be given in sorted order as $L' = (ID_1, ID_2, \ldots, ID_s)$. Since, by construction, no two IDs in L' are adjacent, there are s gaps between the IDs. The i-th gap position $g_i, i \in \{1, \ldots, s\}$ is defined as

$$g_i = \begin{cases} \left\lceil \frac{ID_i + ID_{i+1}}{2} \right\rceil & \text{if } i < s \\ \left\lceil \frac{ID_1 + ID_s}{2} \right\rceil & \text{otherwise} \end{cases} \qquad (4.40)$$

where "+" operates modulo the ring size. Let F_g specify the set of peers chosen as Chord fingers when the gap position g is selected, ordered ascendingly by ID. Moreover, let $d(y)$ return the expected delay from the current peer to peer y as predicted by network coordinates. The chosen Chord ID equals the particular gap position g^* which minimizes the peer's overall delay to its finger targets:

$$g_{i^*} = \arg\min_i \sum_{f \in F_{g_i}} d(f) \qquad (4.41)$$

From the PIS-performing peer's point of view, in a fully populated ring, finger i covers 2^i positions in the identifier space (including its own position) until the next finger position in clockwise direction. Thus, PIS can be refined by weighting the delays accumulated in (4.41). A finger is weighted with the number of identifier space elements for which it would be chosen as the next forwarding hop by the PIS-performing peer. Let $F_{g_i}(j)$ define the $(j+1)$-th finger chosen when gap position g_i is selected as the current peer's identifier. Under the assumption that the identifier space is fully populated, a weighted

PIS formulation is

$$g_{i^*}^{\text{full}} = \arg\min_i \sum_{f=0}^{|F_{g_i}|-1} d\left(F_{g_i}(f)\right) \cdot 2^f \tag{4.42}$$

Since the assumption of complete ring population is rarely expected to hold in practice, a more realistic weighting procedure incorporates the actual super-peers with their true identifiers as specified by the super-peer list. Let the current peer be x. Moreover, let $z\left(F_{g_i}(j)\right)$ be the portion of the identifier space covered by the $(j+1)$-th finger according to F_{g_i}, i. e. the number of identifier space elements in clockwise order for which j is the closest preceding peer and as such, the preferred forwarding target:

$$z\left(F_{g_i}(j)\right) = \begin{cases} \text{dist}\left(F_{g_i}(j), F_{g_i}(j+1)\right) & \text{if } j < |F_{g_i}| - 1 \\ \text{dist}\left(F_{g_i}(j), x\right) & \text{otherwise} \end{cases} \tag{4.43}$$

Since Chord forwarding greedily picks the finger target which is closest but not beyond the actual destination in clockwise order, (4.42) can be generalized with the help of (4.43) to

$$g_{i^*}^{\text{weighted}} = \arg\min_i \sum_{f=0}^{|F_{g_i}|-1} d\left(F_{g_i}(f)\right) \cdot z\left(F_{g_i}(f)\right) \tag{4.44}$$

The super-peer list may temporarily contain outdated information. For this reason, two peers that join the ring concurrently or subsequently with only a brief time span in between could choose the same ID, causing a collision. Hence, ring members need to reject prospective newcomers that request already occupied IDs, providing them with an up-to-date super-peer list instead. Also, ring members should periodically check if their super-peer list contains another peer with the same ID. If the check yields a hit, the detecting peer can ask the remote peer for an ID change, or change its own ID.

The proposed PIS scheme may cause the load to be unevenly distributed. However, since super-peers can promote edge peers in the case of excessive load, the gains are likely to outweigh the non-uniform load. Identifier assignment is a rare event compared to message forwarding. With p super-peers already in the system, the runtime complexity of PIS experienced by the joining peer is the same as with LPRS, but the derivation is different. The PIS-performing peer examines $O(p)$ gaps. For each gap, it needs to assess the placement of $O(\log p)$ fingers. For each finger, $O(p)$ super-peers' identifiers are considered. Thus, the total runtime complexity amounts to $O(p^2 \cdot \log p)$.

When all peers perform PIS, the heightened likelihood of peers occupying ideal finger positions – powers of 2 away from the finger-setting peer in clockwise direction – is expected to lead to a reduced number of routing hops on average as with a randomly scattered distribution of peers over the identifier space. Also, individual fingers are expected to exhibit less delay than in the random configuration due to the delay-sensitive identifier selection scheme. The combination of these effects makes PIS particularly useful to accelerate the propagation of broadcasts. Since the broadcast procedure introduced in Section 4.2.1 uses every finger on every forwarding peer to propagate the broadcast message, picking a location in the identifier space that minimizes finger delays also reduces the delay that broadcast messages experience while being propagated.

4.4.2.4 Experiments

Since the key difference of ChordSPSA over SPSA lies in the establishment of multi-hop routes interconnecting the super-peers through the Chord ring, experiments were conducted to quantify the end-to-end delay overhead incurred by the replacement of direct with multi-hop intra-core connections. To this end, the performance of standard Chord routing, PRS, LPRS and PIS, alone and in combination, was compared to that of direct connections. As with SPSA, it was assumed that all peers wished to communicate with each other to an equal extent.

4.4.2.4.1 Setup

Two experiments were conducted in this context. The first experiment focused on PRS and LPRS. All peers were considered to be super-peers interconnected by a Chord ring, while edge peers were neglected as they have no impact on either PRS or LPRS. To this end, with every available delay matrix, 30 simulated snapshots of a flat Chord ring with randomly picked Chord IDs were created and analyzed. It was assumed that the Chord ring was intact and all finger tables were properly populated. For every combination of randomly chosen IDs, the average delay of end-to-end message paths over all pairs of peers was computed for Chord with standard message forwarding, Chord with PRS, Chord with LPRS, and direct connections between Chord peers. This experiment was conducted not only to assess the performance of LPRS but also to quantify the extra delay incurred by ChordSPSA through the comparison with direct connections. Both SPSA and ChordSPSA add two hops to paths between edge peers when compared to flat topologies. However, while there is only a single link used between super-peers with SPSA, there is a multi-hop route through the Chord ring with ChordSPSA. As there are no edge peers in this experiment, the order of magnitude of the differences in end-to-end delays between SPSA and ChordSPSA could be assessed through the contrast between direct forwarding and the various kinds of Chord-style forwarding.

The computation was performed twice. In the first case, peers were allowed to perform

30 Vivaldi cycles with randomly selected target peers to embed themselves into a 4-dimensional Euclidean space. The second case assumed a flawless embedding to gauge the true performance of the routing algorithms with no influence from potential network coordinates-related embedding errors.

The second experiment concerned the effects of PIS, both alone and in combination with PRS and LPRS. Identifier assignment is a comparatively rare event, and once assigned, an identifier does not change. Hence, there is no way to adapt to fluctuating network coordinates. In this second experiment, a flawless embedding was therefore assumed to assess the performance boost PIS can attain in the best case. Apart from this, the experimental setup matched that of the first experiment. In particular, peers joined in the order prescribed by the respective delay input matrix. While the first peer was free to pick a random ID, since the identifier assignments can be rotated along the ring, all subsequent peers adapted their identifier choice, and as such, this second experiment was not influenced by randomness.

4.4.2.4.2 Results

The first experiment compared PRS, LPRS, and direct connections to original Chord message forwarding. The results are shown in Tables 4.6–4.9, with averages over 30 runs per matrix and weighted averages based on the number of edges ($n \cdot (n-1)$ for a n-node matrix). Table 4.6 shows the results in terms of average end-to-end delay and average path length per peer pair when delays are estimated using Vivaldi. To ease the comparison, these values were normalized with regard to the performance of standard Chord forwarding in Table 4.8. The tables indicate that PRS offers a moderate average improvement of 8 % in end-to-end delay while simultaneously increasing the average path length by 16 %. The effects of LPRS are substantially more pronounced. LPRS lowers the average end-to-end delay by 45 % while leaving the average path length virtually untainted. With LPRS, most networks experience a slightly increased path length (up to 4 %) but the large Meridian matrix lowers the average due to its domineering influence in the computation of the weighted average. Thus, as the path length remains almost unchanged, LPRS provides an efficient permutation of hops taken between source and destination to the benefit of the average end-to-end delay which greatly diminishes in comparison to standard Chord. The less complex PRS procedure yields moderate gains in average end-to-end delay at the expense of more taken hops. In no case did PRS or LPRS produce an average end-to-end delay larger than that incurred by standard Chord routing.

The comparison was repeated with Vivaldi replaced by knowledge of exact pairwise communication delays, disabling potential errors introduced by possibly distorted network coordinates. Table 4.7 shows the outcome of this configuration, emphasizing that the Vivaldi embedding could provide only an approximation of the true delays. The random assignment of Chord IDs caused the minor difference between the weighted averages of standard Chord routing observable from Table 4.6 and Table 4.7. As can also be seen from Table 4.9 which contains the same outcome normalized to the performance of original Chord, PRS brings a mean end-to-end delay improvement of 19 % while increasing the mean path length by 23 % in this configuration. Again, LPRS is superior, lowering the end-to-end delay by 61 % on average. The average path length grows by 12 % with LPRS. These results indicate that while PRS succeeds in reducing the message delay compared to pure Chord, LPRS is considerably more effective than PRS. In the case of the 12-2005 network, LPRS reduced the average end-to-end delay by 71 % which is only slightly worse than all-pairs direct connections saving 77 % but far better than PRS at 42 %. Since neither PRS nor LPRS cause additional messages to be transmitted or require excessive computational effort, the addition of these improvements to Chord message forwarding is worthwhile.

Furthermore, the attained results shown in Tables 4.6–4.9 exhibit the increases in average end-to-end delay that arise through the shift from a fully meshed (SPSA) to a Chord-based (ChordSPSA) super-peer core. The delay increase is the surcharge that multi-hop routing through the Chord ring incurs in exchange for the substantial reduction of the number of connections held by super-peers. With ordinary Chord, the delay approximately quintuples; it increases by a factor of some 4.05. When Chord is augmented through the addition of PRS or LPRS, the increase's extent depends on the network coordinates' accuracy. With the Vivaldi embedding, the delay increases by a factor of 1.75 with LPRS and by a factor of 3.6 with PRS. However, with flawless coordinates and LPRS, the delay increases merely by a factor of 0.95. Thus, a delay increase attributable to the shift from a fully meshed to a Chord super-peer core is clearly observed, but the extent of this increase can be attenuated through the introduction of improvements to Chord's message forwarding procedure, in particular through the addition of LPRS.

Table 4.10 contains the outcome of the second experiment. For most networks, PIS brings significant improvements over standard Chord identifier assignment. This was not the case twice, with 07-2005 and 08-2005. This effect is due to the joining order. Peers joining early have fewer gaps to choose from than peers joining later. Unfavorable delay properties of early peers can significantly worsen the outcome. There are $n!$ possible joining orders in an n-element matrix which makes computing the outcome for all orders intractable even for the smallest matrix, 04-2005. The outcome normalized to PIS performance with no forwarding improvement is shown in Table 4.11. All networks except 09-2005 benefitted from the addition of PRS to PIS; in particular, 07-2005 and 08-2005 overcame their initial penalty and exhibited noticeably reduced end-to-end delays. As before, the effect of LPRS in conjunction with the proposed PIS scheme was significantly larger, reducing the end-to-end delay in the case of 08-2005 by 73%. The action of PRS and LPRS – taking more hops in exchange for reduced end-to-end delay – is clearly visible from Table 4.11 as both PRS and LPRS, when used in conjunction with PIS, took more hops than PIS alone: they circumvented Chord's greedy forwarding scheme, replacing few delay-intensive hops with a sequence of faster hops for improved overall performance.

In total, as Table 4.10 indicates, the combined deployment of LPRS and PIS could greatly reduce the experienced end-to-end delay. In the weighted average case, routing through the Chord ring caused a delay overhead of 67.7% compared to direct links. In the particular case of 12-2005 which was especially amenable to the proposed improvements, the Chord routing delay surcharge amounted to 2.6% only. However, this needs to be put into perspective as a flawless embedding is unavailable in practice. Network coordinates introduce an embedding error whose extent depends on the deployed network coordinates generation scheme and the chosen parameters. Also, delays fluctuate, and changes to the ring composition can render existing identifier choices suboptimal as identifiers are not recomputed when the fingers change. Still, PIS offers promising potential. It is particularly interesting in conjunction with PRS or LPRS that can take advantage of the low-delay finger choices prepared by PIS in the first place.

4.4.2.5 Discussion

This section has suggested the deployment of a super-peer topology that interconnects its super-peers with a Chord ring [170, 219]. Chord is a structured topology with several properties that make it attractive for Desktop Grids, such as scalability, self-organization, and swift message routing with $O(\log n)$ hops on average in an n-peer overlay. However, in Chord, all peers need to be reachable from the outside as other peers will want to set up finger connections to them. This issue is solved through the introduction of super-peers: only super-peers need to be reachable for the topology to work. All edge peers are connected to one super-peer each. Since edge peers initiate the connections to their respective super-peers, firewalls are circumvented.

When compared to pure Chord, the combination of super-peers and Chord also brings other advantages such as faster broadcast propagation and less restructuring efforts on average when an arbitrary peer leaves the overlay. On the other hand, when compared to fully meshed super-peer topologies, the Chord core reduces the number of connections held by an individual super-peer from $O(\sqrt{n})$ to $O(\log n)$. The PRS modification implements a greedy delay-based finger choice in message forwarding that brings moderate gains over standard Chord. PRS is greatly improved by LPRS which provides an approximated lookahead over future forwarding decisions. Moreover, a PIS scheme was suggested that lowers end-to-end latencies through delay-sensitive identifier selection. It can be used in conjunction with PRS or LPRS. When all peers maintain a super-peer list, PIS and LPRS can significantly reduce the end-to-end message delay.

4.4.3 Related work

Research related to the P2P paradigm is abounding. Other structured topologies not elaborated here include VICEROY [154], SYMPHONY [155], KADEMLIA [160], and TAPESTRY [242].

The approach proposed in this thesis endorses a hierarchy through the distinction between super-peers and edge peers. Alternatively, a hierarchy can also be introduced within a DHT. In a hierarchical DHT, lookup messages travel between peers in two dimensions: vertically (across hierarchical borders) and horizontally (from peer to peer within the same layer). The introduction of a hierarchy within a DHT can be performed for various widespread DHTs (including Chord and Pastry) as demonstrated in [92]. Since the flat super-peer Chord ring maintained by ChordSPSA is comparatively small, spreading it over multiple layers is not expected to yield a significant benefit.

Message forwarding within the structured super-peer core benefits from any improvement applied to the core topology. In the context of Chord, the most prominent structural improvement is the introduction of bidirectional finger connections [118]. As TCP operates bidirectionally, using a finger link implemented via a TCP connection in both directions is a natural extension. To this end, [118] suggests to complement Chord's ordinary finger table with a *reverse finger table*. It is shown that the lookup path length declines significantly with this extension.

The notion of self-organizing algorithms for the purpose of P2P topology construction has been adopted elsewhere. In [208], the RING NETWORK (RN) distributed algorithm is proposed that transforms an arbitrary topology to a ring-shaped topology in a self-stabilizing way. RN requires a unique ID for every peer. Moreover, it assumes the presence of a bootstrapping system which keeps track of a subset of the peers, and those peers need to be weakly connected at least. ChordSPSA differs from RN in that it maintains a super-peer topology backed by a Chord ring, and returns to this state in a self-stabilizing way upon disruption, while RN concentrates on flat ring topologies.

In [150], the SPSP is compared to the *dominating set* problem (the super-peers make up the dominating set) and the *p-center* problem from the group of facility location problems. In the p-center problem, the minimum or total distance between edge peers and super-peers is to be minimized, but unlike Hub Location, multi-hop end-to-end delays are not taken into account. Three distributed algorithms for super-peer selection are presented, neither of which actively pursues delay minimization to the end of improving application performance. The first is SOLE which picks super-peers from within a structured topology underlying a DHT such that both super-peers and edge peers reside within the same flat topology. The hierarchical distinction is achieved by partitioning the identifier space into two parts: one portion for edge peer identifiers and another for super-peer identifiers. Super-peers are selected at the discretion of the SOLE initiator which can be any peer. Information required for SOLE to work is stored within the DHT. Another proposal is PoPCORN which requires network coordinates to operate. Its primary objective is the maximum dispersal of super-peers which is pursued through maximizing the sum of inter-peer distances between the super-peers. This is implemented in a distributed way by a gossip approach that distributes p tokens among all peers, where p is the desired number of super-peers. Each token holder is a super-peer for the time it keeps the token. Once no tokens are passed to other peers any more, the system is in a stable state. The third suggested algorithm is H_2O which is exclusively devoted to creating two-layer hierarchies in unstructured topologies. Its distributed implementation uses advertisements that are propagated through Gnutella-style flooding. A TTL constraint defines the flooding horizon. While [150] also addresses the SPSP, the approach proposed in this thesis differs significantly from it. In [150], the optimum number of super-peers is not determined. There are no simulations or live experiments to evaluate the fitness of SOLE, PoPCorn and H_2O. Additionally, the problem of assigning edge peers to super-peers in a distributed way is not addressed, and the pursued objectives are substantially different. Although the p-center model can be used to capture the issue of super-peer selection, it does not tackle the end-to-end delays when messages are routed between edge peers, passing through the super-peer core.

The importance of proximity awareness in P2P topology management is stressed in [43, 103] which point out that proximity-related optimizations can be performed during routing and identifier assignment. Specifically with a focus on Chord, [115] introduces a proximity-aware variant of Chord called HP-CHORD that modifies Chord's routing component. The scalability of the HP-Chord approach remains questionable as it explicitly relies on live delay measurements via ping messages with no use of network coordinates.

With a focus on performance, properties of gossip variants were analyzed in a survey [213]. This survey also contains the generic deterministic round-robin scheme which has been modified for use within a Chord ring (cf. Section 4.4.2.2).

The notion of super-peers supporting P2P applications was introduced in [237], albeit in a filesharing context and without explicit topology optimization. There is a substantial number of more recent efforts pertaining to super-peer topology construction. For the sake of readability, the following compilation of related work is divided into two parts. The first part outlines efforts that refer to arbitrary non-structured topologies interconnecting the super-peers, while the second part concentrates on work focusing on structured super-peer interconnection topologies.

4.4.3.1 Unstructured or undefined super-peer interconnection topologies

SG-2 proposes the construction of a super-peer topology with the aid of 5-dimensional network coordinates provided by Vivaldi [117]. SG-2 mimics the social behavior of insects to promote particular peers to super-peer level and vice versa. Peers observe local capacity constraints and a maximum tolerable latency threshold. SG-2 strives to minimize the number of super-peers, however according to [117], this number is on the order of $O(n)$ while SPSA achieves $O(\sqrt{n})$, with n being the total number of peers. Moreover, because of the spatially limited zones of influence, SG-2 does not ensure overlay connectivity, and since every peer is assumed to be reachable from the outside, firewalls represent an obstacle to SG-2 operations.

Another procedure to create super-peer topologies is based on *Yao graphs* and a clustering-based network coordinates generator [131]. It determines the role of a peer statically upon entrance into the overlay. Peers are placed in a geometrical space with common peers attaching themselves to the closest super-peer. The overlay size and the number of super-peers are unrelated, however, and message forwarding load among the super-peers is unevenly distributed, with super-peers close to the Yao graph's edge bearing less load than those in its center.

A global-view strategy to pick the most suitable super-peer for an edge peer to connect to in unstructured super-peer topologies is presented in [172]. It consists of a weighted mixture of GNP-based delay estimation, CPU load smoothed over time using exponential averaging, and a content similarity measure which is useful only in scenarios where data is shared (e. g. filesharing). While this strategy incorporates proximity awareness and deploys network coordinates, the super-peers are assumed to be known and fixed, a global view is required, and there is no distributed algorithm to create a super-peer topology.

The SCALABLE UNSTRUCTURED P2P SYSTEM (SUPS) interconnects the super-peers with a random graph created and maintained by a distributed algorithm [191]. SUPS achieves a network diameter of $O\left(\frac{\log n}{\log \log n}\right)$ which is better than ChordSPSA's at $O(\log n)$ but worse than SPSA's at $O(1)$. Similar to ChordSPSA, it places $O(n \cdot \log n)$ edges among the super-peers, and like Chord in its original version, it aims for a low average path length irrespective of a hop's actual delay. While SUPS has a low network diameter and attempts to balance the load by equalizing the super-peers' node degrees, SUPS does not incorporate locality, does not specify a super-peer selection criterion, and due to the stochastic nature of its random graph approximation process, does not provide deterministic performance guarantees.

The DYNAMIC LAYER MANAGEMENT (DLM) distributed algorithm maintains an unstructured super-peer topology [235]. An edge peer may be connected to an arbitrary number of super-peers, and the super-peers' subgraph may be disconnected. The optimal number of super-peers, given as the ratio between edge peers and super-peers, is derived analytically. Like SPSA and ChordSPSA, the DLM algorithm promotes edge peers to super-peer level and vice versa. Instead of proximity, DLM measures peer capacity and lifetime as super-peers are desired to be capable and durable. Every peer samples its neighborhood with these metrics and compares its own performance to the sample. If an edge peers finds itself more capable than most sampled super-peers, it upgrades itself, while a super-peer that finds sufficiently many edge peers more capable than itself downgrades. The main issue with DLM is that it sticks with an unstructured super-peer core topology. Other issues include the absence of proximity awareness and the assumption that a peer's capabilities (including bandwidth, CPU load, and storage space) do not change throughout its lifetime. An improved variant of DLM is SRM which increases the accuracy of the super-peer ratio estimation and prevents edge peers from causing a super-peer downgrade [15]. SRM formulates the task of ratio estimation as an optimization problem that can be solved heuristically with *Particle Swarm Optimization*, a procedure which is similar to that employed by BBS for determining network coordinates (cf. Section 3.3.3). However, while SRM improves particular aspects of DLM, there is still an unstructured topology and no notion of proximity awareness.

A self-organizing approach to creating a super-peer topology using SCHELLING'S MODEL was proposed in [212]. Like the Hub Location model underlying SPSA, this approach is inspired by an economic model, in this case through one created by economist Thomas Schelling. Originally, Schelling's model was supposed to capture the self-organizing creation process of segregated neighborhoods in U.S. cities during the 1960s. Citizens are assumed to strive for a neighborhood in which at least a given minimum number of other citizens are similar to themselves. The model considers the world as a grid made of $m \times n$ cells. Cells are either empty or inhabited by turtles which are blue or red. In the beginning, about $\frac{2}{3}$ of the grid's cells are populated by randomly distributed blue or red turtles, one turtle per cell. As each turtle desires a certain percentage of its neighbors to match its color, it moves randomly to an adjacent empty cell if this desire is not satisfied. The system converges to a stable state once all turtles are content with their current positions. Interpreting turtles as peers, every peer has a predefined radius of sight around its position, and will connect to peers within this radius only. Super-peers are satisfied as long as there are enough common peers in their vicinity that can connect to it, while common peers are satisfied as long as there is at least one super-peer close by. However, this approach merely represents a framework that can be implemented by various algorithms. While Schelling's model defines the connections between peers, the rule according to which peers are assigned the super-peer role is left unspecified.

4.4.3.2 Structured super-peer interconnection topologies

A fundamental partition of work concerning structured topologies to link the super-peers divides the reviewed efforts into those focusing on frameworks and others related to design blueprints and implementations of tangible systems.

4.4.3.2.1 Frameworks

Hierarchical structured topologies with super-peers as the interconnection points between the hierarchy layers are explored in [93]. The proposed framework relates hierarchical structured topologies to routing between two autonomous systems (AS) in the Internet. According to this model, super-peers correspond to AS gateways while edge peers are common nodes or routers within an AS. A two-layered DHT is conceived. First, peers may join groups whose members are interconnected by an arbitrary structured topology. Every group has one or more super-peers which serve as gateways to other groups. The super-peers are interconnected with a Chord ring. Looking up a key is a two-stage process: first, the group which is responsible for the key is determined and the query is sent to one of the group's super-peers. Subsequently, the query is forwarded to its true destination within the group. Like ChordSPSA, this approach fosters locality and accelerates message forwarding. At the same time, it is more complex and, as a framework, it does neither explicitly specify the selection rule for super-peers nor the nature of the proximity measurement process.

In an effort similar to that of [93], a framework for the hierarchical design of structured topologies was proposed along with a cost-based analysis of such structures in [14]. It is argued that hierarchical designs can alleviate the bottleneck effects of weak members in flat topologies. Moreover, it is stressed that hierarchical designs foster the locality-aware creation of edge peer clusters around super-peers. [14] contrasts flat designs that consider all peers equal to super-peer approaches in which super-peers care for a large number of potentially unstable edge peers. In the super-peer case, unlike the approach proposed in this chapter, it is assumed that both the super-peers and all peers within a cluster are interconnected by Chord rings. Moreover, [14] cites a diminished fault tolerance compared to flat structures as the loss of a super-peer must be compensated. However, this needs to be put in perspective. As discussed in Section 4.4.2 and in [32], the departure of any peer in a flat Chord ring forces other peers to repair their finger tables while in super-peer structures, only the loss of a super-peer requires significant reorganization efforts.

Extending [14] and [93], [248] concentrates on two-tier super-peer structures with structured topologies to hold the super-peers. While the super-peers are interconnected by a structured topology (with a focus on Chord), various alternatives for connecting the edge peers are discussed, and a formal metric to compute the operational cost is presented to evaluate the alternatives. As in the approach proposed in Section 4.4.2, every super-peer manages a cluster of edge peers. In [248], three options for interconnecting the peers in such a cluster are considered: a clique, a structured topology, and a star-shaped topology in which every edge peer maintains exactly one connection, the one to its assigned super-peer. It is confirmed that the topology created by ChordSPSA – a structured topology to hold the super-peers, while each edge peer maintains a link only to its assigned super-peer – performs better than the other alternatives mainly because under realistic operating conditions, it incurs the least volume of traffic. Additionally, it is found that in heterogeneous systems, a hierarchical topology is superior to a flat one. This is consistent with the conclusion reached by [247], published by the same authors as [248]. The contribution of [247] is a cost-based framework to evaluate the operational costs for super-peer topologies in which the super-peers are interconnected by a structured topology (with Chord as the preferred one), while the edge peers are connected to one super-peer each. With Chord, this equals the topology that ChordSPSA builds and maintains. The conclusion of [247] also contains the insight that maintaining a star-shaped topology is least expensive in terms of network traffic, but overburdens the single super-peer. Hence, under the assumption that a super-peer is willing to bear a limited amount of load only, more than one super-peer is required to maintain the topology. However, the presented analysis focuses on the storage-related (DHT) use of structured topologies, with data items stored by individual peers. Also, it neglects churn, and it assumes a Chord ring fully populated with super-peers. The work presented in this thesis complements the analysis of [247] to the end of providing a distributed topology construction algorithm whose existence the authors of [247] assume.

4.4.3.2.2 Tangible systems

BROCADE has pioneered the idea of interconnecting super-peers with a structured topology [62, 241]. Brocade selects one highly capable super-peer per AS in the Internet and uses Tapestry to interconnect these super-peers. They are elected or picked by ISPs in a comparatively static process. However, the number of super-peers is not automatically adapted to the overlay size as with SPSA, and locality is provided merely by attaching edge peers to the particular super-peer which is located in their AS.

The cost of lookups in DHTs is reduced by a super-peer approach that exploits the heterogeneity inherent to P2P networks [174]. It corresponds to a super-peer-mediated DHT structure with a fixed diameter. As conventional DHTs like Chord have a diameter on the order of at best $O(\log n)$ with n being the number of peers in the overlay, the cost of a query increases logarithmically with the overlay size. In contrast, lookups in client/server systems can be handled in $O(1)$ time at the expense of scalability and robustness. The approach proposed in [174] appoints the small fraction of highly capable participants super-peers, following a hybrid design that uses super-peers as the silver bullet between centralized and fully decentralized systems. The super-peers carry additional state on the order of $O(\sqrt{n})$ to allow $O(1)$ lookups. The topology is made of two nested rings: the inner ring contains the super-peers, while the outer ring carries all edge peers in a Chord DHT and is split into as many equal-sized arcs as there are super-peers. Every super-peer is assigned to an arc; a super-peer is responsible for handling the edge peers located in its arc of the outer ring. Super-peers know about their edge peers' Chord IDs and IP addresses. A lookup for x is performed by querying the local super-peer for the peer on the outer ring responsible for x. If x is within the super-peer's arc, it can resolve the query directly and return the destination's IP address. Otherwise, the super-peer contacts the responsible super-peer which then returns the destination's IP address to the query issuer. Thus, the overlay diameter amounts to 3 hops. However, this approach relies on peers being reachable from the outside, precluding the use of firewalls. It shares some properties with SPSA as the super-peers are fully meshed, and the maximum number of hops to travel for a query message is 3. Super-peers can directly contact all other super-peers. If TCP connections are used, super-peers will be busy creating and closing connections to edge peers which is a costly effort. Therefore, SPSA and ChordSPSA, which keep up existing connections as required, are preferable for the purposes of Desktop Grids.

While not an explicit hybrid P2P system, eQuus fosters proximity awareness and supports a large degree of overlay dynamics [151]. It is built on a structured topology in which peers that are close to each other in the underlying network form clusters. Unlike Chord, Pastry, and other conventional DHT systems, there is more than one peer responsible for an ID. Every peer in a cluster has the same ID, and the peers in a cluster make up a clique. In addition, every peer maintains links to peers in other clusters. While eQuus offers a high degree of resilience to churn and low maintenance overhead, it requires every peer to be reachable from the outside, excluding peers behind firewalls from participation.

The CHORDELLA hierarchical DHT features the same structure as proposed in this thesis: a super-peer topology in which the super-peers are interconnected by a Chord ring, and a self-organizing algorithm to minimize the total cost [114]. The Chordella algorithm downgrades super-peers and upgrades edge peers to super-peer level based on local estimates of global system parameters. There are two key differences between the approach proposed in this thesis and Chordella. First, Chordella is geared towards wireless networks, considering the edge peers to be resource-constrained devices such as mobile phones. Second, Chordella aims for equalizing the load burden carried by the super-peers only but does not consider the average end-to-end communication delay.

The STEALTH DHT is another approach at creating a super-peer topology [32]. On the basis of an existing DHT structure (Pastry is used in [32]), the set of peers is divided into a small number of *service nodes* (super-peers) and a large number of *stealth nodes* (edge peers). The service nodes make up the core of the DHT which the stealth nodes rely on. While the stealth nodes are part of the DHT, they are not involved in routing or forwarding operations, and they do not receive any queries either. There is no explicit selection criterion for the service nodes. In fact, [32] states that this criterion should be picked and handled by the application. Moreover, while the locality issue is addressed, there is no explicit topology optimization process, and super-peers are assumed to be capable and stable, possibly provided by a single entity. Thus, the Stealth DHT approach is of limited use for a Desktop Grid.

A peculiar structured topology is the MINIMUM-DELAY TREE (MDTree) topology. While its peers are not equipped with topology-specific identifiers, the MDTree topology fulfills the criterion of being a structured topology as peers are not free to forge arbitrary links to other peers but need to adhere to a prescribed tree structure. The MDTree approach defines a super-peer topology specifically geared for an open, self-organizing Grid with heterogeneous resources [240]. Its purpose is to facilitate the selection of variable-sized clusters of workers for distributed computing, clustered according to network proximity. A MDTree is a particular kind of tree. Edges in the MDTree imply links in the actual topology. Each of a MDTree's nodes refers to up to a constant value of K fully meshed peers (called *neighborhood*), and each of the tree's levels contains peers that experience low delay to each other. A node on a tree level refers to a peer which is a super-peer for a neighborhood of peers on the level below, and also belongs to that neighborhood. Hence, all peers represented by the tree's inner nodes are super-peers. A MDTree contains subtrees rooted at super-peers. A super-peer considers all peers on its tree level and all its children as close to itself in terms of network delay. Every super-peer maintains its subtree. In addition, all super-peers besides the root keep a link to their respective parent super-peer. To select a cluster of workers, a super-peer considers the subtree it locally maintains. If the tree contains enough peers, these are chosen as worker candidates. Otherwise, a request for workers is forwarded recursively via the chain of parent super-peers. The forwarding process stops once enough worker candidates have been found or the root node's MDTree is too small to satisfy the request. A neighborhood of K peers that needs to accommodate a new peer in the MDTree exceeds its capacity limit, and is hence split into two neighborhoods with a common super-peer. Since optimal bi-partitioning is NP-hard, [240] deploys a genetic algorithm for an approximate solution.

The MDTree approach's motivation, in particular its focus on proximity, and the necessity to split overcrowded neighborhoods (the counterpart to the super-peer promotion step in SPSA and ChordSPSA) resemble the procedure proposed in this thesis. However, the MDTree approach is flawed in several respects. Since delays fluctuate, the tree needs to be updated accordingly, and the large number of ping messages required to insert a new peer into the tree entails non-negligible overhead in the face of overlay dynamics. All super-peers (considerably more than with SPSA or ChordSPSA) need to be reachable from the outside, and since new peers enter the overlay via the MDTree's root node, the peer referenced by the root node should not fail. While a new root node could be elected in a distributed way, no new nodes can join in the meantime, and the tree must be reorganized. Furthermore, to select a cluster of workers, an initiator needs to send ping messages to all candidates. Besides the network load, there is no way to determine the delay between any two workers with this approach. Network coordinates can solve this issue, and in the case of dynamic generation algorithms, adapt to fluctuating delays. Also, PeerGrid exhibits none of the other issues as a small number of super-peers can act as proxies for a large number of edge peers that potentially operate from behind firewalls, and there is no single bootstrap peer. While the MDTree topology is structured in a tree-like shape, its peers have no distinct identifiers, and the topology is built mainly for picking clusters of peers, not for actual message propagation.

Network	Size	Standard		PRS		LPRS		Direct	
		Delay	Hops	Delay	Hops	Delay	Hops	Delay	Hops
01-2005	127	850.23	4.40	777.92	5.32	468.58	4.58	251.41	1.00
02-2005	321	834.28	5.04	782.10	5.92	461.27	5.15	204.43	1.00
03-2005	324	900.05	5.05	818.33	5.97	465.86	5.17	221.53	1.00
04-2005	70	506.98	4.00	463.71	4.72	300.01	4.07	165.28	1.00
05-2005	374	866.05	5.16	825.63	6.02	478.35	5.24	208.56	1.00
06-2005	365	949.31	5.13	842.52	6.08	507.09	5.25	224.94	1.00
07-2005	380	1,126.52	5.17	889.97	6.05	549.34	5.22	269.98	1.00
08-2005	402	1,057.23	5.20	890.53	6.11	544.46	5.26	247.22	1.00
09-2005	419	998.13	5.24	850.27	6.14	522.96	5.29	237.75	1.00
10-2005	414	1,152.18	5.23	924.29	6.12	579.68	5.24	270.52	1.00
11-2005	407	891.69	5.21	827.43	6.10	509.37	5.26	211.00	1.00
12-2005	414	1,650.70	5.23	1,198.86	6.20	800.50	5.33	388.42	1.00
King	1,740	969.33	6.25	904.77	7.28	493.45	6.37	184.00	1.00
Meridian	2,500	432.25	6.51	409.21	7.53	261.11	6.42	79.67	1.00
Weighted average		670.03	6.25	615.38	7.26	366.32	6.24	132.92	1.00

Table 4.6: Average delay and average path length (absolute values) with PRS and LPRS for all evaluated networks. Inter-peer delays were estimated with Vivaldi.

Table 4.7: Average delay and average path length (absolute values) with PRS and LPRS for all evaluated networks. Inter-peer delays were known exactly.

Network	Size	Standard		PRS		LPRS		Direct	
		Delay	Hops	Delay	Hops	Delay	Hops	Delay	Hops
01-2005	127	834.99	4.40	699.39	5.81	397.97	4.99	251.41	1.00
02-2005	321	814.74	5.04	672.02	6.48	358.62	5.65	204.43	1.00
03-2005	324	905.20	5.06	736.69	6.52	379.86	5.77	221.53	1.00
04-2005	70	503.77	4.00	425.74	5.03	258.09	4.30	165.28	1.00
05-2005	374	871.22	5.15	708.33	6.65	371.49	5.80	208.56	1.00
06-2005	365	910.20	5.14	664.22	6.62	353.23	5.83	224.94	1.00
07-2005	380	1,144.78	5.16	775.94	6.63	418.12	5.82	269.98	1.00
08-2005	402	994.44	5.20	732.30	6.65	385.88	5.86	247.22	1.00
09-2005	419	996.97	5.24	722.17	6.73	384.00	5.97	237.75	1.00
10-2005	414	1,108.61	5.22	762.00	6.71	413.33	5.89	270.52	1.00
11-2005	407	897.50	5.22	695.46	6.68	363.94	5.95	211.00	1.00
12-2005	414	1,697.92	5.22	992.49	6.70	491.58	5.92	388.42	1.00
King	1,740	967.24	6.25	837.18	7.57	402.39	6.56	184.00	1.00
Meridian	2,500	433.66	6.51	344.40	7.97	165.01	7.46	79.67	1.00
Weighted average		669.11	6.25	539.18	7.68	263.53	6.98	132.92	1.00

Network	Size	PRS Delay	PRS Hops	LPRS Delay	LPRS Hops	Direct Delay	Direct Hops
01-2005	127	0.91	1.21	0.55	1.04	0.30	0.23
02-2005	321	0.94	1.17	0.55	1.02	0.25	0.20
03-2005	324	0.91	1.18	0.52	1.02	0.25	0.20
04-2005	70	0.91	1.18	0.59	1.02	0.33	0.25
05-2005	374	0.95	1.17	0.55	1.02	0.24	0.19
06-2005	365	0.89	1.18	0.53	1.02	0.24	0.19
07-2005	380	0.79	1.17	0.49	1.01	0.24	0.19
08-2005	402	0.84	1.17	0.51	1.01	0.23	0.19
09-2005	419	0.85	1.17	0.52	1.01	0.24	0.19
10-2005	414	0.80	1.17	0.50	1.00	0.23	0.19
11-2005	407	0.93	1.17	0.57	1.01	0.24	0.19
12-2005	414	0.73	1.19	0.48	1.02	0.24	0.19
King	1,740	0.93	1.17	0.51	1.02	0.19	0.16
Meridian	2,500	0.95	1.16	0.60	0.99	0.18	0.15
Weighted average		0.92	1.16	0.55	1.00	0.20	0.16

Table 4.8: Average delay and average path length (relative values) with PRS and LPRS for all evaluated networks. Inter-peer delays were estimated with Vivaldi. This table contains the data from Table 4.6 normalized to the performance of original Chord.

Network	Size	PRS Delay	PRS Hops	LPRS Delay	LPRS Hops	Direct Delay	Direct Hops
01-2005	127	0.84	1.32	0.48	1.13	0.30	0.23
02-2005	321	0.82	1.28	0.44	1.12	0.25	0.20
03-2005	324	0.81	1.29	0.42	1.14	0.24	0.20
04-2005	70	0.85	1.26	0.51	1.08	0.33	0.25
05-2005	374	0.81	1.29	0.43	1.13	0.24	0.19
06-2005	365	0.73	1.29	0.39	1.13	0.25	0.19
07-2005	380	0.68	1.29	0.37	1.13	0.24	0.19
08-2005	402	0.74	1.28	0.39	1.13	0.25	0.19
09-2005	419	0.72	1.29	0.39	1.14	0.24	0.19
10-2005	414	0.69	1.29	0.37	1.13	0.24	0.19
11-2005	407	0.77	1.28	0.41	1.14	0.24	0.19
12-2005	414	0.58	1.28	0.29	1.13	0.23	0.19
King	1,740	0.87	1.21	0.42	1.05	0.19	0.16
Meridian	2,500	0.79	1.23	0.38	1.15	0.18	0.15
Weighted average		0.81	1.23	0.39	1.12	0.20	0.16

Table 4.9: Average delay and average path length (relative values) with PRS and LPRS for all evaluated networks. Inter-peer delays were known exactly. This table contains the data from Table 4.7 normalized to the performance of original Chord.

Network	Size	PIS Delay	PIS Hops	PIS+PRS Delay	PIS+PRS Hops	PIS+LPRS Delay	PIS+LPRS Hops	Direct Delay	Direct Hops
01-2005	127	775.67	4.00	528.88	5.72	338.27	4.76	251.41	1.00
02-2005	321	535.42	4.65	525.10	6.42	284.91	5.50	204.43	1.00
03-2005	324	678.97	4.70	581.47	6.46	302.42	5.60	221.53	1.00
04-2005	70	425.37	3.37	410.91	4.79	263.47	4.01	165.28	1.00
05-2005	374	694.59	4.77	633.02	6.56	293.91	5.82	208.56	1.00
06-2005	365	630.60	4.80	617.39	6.75	284.60	6.20	224.94	1.00
07-2005	380	1,167.41	5.03	740.38	6.83	353.59	6.26	269.98	1.00
08-2005	402	1,260.62	5.02	739.00	6.81	344.28	6.17	247.22	1.00
09-2005	419	708.32	5.06	745.42	6.95	323.14	6.10	237.75	1.00
10-2005	414	832.70	5.11	792.81	6.86	366.00	5.93	270.52	1.00
11-2005	407	698.92	4.95	626.26	6.68	298.54	6.31	211.00	1.00
12-2005	414	988.27	4.98	917.33	6.67	398.61	6.00	388.42	1.00
King	1,740	804.76	6.46	680.32	8.01	349.12	7.25	184.00	1.00
Meridian	2,500	382.43	6.44	328.40	8.76	136.46	9.08	79.67	1.00
Weighted average		563.84	6.24	479.30	8.27	222.87	8.14	132.92	1.00

Table 4.10: PIS performance (average delays and path lengths) for all evaluated networks, alone and in combination with PRS and LPRS.

Network	Size	PIS+PRS Delay	Hops	PIS+LPRS Delay	Hops	Direct Delay	Hops
01-2005	127	0.68	1.43	0.44	1.19	0.32	0.25
02-2005	321	0.98	1.38	0.53	1.18	0.38	0.21
03-2005	324	0.86	1.38	0.45	1.19	0.33	0.21
04-2005	70	0.97	1.42	0.62	1.19	0.39	0.30
05-2005	374	0.91	1.38	0.42	1.22	0.30	0.21
06-2005	365	0.98	1.41	0.45	1.29	0.36	0.21
07-2005	380	0.63	1.36	0.30	1.24	0.23	0.20
08-2005	402	0.59	1.36	0.27	1.23	0.20	0.20
09-2005	419	1.05	1.37	0.46	1.21	0.34	0.20
10-2005	414	0.95	1.34	0.44	1.16	0.32	0.20
11-2005	407	0.90	1.35	0.43	1.27	0.30	0.20
12-2005	414	0.93	1.34	0.40	1.20	0.39	0.20
King	1,740	0.85	1.24	0.43	1.12	0.23	0.15
Meridian	2,500	0.86	1.36	0.36	1.41	0.21	0.16
Weighted average		0.85	1.33	0.40	1.31	0.24	0.16

Table 4.11: PIS performance (average delays and path lengths) for all evaluated networks, alone and in combination with PRS and LPRS. This table contains the data from Table 4.10 normalized to the performance of PIS alone.

4.5   Summary

In this chapter, the needs of Desktop Grids with regard to the underlying P2P structure were analyzed. Unstructured and centralized topologies lack the scalability of structured topologies. A structured super-peer core topology provides the ground for an efficient broadcast mechanism which is the backbone for propagating super-peer beacon information and calls for workers in a Desktop Grid. Both flat and hierarchical variants of structured topologies were considered. While a Chord topology satisfies most of a Desktop Grid's communication-related requirements, its peers must be reachable from the outside to permit the creation of finger connections. This drawback affects the other flat topologies discussed in this chapter in similar ways: Pastry, Meridian and CAN.

Hybrid P2P topologies can solve the issue by introducing super-peers. Parallels exist between the super-peer topology construction problem and a family of facility location problems, the Hub Location family. A particular Hub Location problem and SPSA, a distributed algorithm for making super-peer topologies with a fully meshed super-peer core, were presented in a first step. The Hub Location problem can be solved exactly for small instances only, but it is helpful to obtain lower bounds and provide a formalized understanding of the topology's characteristics. It was shown that for this topology type and the goal of minimizing a super-peer's connection count, the optimum number of super-peers in an n-peer overlay is $\sqrt{n}$. The associated distributed algorithm, SPSA, strives for an equilibrium of $\sqrt{n}$ super-peers and $\sqrt{n} - 1$ edge peers per super-peer.

In spite of its benefits, the complete subgraph holding the super-peers is an obstacle to scalability. Replacing it with a Chord ring creates multi-hop routes between super-peers but decreases the number of connections held by a super-peer to $O(\log n)$. The ChordSPSA algorithm constructs and maintains a super-peer topology of this kind. Also, efficient broadcast with only $O(\log n)$ messages sent by a forwarding peer becomes possible. ChordSPSA's properties were examined analytically and through simulation. Compared to keeping all peers in a flat Chord ring, the need for Chord ring reorganizations becomes rare. Moreover, in this type of super-peer topology, there is a distinctive potential for accelerating message forwarding procedures through shifting the objective from minimizing the average path length to minimizing the average end-to-end delay. Three methods, PRS, LPRS and PIS, were introduced and evaluated in this context. All three methods operate in a fully distributed way, can be implemented to run in polynomial time, and require no extra messages to be sent. The PeerGrid middleware on which Chapter 6 will elaborate resorts to ChordSPSA as its topology maintenance mechanism.

The Hub Location model and a description of SPSA have been published in [168]. Additional work on SPSA has been released in [169]. ChordSPSA, the vital aspects of PIS and PRS, and the deterministic gossip scheme have been published in [170].

5

Peer behavior

Unlike Grid computing, there are no pre-made trust relationships in Desktop Grids. Since a peer's owner in a Desktop Grid usually has no knowledge about the entity operating another peer, the anonymity precludes inherent trust. This chapter provides an overview over common behavioral types of peers and presents a distributed reputation system that shields cooperative participants from exploitation.

5.1   Behavioral types

Every peer is modelled to have a private *type* which determines its behavior. The behavioral model distinguishes between three major types of peers [4, 49, 80, 99, 182]:

- *Altruists* serve to the best of their capabilities every request issued by other peers without asking for reciprocity.

- *Collaborators* expect to receive a benefit from the Desktop Grid, but are generally willing to cooperate if they can trust their counterpart to eventually reciprocate.

- *Free-riders* are selfish participants that do not wish to contribute resources to the Desktop Grid. Rather, they try to exploit the computational resources of unsuspecting or exposed peers.

The properties of these types are now discussed in more detail.

5.1.1 Altruism

Exhibiting the opposite behavior to complete selfishness, altruists always obey and co-operate with other peers regardless of external rewards [16, 182, 226]. Their utility rises when they increase the welfare of others [16, 80].

Altruism is a widespread assumption in P2P system design [69]. For instance, routing mechanisms frequently assume that peers will expend resources to forward traffic to other peers even if the forwarding peer does not have any advantage of the act of forwarding. With regard to P2P filesharing applications, a study considered peers' varying degrees of intrinsic altruism, differentiating between *realistic altruism* (an altruistic peer i's utility grows with the utility increase of other peers caused by the donations of i) and *selfish altruism* (the utility of i grows with the amount of resources it provides, no matter the consumers' utilities) [226]. The study finds altruism to be an endogenous incentive, causing altruists to join the system because they wish to contribute.

The notion of altruism is not limited to being a model assumption. It can be observed in reality. Human societies are based on cooperation and a certain level of altruism [129]. In the context of distributed computing, volunteer computing systems like SETI@home rely on large numbers of peers willing to donate cycles, bandwidth, and power for no material return. Dingledine et al. find the roots of P2P altruism in a reversed *tragedy of the commons*: "when the cost of contributing to a system is low enough, people will contribute to it for reasons not immediately beneficial to themselves" [69]. Altruistic individuals supply OpenStreetMap with geographic information for use by others [105], a similar principle as pioneered by Wikipedia [33]. These findings suggest that it is fitting and proper to incorporate the concept of altruism into a model that captures peer behavior.

5.1.2 Free-riding

P2P systems rely on cooperation among the peers. A free-rider is an individual who does not provide any resources to a system but exploits it selfishly [4, 5, 8, 49, 80, 81, 82, 124, 182, 234]. Free-riding is a consequence of rational behavior which is usually interpreted as utility-maximizing. The following assertion originates from [49]:

> The fundamental premise of peer-to-peer systems is that individual peers voluntarily contribute resources to the system. However, the inherent ten-sion between individual rationality and collective welfare produces a mis-alignment of incentives in the grassroots provisioning of P2P services. What makes free-riding a particularly difficult problem is the unique set of chal-

lenges that P2P systems pose: large populations, high turnover, asymmetry of interest, collusion, hidden actions, and zero-cost identities.

In the Gnutella filesharing network, approximately 70 % of the peers were found to be free-riding [4]. In Desktop Grids, free-riding behavior could be expected as some peers might join the system exclusively to the end of submitting a job but not for providing resources to others. Once the job's result is available, a free-rider immediately leaves the system. This behavioral scheme is consistent with the empirical observation made in the MAZE P2P filesharing system that a free-rider's sojourn time is approximately one third of the session length of an ordinary, non-free-riding user [238]. While an altruistic setting may support a certain extent of free-riding, it is expected to collapse if exceedingly many peers choose to act as free-riders [182]. Therefore, Desktop Grids benefit from mechanisms which curb free-riding.

5.1.3 Collaboration

Collaborators are willing to reserve resources for use by others provided they are not exploited by free-riding users. Collaborators seek other collaborators (or alternatively, altruists) for interaction: they are willing to cooperate if the other player cooperates, too. Since free-riders do not accept to work for others and altruists do not mind being exploited, collaborators are the only kind of peers that require protection from exploitation. This kind of protection is the key feature of the distributed reputation system discussed in Section 5.3.

Without protection, collaborators cannot tell about the past behavior of peers they are about to interact with. Hence, their resources are easily occupied by free-riders that exploit this lack of protection. Technically, while both accept any job, altruists and exposed collaborators differ in that altruists do not mind being exploited because they gain utility from the mere act of unconditionally donating their resources to others [80,99]. On the contrary, collaborators seek reciprocity and shun exploitation.

Collaborating peers exhibit a limited amount of selfishness. Unlike altruists, they are not always willing to obey, and unlike free-riders, they are generally willing to share their resources if they have a reason to believe the remote peer will eventually reciprocate.

5.1.4 Interaction among peers

Considering all peers to be either altruistic or rational may lead to an overly coarse model that fosters biased conclusions. A peer's individual motivation may be arbitrarily selfish, creating a mixture of motivations within a peer population which is composed of individuals represented by the three introduced behavioral types. In the remainder of this chapter, it is assumed that every direct interaction in a P2P system involves two peers. This section first reviews a model that describes the interaction between selfish peers, then continues with a description of peer interactions when arbitrary combinations of the introduced peer types interact.

5.1.4.1 The Prisoner's Dilemma

The interaction between two selfish peers is frequently modelled as an instance of the PRISONER'S DILEMMA game where both players can pick one of the strategies *cooperate* or *defect* independently from each other [16, 49, 90, 182]. The first strategy will lead to reciprocation while the latter strategy will lead to the attempt of exploiting the other player. Each of the four strategy combinations is a distinct *outcome* of the game, and every outcome is linked to a *payoff* for each player. Let $p_i(s,t) \in \mathbb{R}$ be the payoff player $i \in \{1,2\}$ receives when he plays strategy s while the other player plays strategy t. In the Prisoner's Dilemma, payoffs are symmetric: $p_1(s,t) = p_2(s,t)$. Strategies and payoffs for all players are known to every player beforehand. The dilemma situation is enabled through the particular allocation of payoffs to the various strategy combinations.

From the first player's point of view, there are three possible outcomes in a Prisoner's Dilemma game (the situation is analogous for the second player):

- In case both players cooperate, they are able to attain the highest cumulative payoff: $p_1(\text{cooperate,cooperate}) + p_2(\text{cooperate,cooperate})$ is maximum.

- When the first player cooperates and the second defects, the defector exploits the cooperativeness of his opponent. His payoff is higher than what he would have gained if he had cooperated ($p_2(\text{defect,cooperate}) > p_2(\text{cooperate,cooperate})$), but the joint payoff diminishes: $p_1(\text{cooperate,cooperate}) + p_2(\text{cooperate,cooperate}) > p_1(\text{cooperate,defect}) + p_2(\text{defect,cooperate})$. The payoff $p_1(\text{cooperate,defect})$ of player 1 is at its minimum as he is exploited by player 2. This case is symmetrical to the case of player 1 exploiting a cooperative player 2.

- When both players defect, the combined payoff $p_1(\text{defect,defect}) + p_2(\text{defect,defect})$ is lower than in the other cases, but player 1 no longer pays the price of exploitation: $p_1(\text{defect,defect}) > p_1(\text{cooperate,defect})$, while $p_2(\text{defect,defect}) < p_2(\text{defect,cooperate})$.

When both players try to maximize their respective payoff, there are solution concepts that predict the outcome. Each outcome represents an *equilibrium* from which neither player wishes to deviate. An *equilibrium in dominant strategies* exists if for each player there is a strategy that yields at least as much payoff as any other strategy, no matter what strategy the other player chooses. If no equilibrium in dominant strategies exists, a weaker solution concept that might identify more than one possible outcome per game is the *Nash equilibrium*. For a Nash equilibrium, every outcome qualifies in which a player's strategy choice cannot be improved with respect to the payoff given the assumption that the other player will not deviate from its strategy. An equilibrium in dominant strategies always is a Nash equilibrium [90].

The Prisoner's Dilemma depicts a conflict between group rationality and individual rationality. To maximize the group utility (cumulative utility), both players need to cooperate. Given the strategy combination (cooperate,cooperate), either player would be better off by exploiting the other player's cooperativeness. Enabled by selfishness, this temptation to increase the individual utility at the expense of the group's welfare fuels the dilemma situation. Since all strategies and payoffs are known to everyone, each player will anticipate the other player's desire to defect and see the own benefit in defection. At this point, the equilibrium becomes (defect,defect). In addition to the own gains attained through defection if the other player cooperates, the only way to protect oneself against being exploited is to defect oneself. No matter the strategy of the other player, it is always better to defect to maximize the individual utility. Thus, two rational players will make the game result in the game's equilibrium in dominant strategies (defect, defect) which also is the game's only Nash equilibrium. This outcome is individually rational but not Pareto efficient since both players would enjoy more utility if they had played (cooperate, cooperate).

When the same pair of players repeatedly interacts, each iteration can be modelled as a distinct Prisoner's Dilemma game. If time is discrete, divided into rounds, the outcome of each game depends on the previous game and the expectation of future behavior in the upcoming rounds. A sequence of ordinary Prisoner's Dilemma games augmented by strategies that take future games and past behavior into account is modelled through the *Repeated Prisoner's Dilemma* [90]. [38]

The Prisoner's Dilemma model does not always fit the peculiarities of interactions in a P2P system. Its requirement of total knowledge of strategies and payoffs, including those of the other player, and its assumption of exclusively selfish behavior cannot be upheld in the context of Desktop Grids. The next section will inquire on the characteristics of P2P interactions in a Desktop Grid given the various behavioral types of peers.

5.1.4.2 Type-dependent peer interactions

The outcomes of interactions between peers depend on the behavioral types of the in-volved peers. Altruists will always choose to cooperate while free-riders will always

---

[38] A synonym for the Repeated Prisoner's Dilemma is *Iterated Prisoner's Dilemma* [182].

choose to defect. Hence, two altruists will cooperate, two free-riders will not cooperate, and a free-rider will occupy the resources of an altruist but neither will mind. Collaborators will interact with anyone they deem trustworthy. In the conventional Prisoner's Dilemma or when the number of dilemma iterations is known beforehand, defection is the rational strategy to play for selfish individuals. However, if the number of played rounds is unknown, cooperation becomes the rational strategy. When rational players cannot assess the negative consequences of defection, they are better off by choosing cooperation [16].

Collaborators are inclined to play a *tit-for-tat* strategy [16, 26, 145]. Tit-for-tat players always cooperate in the first round. In all subsequent rounds, they replicate their counterpart's behavior from the previous round. Tit-for-tat exhibits a number of desirable properties as it is initially friendly, reactive, maintains mutual cooperation, and is ready to retaliate immediately when provoked [16]. However, tit-for-tat is vulnerable in P2P environments through the availability of cheap identities, as will be discussed below.

In Desktop Grids, there are no enforced policies – rules that define acceptable behavior – as in a conventional Grid. In the absence of public-key infrastructures (PKI) that could provide peers with persistent identities, peers may obtain non-persistent (transient, *weak*) identities at virtually zero cost [69, 89, 142]. These circumstances lead to the *whitewashing* phenomenon [80]. It describes the situation that a selfish peer is tempted to leave and rejoin the overlay with a new identity after having performed actions that are detrimental to its reputation in the first place. The particular peer is whitewashing its standing [80, 81, 82]. Whitewashing free-riders play the *always defect* strategy that exploits any other peer at the first opportunity. It threatens tit-for-tat players as *always defect* capitalizes on tit-for-tat's leap of faith in its first round. This strategy is possible only because identities are cheap.

With non-persistent identities, there is no definitive means to distinguish a true newcomer from a whitewasher. Placing general mistrust in newcomers is one way to discourage whitewashing [9, 80, 89]. However, honest newcomers suffer from such mistrust. The social cost of this approach was assessed in [89]. An alternative to general mistrust was suggested in [81]. It consists of an adaptive stranger policy that judges new peers on the basis of new peers' behavior in the past by maintaining a *stranger account* that accumulates recent experience with new peers. A large number of free-riders joining the Desktop Grid will tend to decrease the stranger account's value, while a majority of collaborators or altruists will increase it. Hence, the stranger account may serve as a predictor for an unknown peer's trustworthiness.

5.2   Reputation

Reputation conveys information about a peer's past conduct to influence expectations of its future behavior [89, 142]. It quantifies the risk in trusting others. Reputation may also serve as a currency replacement. Workers charge initiators a payment for the work they have accomplished on behalf of the respective initiator. The payment depends on the work's volume and is deducted from the initiator's local reputation account held by the worker. This way, reputation may be built by serving others and spent by straining others. It supports the notion of reciprocity which requires peers to track the behavior of others in order to gauge their willingness to reciprocate [80].

In a Desktop Grid setting, peers prefer to cooperate with other peers that have high reputation, and they wish to establish and maintain the potential to become a successful initiator. This requires the capability to attract a sufficient number of workers to have the job computed in a reasonable period of time. As the level of attraction is linked to the reputation, peers benefit from behaving in a way that earns them positive reputation, creating an incentive for cooperation.

A *reputation system* collects information on the past behavior of other peers to allow predictions on their future conduct [45, 69, 142, 197]. It enables cooperative peers to identify other cooperative peers, and it creates incentives for peers to act cooperatively by providing rewards for cooperative behavior [45, 129]. It enables casting the *shadow of the future* which ensures that selfish peers need to consider the consequences of defection [16]. Cooperative peers learn about the true willingness of others to reciprocate only when requesting remote resources themselves, but by resorting to a reputation system, they can reduce the risk of erroneously donating resources to uncooperative peers, and they can limit their level of involvement with other parties to the particular level of trust they place in the respective other party [142]. By disseminating aggregated information on peer behavior, a reputation scheme encourages selfish peers to act in a fair manner [5].

Reputation systems differ in the way reputation is recorded. If a peer records reputation ratings only on those peers with which it has directly interacted in the past, the recorded information is unforgeable, but in large dynamic systems with substantial turnover, peers rarely encounter the same peer twice. A simple reputation system that relies on direct observations is the tit-for-tat strategy as it considers the rated peer's most recent action only [145]. In contrast, shared-history reputation systems additionally incorporate experiences made by other peers [81]. Generally, reputation aggregates feedback information. Without a shared-history reputation mechanism, a peer's abusive behavior toward a certain peer will not harm the misbehaving peer when interacting with other peers.

In this model, it is assumed that free-riders will not compute any tasks for others. When collaborators refuse to compute tasks for free-riders, free-riders are left with the choice to switch to cooperative behavior or to leave the Desktop Grid. Due to their cooperativeness, collaborative peers are assumed to provide feedback on other peers, while ordinary free-riders issue no feedback at all.

5.2.1 Attacks

There is a special form of free-riders that spread spoof reputation ratings. In the context of Desktop Grids, the transmission of spoof ratings, which consists of faulty or purposefully forged opinions on other peers, is the most prominent kind of attack on shared-history reputation systems [29]. In particular, a shared-history reputation system may face *collusion*, the phenomenon of interacting selfish peers (*colluders*) that mutually forge ratings to benefit fellow peers in the colluder group and harm those outside it [80]. It is assumed that a colluder always attempts to free-ride.

Due to its purposeful, organized and durable nature, collusion is a severe form of spoof feedback. When a group of colluding peers agrees to spread only positive information on the group's members to other peers, ordinary peers need to remain vigilant when receiving shared-history feedback from a remote peer. Systems in which all peers agree on a common (objective) reputation rating for every peer are especially vulnerable to collusion [81].

The severity of collusive behavior on P2P systems increases with the *Sybil attack*. This attack constitutes a particularly intense case of collusion [72, 145]. It can occur in systems where identities cannot be verified due to the lack of a trustworthy authority, and it is encouraged through the availability of cheaply replenishable identities. In the Sybil scenario, a group of colluding peers is controlled by the same entity. However, to the remaining peers, the Sybil colluders pretend to be controlled by distinct entities. Thus, the assumption of administrative autonomy and independence of peers does not hold for the colluders in the Sybil attack. There is no generally effective defense to this attack in distributed systems that satisfies the requirements of efficiency and scalability, but a number of approaches exist to limit the attack's effects in various application domains [143]. In Desktop Grids, besides weighting remote feedback with the submitting peer's credibility [81], a *similarity measure* can alleviate the effects of spoof feedback [129, 216]. When using a similarity measure that quantifies the consistency of two peers' ratings, peers pay more attention to peers reporting similar opinions as their own.

Similar to the Sybil attack, an issue affecting distributed systems with zero-cost identities and selfish peers is the theft of identities. This issue is called the *impersonation attack*. A selfish peer, by claiming to be another peer with high reputation, can trick other peers into believing that they deal with a highly reputed peer. The general solution to thwarting the impersonation attack is to have a trustworthy entity vouch for the identity in question. Since in distributed systems, no single trustworthy component exists (this includes the absence of PKIs), this solution cannot be implemented. A *random visitor* alternative based on a DHT was proposed in [102]. To solve the authentication problem under the given circumstances, it suggests to let peers embed identifiers into cryptographically secure *bindings* to remote peers which are called *delegates*. When the demand for identifier authentication of a remote peer arises, the peer picks a randomly chosen delegate which then delivers a credential to the authentication target peer. The target peer can use the credential to deliver proof of its sincerity to the proof-requesting peer. The key idea of this approach is to use asymmetric cryptography and identifiers that are built from public keys, and to replace the PKI with randomly selected delegates. Besides combatting identity theft, the concept is reported to repel Sybil attacks with high probability in fully distributed P2P systems [102].

The reputation system presented in this chapter serves the purpose of enabling collaborative peers to detect free-riders in order to prevent them from donating resources to peers that are unwilling to reciprocate. A possible future extension would discourage colluders from occupying super-peer positions. When colluders become super-peers, they may exert malevolent influence on their edge peers. For instance, a super-peer which participates in a collusion could decide to forward only messages from fellow colluders and drop all others, or distribute forged reputation ratings to its possibly unsuspecting edge peers. To assess threats of this kind, it is helpful to consider the worst case that all free-riders know each other and form a single collusion group. In a fully meshed super-peer topology, let n be the number of peers in the overlay out of which $\sqrt{n}$ are super-peers as selected by SPSA. Moreover, let p be the probability that an arbitrary peer is a colluder. The number of super-peers which belong to the colluder group follows the binomial distribution with parameters $\lceil \sqrt{n} \rceil$ and p. Let X be a random variable with this distribution. Its cumulative distribution function is

$$Pr(X \leq x) = F(x) = \sum_{i=0}^{x} \binom{\lceil \sqrt{n} \rceil}{i} \cdot p^i \cdot (1-p)^{\lceil \sqrt{n} \rceil - i}$$

Hence, the probability that at least one of the super-peers is a colluding free-rider amounts to

$$Pr(X \geq 1) = 1 - Pr(X \leq 0) = 1 - (1-p)^{\lceil \sqrt{n} \rceil}$$

For a network of $n = 100$ peers and $p = 0.1$, this probability equals 65.13 %; at $p = 0.2$, it reaches 89.26 % and at $p = 0.3$, 97.18 %. To attain a probability of 50 % that a colluder is among the super-peers, the fraction of free-riders in the 100-peer system need only be $p = 0.067$, i. e. 7 colluding peers are already sufficient. In a 10,000-peer system, it is $p = 0.007$, requiring 70 colluders to achieve the same effect. These results show that it is feasible for a comparatively small number of colluding peers to get hold of a part of a super-peer overlay's infrastructure. SPSA and ChordSPSA use network proximity as the main criterion for selecting new super-peers from the set of edge peers. An overloaded super-peer that wishes to promote an edge peer can additionally take the candidates' reputation ratings into account before picking the particular edge peer to be promoted. Since super-peers are linchpins in the overlay, future research may want to consider extensions to the reputation system to prevent colluders from being promoted to super-peer level.

5.3   A reputation system for Desktop Grids

In this section, a distributed reputation system is presented that incorporates the presence of super-peers, protects collaborative peers from exploitation, and imposes no barriers on the scalability of the accompanying Desktop Grid. Every collaborative peer is supposed to run an instance of this reputation system within the suggested PeerGrid middleware, and colluders are expected to pretend being cooperative as a camouflage for the attempt to spread forged ratings. Portions of this section are based on the results of [132].

5.3.1 Procedures

Collaborative peers spread ratings on the behavior of other peers they have interacted with. In particular, this concerns the initiator-worker relationship. For this purpose, every peer maintains a list of recent contacts, i. e. peers with which successful interaction has taken place in the past. Additionally, peers maintain reputation records (*ratings*) on arbitrary other peers by keeping a *reputation list* of weighted positive (a) and weighted negative (b) experiences per remote peer. From these parameters, a peer may set up a β-distributed random variable $\beta(a, b)$ for every remote peer and use its mean to reflect the respective remote peer's trustworthiness. While raw feedback is binary (0 equals poor, 1 equals good performance), reputation may assume any value $v \in [0, 1)$ due to feedback weighting and aggregation. Both a and b will be initialized with 1 such that the distribution mean $\frac{a}{a+b}$ equals the neutral reputation value, 0.5, in the beginning [119]. This may be overridden by the stranger account. Since $b \geq 1$, $\frac{a}{a+b}$ cannot reach 1, but in the asymptotic case for a perfectly well-behaving peer with $a \to \infty$ and $b = 1$, the rating gets arbitrarily close to 1 as $\lim\limits_{a \to \infty} \frac{a}{a+b} = 1$.

To keep the reputation list size manageable, there shall be a time window that will remove outdated peers (i. e. those with no recent sign of activity). The list is split in two: one direct interaction history and one holding shared-history information received from other peers. Let $r_{local}(i) \in [0, 1]$ be the local rating on peer i accrued by the current peer through direct interactions with i, and $r_{shared}(i) \in [0, 1]$ the shared-history rating regarding i that has been acquired through ratings received from other peers. More weight can be placed on own observations than on those received from others, however, remote reputation may be aggregated over several observations such that the choice of equal weights can be appropriate. When computing a joint rating on another peer, let $w_{local} \in [0, 1]$ be the weight placed on local ratings and $w_{shared} = 1 - w_{local}$ the weight placed on shared-history ratings. In this way, when peer j computes the joint rating for a peer i, j takes both local and shared-history reputation information into account by computing the weighted average:

$$r_{ji} = w_{local} \cdot r_{local}(i) + w_{shared} \cdot r_{shared}(i) \tag{5.1}$$

Reputation is periodically spread to the last batch of peers with which a peer has interacted in the past. Stored reputation is subject to a periodically applied exponential decay using a weighting factor $z \in (0, 1)$ to focus on the rated peer's recent behavior, effectively leading to a short-term history [81, 119, 142]. Essentially, for every remote peer i on which reputation information is available, the decay process performs the following update:

$$a_i := 1 + (a_i - 1) \cdot z$$

$$b_i := 1 + (b_i - 1) \cdot z$$

That way, past reputation will fade out over time, gradually taking the distribution's parameters back to the initial setting unless new reputation ratings arrive.

When a request for participation as a worker from an initiator i with reputation r_{ji} arrives at a peer j, j will check with its reputation list if i is acceptable. Peer j instantly agrees to become a worker for i if j's directly observed reputation about i exceeds 0.5, or j's combined weighted local and remote observations about i reach or exceed the neutral value of 0.5. The neutral value's inclusion at this point supports bootstrapping the system in the beginning when no worker-initiator interaction has taken place yet.

If i is rejected according to the aforementioned rule, j switches to *random-acceptance* mode: i's reputation with j is compared to the moving average m of the last f seen initiators' ratings with a tolerance factor $\tau \in [0, 1]$. The random-acceptance mode is based on three rules which are sequentially evaluated:

- If $r_{ji} > (1 + \tau) \cdot m$, i is accepted.

- If $r_{ji} \leq (1 - \tau) \cdot m$, i is rejected.

- If $(1 - \tau) \cdot m \leq r_{ji} < (1 + \tau) \cdot m$, j makes its decision on a randomized basis by drawing a random number $d \in [0,1]$ from a uniform distribution. If $d < r_{ji}$, i is accepted, otherwise it is rejected.

The random-acceptance mode supports the emergence of cooperation in environments with many free-riders. With a modest probability, it permits unknown peers – which could be collaborative – to be accepted as initiators. However, the higher the tolerance level, the more free-riders are likely to pass through. It is for this reason that τ needs to be chosen carefully to avoid an adverse impact on the reputation system's effectiveness. In all cases where no reputation information is available on an initiator, the potential worker resorts to the stranger account.

Every peer i individually specifies an interval length t_i which defines the frequency of its reputation exchange with other peers.[39] After a period of length t_i has elapsed, i transmits its stored reputation information (the weighted average of the distribution means for both the local and the remote observations) to the members of its recent contacts list. Since reputation information basically consists of one peer ID and one floating point number per rated peer only, the reputation-related message volume remains reasonable. Peer i expects its contacted peers to reciprocate by replying with their respective reputation information. If a contacted remote peer fails to fulfill this expectation multiple times in a row, i removes it from its contact list. That way, the reputation exchange cycle encourages mutual updates.

When j receives a reputation list from i, let $\mathcal{K}$ be the set of all peers for which both i and j can provide ratings. If $\mathcal{K} = \emptyset$, j discards the received reputation set and aborts the current reputation exchange. Otherwise, j normalizes i's reputation ratings for every peer $k \in \mathcal{K}$. To this end, for every rating v_{ik} submitted by i about a peer $k \in \mathcal{K}$, j computes

$$v_{ik}^* = \frac{v_{ik} - 0.5}{\sum\limits_{k \in \mathcal{K}} |v_{ik} - 0.5|}$$

which yields the normalized rating $v_{ik}^* \in [-1,1]$. Analogously, i also computes normalized variants of its own ratings about every peer referred by $\mathcal{K}$.

Provided that $\mathcal{K} \neq \emptyset$ holds, a *similarity measure* $s_{ij} \in [0,1]$ quantifies the similarity between the ratings of i and j on all peers indicated by $\mathcal{K}$ [216]:

$$s_{ij} = s_{ji} = 1 - \sqrt{\frac{\sum\limits_{k \in \mathcal{K}} (v_{ik}^* - v_{jk}^*)^2}{4 \cdot |\mathcal{K}|}} \tag{5.2}$$

If $\mathcal{K} = \emptyset$, s_{ij} may be assigned a default value $s_{\text{default}} \in [0,1]$. Large values of s_{ij} indicate a high degree of similarity and vice versa. The factor of 4 in the denominator in (5.2)

---

[39] t_i need not equal the reputation decay interval length.

serves a normalization purpose. It accounts for the fact that $-2 \leq v_{ik}^{*} - v_{jk}^{*} \leq 2 \Leftrightarrow 0 \leq (v_{ik}^{*} - v_{jk}^{*})^2 \leq 4$, i.e. a mapping from $[0, 4]$ to $[0, 1]$ is required which is provided through the division by 4.

The presented similarity measure repulses collusion attempts [216]. It does so at the expense of some mistrust exerted towards honest peers which make observations that are inconsistent with the judging peer's information. If a truthful peer has one deviant opinion, there is a small degree of dissimilarity. In this sense, honest peers are discouraged by the similarity measure to report news. However, this is considered acceptable in the face of possibly massive collusion in the system. If all ratings regarding the remaining peers in $\mathcal{K}$ agree, the penalty is tiny, and the similarity between ratings will eventually increase. Collaborative peers can deploy the similarity measure to counteract attempts of collusion (including the Sybil attack) while still allowing truthful ratings to be incorporated, albeit possibly at a slower rate.

Besides the similarity measure, a natural way to gauge i's credibility is to use i's reputation with j, quantified by r_{ji}. To this end, let

$$r_{ji}^{*} = \alpha + \max\left\{0, \, 2 \cdot (1 - \alpha) \cdot (r_{ji} - 0.5)\right\} \tag{5.3}$$

with $\alpha \in [0, 1]$ being the minimum weight that j applies to remote opinions. $r_{ji}^{*} \in [\alpha, 1]$ expresses the particular weight which j associates with i's ratings.

Peer i's ratings will be incorporated into j's shared-history reputation list if i's credibility with j is found to be sufficiently large. This is true if i's reputation with j, r_{ji}, or s_{ij} exceed the neutral value of 0.5. If i passes the credibility test, j continues to process i's reputation list, otherwise i's information is discarded. In the first case, let g_{ji} be the weight j applies to each of i's votes, composed of both similarity and rater reputation: $g_{ji} := s_{ji} \cdot r_{ji}^{*}$. Ultimately, for every $v_{ik'}^{*}$ j updates its remote observation list: if $v_{ik}^{*} > 0$, i's opinion on k is positive, hence j sets $a_{jk} := a_{jk} + g_{ji} \cdot v_{ik}^{*}$. If $v_{ik}^{*} < 0$, i's opinion on k is negative, so j sets $b_{jk} := b_{jk} + g_{ji} \cdot v_{ik}^{*}$. A default value of 1 for s_{ij} in case of $\mathcal{K} = \emptyset$ effectively disables the similarity measure in the computation of g_{ji}.

While shared-history reputation information arrives from other peers, local reputation information is influenced by the outcomes of worker-initiator relationships. An initiator i determines a worker's reputation gain primarily by the computation time the worker has expended. Concisely, let w be the worker in question, t the number of i's reputation exchange cycle periods – including fractions – of length t_i the task has occupied computational resources on w, and power$_x$ the local power index of peer x. Now, i quantifies w's work effort h_{iw} as

$$h_{iw} = \frac{\text{power}_w}{\text{power}_i} \cdot t \tag{5.4}$$

Peer i recomputes the β-distribution parameters it keeps for w, a_{iw} and b_{iw}. If w has completed its task in time, i sets $a_{iw} := a_{iw} + h_{iw}$, otherwise $b_{iw} := b_{iw} + 2 \cdot h_{iw}$, as a direct observation. The factor of 2 serves as a penalty for the failed completion of a task. Neither i's choice of its reputation update interval length t_i nor the worker-initiator power ratio biases the reputation propagation as reputation information transmitted to other peers is processed in an aggregated form only (by means of the distribution mean) which is normalized by the receiver.

Workers charge initiators reputation as the price of computation by adding negative feedback to the respective initiator's local reputation account. Since free-riders do not accrue positive reputation on their own, subsequent requests for workers by free-riders will be declined.

5.3.2 Incentives

A self-sustaining system with a mutual reputation exchange is a desirable goal. To this end, a reputation-based incentive scheme that operates without the need to exchange virtual money works towards the defined goal. Rather than resorting to money, it fosters reciprocity in a dynamic environment. This scheme is built on the notion of positive reputation that may be obtained by adequate behavior. Positive reputation can be earned only through the accomplishment of work, boosting the willingness of peers to become workers. There are two aspects where the reputation system or the peer type provide implicit incentives to behave in a decent, cooperative way. These concern the distribution of reputation ratings and the establishment of super-peers. These aspects will now be discussed.

Workers and initiators have established a trustful relationship after having successfully cooperated. Afterwards, they begin to exchange reputation information periodically. In the model proposed here, successfully completing a worker-initiator cycle is the only way to exchange reputation ratings with another peer because both roles confirm that a degree of cooperativity must have been present. An initiator needs high reputation ratings with other peers to attract a sufficiently large number of workers; conversely, low-reputed peers are unlikely to be accepted as initiators. It is for this reason that peers which successfully assume the initiator role can generally be considered cooperative, as only cooperation can build reputation. On the contrary, a worker must complete a task which requires more effort than a free-rider is willing to sustain. If the worker cheats, the initiator will consider the relationship not to be a success. Successfully interacting over a longer period of time builds mutual trust. This also hampers collusion as any peer wanting to spread false feedback will first need to complete a worker-initiator cycle. The single exception is in the very beginning when a peer enters the system, its stranger account is at its default value and it has not accumulated any reputation. In this special situation, some free-riders might temporarily exploit the circumstances and slip by the defensive measures of a new peer's reputation system. In the long run, the system is expected to stabilize.

Peers will stop transmitting reputation information to other peers if these remote peers do not provide reputation information themselves. This approach resembles the tit-for-tat reputation exchange strategy used in [29]. The reputation exchange between two peers should be alternately initiated. This prevents peers from cheating continuously by replying with the same reputation ratings they have just received. It also prevents the similarity measure from being tricked, because with equal reputation ratings, the similarity is maximum (1). Moreover, it is reasonable to assume that collaborators will behave in the expected way. Collaborators are the only type of peers that need to spread reputation ratings for a reputation system to work. In comparison to processing a task for a remote peer, it is virtually effortless to spread reputation ratings to other peers. Thus, the general willingness to compute for others can be assumed to imply the general willingness to spread ratings. If a peer generally declines to work for others, its only reason to join the Desktop Grid is to exploit others, hence it is a free-rider. Furthermore, collaborators do not benefit from spreading false ratings, but if they did, the rating receiver's similarity measure defined in (5.2) would reduce their influence.

Super-peer activity is considered a specific computation job with unknown duration. All edge peers are considered initiators and their respective super-peer is the single worker of their job. Consequently, super-peers charge their edge peers reputation while edge peers grant their super-peers positive ratings. At join time, a peer has neutral reputation with all other peers, only modified by the stranger account. When super-peers regularly charge their edge peers reputation for the super-peer service and spread this reputation information to other peers, an edge peer's reputation will almost instantly drop below the neutral threshold. It continues to decline unless the edge peer performs work for other peers or becomes a super-peer itself. However, to become a super-peer, the SPSA and ChordSPSA algorithms both require an edge peer to be appointed by a super-peer. Edge peers are technically unable to promote themselves unless they are the first peer in the overlay. This way, a super-peer is free to limit the set of upgrade candidates to its trustworthy edge peers. Since the reputation system in its presented configuration does not affect the formation of links between super-peers and edge peers, both groups of peers may want to refrain from exchanging reputation ratings with each other as no true worker-initiator relationship (as in the computation of a job) had been completed.

Peers can receive an additional incentive to become super-peers by granting a super-peer the right to require its attached edge peers to compute a task for it. Every edge peer takes its turn in a round-robin or randomized fashion, and the turn length equals the length of the super-peer's reputation exchange interval. That way, every edge peer expends some computation power to the super-peer once in a while. If a super-peer attempts to cheat by requiring one edge peer too often to compute a task, that edge peer may disconnect at any time and seek another super-peer. Conversely, if an edge peer refuses to compute, the super-peer itself disconnects the link. The job may concern the computation of an arbitrary problem, or in the default case, be a dummy job which returns proof-of-work messages to the super-peer.

5.3.3 Experiments

A reputation system faces the challenge of distinguishing cooperative from free-riding peers. In the beginning, all peers consider all other peers equal due to their lack of experience. With time passing, collaborators interact with other collaborators. Hence, the reputation system is expected to adapt to its environment in the course of time, accepting a limited number of free-riders in the beginning but repelling them after having swung in. To assess the performance of this approach, a number of experiments were conducted in a NetSim environment executing SPSA.

5.3.3.1 Setup

Initiators are anticipated to submit computationally intensive jobs only since small jobs may be computed locally without needing to deal with the additional complexity of a Desktop Grid [8]. Hence, a Desktop Grid is likely to be exposed to jobs that would otherwise be processed by supercomputer-class systems. To model the volume of such jobs, the experiments resorted to real-world workload traces [40] of jobs processed by a Linux cluster at the OHIO SUPERCOMPUTING CENTER. After data sanitization, the data of $30,414$ jobs were available. Since ITA jobs tend to exert more negative influence on the average makespan than CP jobs due to their unknown runtime, jobs were considered to be of the ITA type. Cooperative peers initiated jobs independently from their current local load. The interarrival time between two jobs submitted by the same cooperative peer was modelled by a uniformly distributed random variable $U(0; 4 \cdot$ average single-machine CPU time per job$)$. The makespan computation exclusively concerned jobs initiated by cooperative peers. The computational speedup experienced by free-riders has not been taken into account as the utility of free-riders is considered irrelevant in this context. The sample network consisted of the 127 nodes whose inter-node delays were given by the 01-2005 matrix. The simulation environment

---

[40] from http://www.cs.huji.ac.il/labs/parallel/workload/l_osc/index.html

included a SPSA super-peer overlay optimization process running on every peer which
reshaped the overlay for low end-to-end communication delay.

The reputation spreading scheme pushed reputation information to the elements of
its recent contacts list (workers and initiators) once a minute of simulated time. The
reputation aggregation mechanism placed a weight of 0.75 on local and a weight of 0.25
on remote observations. The history decay factor z was set to $z = 0.999$ to enable a
graceful decay and long history of positive reputation accrued through previous work
for other peers. To limit the load, the recent contacts list was restricted to $q = 10$ elements
and the unique initiator reputation history also to $f = 10$ elements. The minimum
granted reputation weight α was set to 0.1, the random-acceptance tolerance level τ to
0.02. After having completed a task, worker j modified an initiator i's local reputation
by setting $a_{ji} := a_{ji} + \frac{1}{4} \cdot t_c$ and $b_{ji} := b_{ji} + \frac{3}{4} \cdot t_c$, where t_c is the number of reputation
intervals – including fractions – that j has spent computing i's task.

Free-riding behavior has been modelled as the refusal to accept foreign tasks for local
computation, the desire to submit a job for distributed computation upon entry, and
the departure from the system as soon as the job was completed. Additionally, free-
riders in the super-peer role discarded calls for workers received from other peers. Once
a free-rider left the system, a very brief period of simulated time (3 seconds) elapsed
until it was replaced by another free-rider which immediately attempted to submit a
new job. This aggressive behavior partially suppressed the establishment of reputation-
backed cooperative relationships and spread mistrust in the system due to the large
amount of jobs initiated by free-riders; it strained the reputation system, testing a case
which is substantially more severe than is likely to be encountered in practice due to
the exceedingly high volume of jobs submitted by free-riders. Free-riders attempted 10
times to distribute their job before giving up on that job.

Moreover, free-riders could collude. Collusion was modelled to extend free-riding behavior with the desire to spread reputation information which maximally benefits all
members of the colluding peer group while at the same time, maximally debases all
other peers to reduce their capability to initiate a job of their own. Hence, a colluder's
feedback on fellow colluders was quantified as 1, while feedback on other peers was
quantified as 0. After a colluder's job was completed, the colluder lingered for up to
30 minutes in the system (the exact timespan was drawn from a uniformly distributed
random variable) to be able to spread its forged ratings to the workers in its recent
contacts list, before leaving the system for whitewashing. A worst-case evaluation approach was adopted with regard to collusion, assuming that all free-riders in the system
were colluders, and there is only one colluder group in the system, i. e. every colluder
knew all remaining colluders. In the non-collusion scenario, free-riding initiators did
not exchange reputation information with their collaborating workers since by model

assumption, ordinary free-riders left the overlay immediately upon completion of their job and returned with a whitewashed identity.

While the model supports heterogenous worker capabilities, identical peer equipment was assumed in these experiments to facilitate comparisons. The willingness of peers to process tasks was limited to a maximum of 12 hours of computation time per task. The simulation lasted for 7 days of simulated time. The admission of jobs was narrowed to those of 10 days or less of total computation time on a single CPU. Moreover, jobs with very short CPU time requirements (less than one hour on a single CPU) were ignored because such jobs are unlikely to be submitted to a Desktop Grid. In total, $13,748$ jobs matched the admission requirements and were made available to the simulation environment. The longest job required 8 days, 5 hours and 22 minutes on a single CPU, the shortest one exactly one hour. Median job CPU time consumption equalled 11 hours, 24 minutes, while some long-running jobs boosted the mean to amount 25 hours and 10 minutes.

Workloads were drawn randomly from the set of admitted jobs. For every experimental scenario, 30 runs were performed.

5.3.3.2 Results

The first experiment examined the impact of free-riding behavior on a Desktop Grid with cooperative workers not protected by a reputation scheme. The system was exposed to free-rider fractions of various sizes prior to measuring the average makespan experienced by cooperative peers. Figure 5.1 shows the outcome, confirming that the makespan grows with the fraction of free-riders. This reflects the negative impact of free-riders on system performance, highlighting the necessity to introduce countermeasures that inhibit free-riding. Two main factors contribute to the negative impact on the makespan as shown in Figure 5.1. In addition to the free-riders occupying the resources of unsuspecting peers, the number of generally available computational resources decreases as the fraction of free-riders grows. For instance, with 30 % free-riders in the system, only 70 % of the peers can act as workers. Hence, the makespan increases for this reason alone. Compared to the case of no free-riders and n peers, a system with $\lambda \cdot n$ cooperative peers, $\lambda \in (0,1)$, and no free-riders is expected to attain a makespan which is $\frac{1}{\lambda}$ times as long as the original n-peer system's makespan. In the following figures, adjusted makespans are included to account for this fact.

The performance of a free-riding-resilient Desktop Grid which uses the presented reputation system was compared to an unprotected but otherwise identical Desktop Grid. Figures 5.2, 5.3, and 5.4 show the outcome for free-rider fractions of 10 %, 30 %, and 50 %, respectively. The makespan is considerably lower when the reputation system is

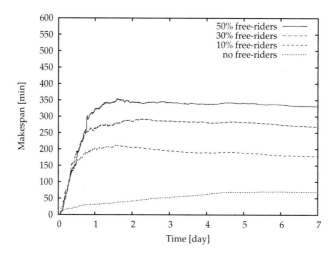

Figure 5.1: Effects of free-riding on the average makespan

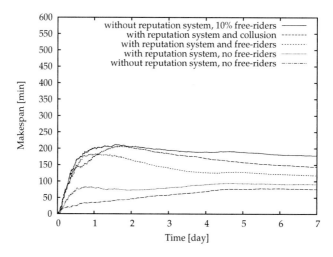

Figure 5.2: Average makespan with 10 % free-riders in the Desktop Grid

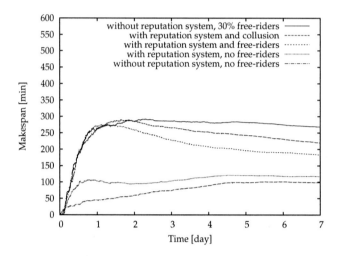

Figure 5.3: Average makespan with 30 % free-riders in the Desktop Grid

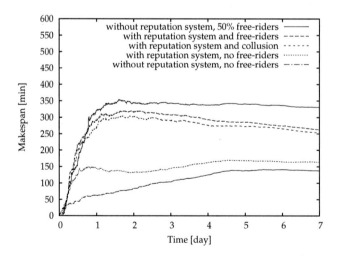

Figure 5.4: Average makespan with 50 % free-riders in the Desktop Grid

available to the collaborating peers than in the exposed setting where unprotected collaborating peers cannot detect free-riders. In all plots, the two lowermost curves show the makespans adjusted to the respective fraction of collaborators when no free-riders are present. The lowest makespan is attained when no overhead from the reputation system applies, while the second-lowest makespan incorporates the overhead.

With free-riders in the system, the reputation system takes time in the beginning to adapt to the environment but then swings into stabilizing the average makespan at a low level in the long term. This fact implies that the proposed concept actually exhibits the desired resilience towards free-riders. An interesting particularity can be observed in Figure 5.4. There, the makespan with colluders falls short of that seen when ordinary free-riders are present. This is due to the fact that colluders linger for up to half an hour and do not submit any jobs in this period. In contrast, a large number of free-riders (in this setting, half the network) aggressively tries to submit jobs in short intervals, and occasionally succeeds in finding a loophole through the random-acceptance mode. This effect is not observed with smaller fractions of colluders and free-riders because of the reduced overall penetrance of free-riders in those scenarios.

The handling of requests for participation in a scenario with 30 % free-riders is illustrated by Figure 5.5. It shows the cumulative numbers of tasks accepted and declined by worker peers, differentiated between free-riders and collaborators, the latter being either exposed or protected by the reputation system. The figure proves that in the unprotected case, collaborators' resources are quickly exhausted by the requests of free-riders, hence few resources remain for computing tasks initiated by other collaborators. In contrast, collaborators protected by the reputation system decline the vast majority of free-riders' requests. As desired, this behavior enables them to dedicate their resources to other collaborators.

The speedup of jobs is depicted in Figure 5.6. This experiment was conducted to quantify the general benefit of Desktop Grids. As also seen in Figure 5.2, the speedup of jobs drops to a low level already with as little as 10 % of free-riding peers if protection against free-riders is unavailable. The experimental results confirm that in the optimal case with all peers being altruists and zero overhead from a reputation system, a 127-peer Desktop Grid can deliver a peak speedup of approximately 96 on average. This situation arises in the very beginning when the first job is introduced into the system by an initiator, and all remaining (altruistic, exposed) peers are free to join as workers. The speedup is attenuated over time as more jobs are submitted, causing the mean number of workers per job to decline which in turn also causes the speedup to decrease. In the long run, Figure 5.6 also confirms that the overhead generated by the reputation system exerts only a small influence on the speedup.

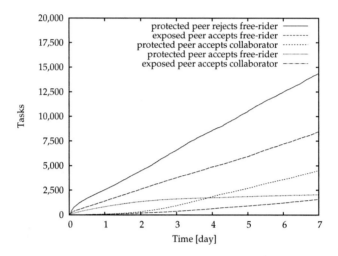

Figure 5.5: Cumulative numbers of accepted and declined tasks

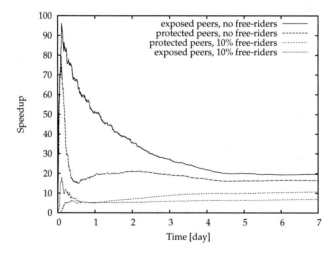

Figure 5.6: Average speedup through distributed computation

5.3.4 Related work

The free-riding phenomenon affects distributed systems whose utility relies on voluntary contributions from its selfish participants. Free-riding has been observed in P2P filesharing systems as a cause for performance degradation [4, 81, 124]. Due to a different nature of resources in Desktop Grids, solutions for free-riding prevention in filesharing systems need to be modified for Desktop Grid settings. While files may be distributed and stored, CPU cycles are volatile and can neither be stored nor replicated.

A survey of approaches that attempt to overcome free-riding is provided in [80]. It includes a brief summary of the principles of monetary payment schemes that implement a market economy, under the constraint that payments require a virtual currency and a secure payment infrastructure.

With respect to reputation systems, [45] distinguishes symmetric from asymmetric approaches. In symmetric systems, the computation of a remote peer's reputation happens under anonymity. Peer identities can be exchanged as long as the trust graph's topology remains unmodified. Except for the trivial constant variant, symmetric reputation functions are vulnerable to collusion. In contrast, asymmetric reputation functions apply when every peer computes remote peer ratings by itself, and can be shown to resist Sybil attacks under certain conditions. The distributed reputation system discussed in this chapter uses an asymmetric approach.

The reputation scheme proposed in [121] incorporates the notion of incentive compatibility from the field of mechanism design. It solves the problem of forged feedback on other peers' past performances by seeing to it that telling the truth is in the best self interest of the reporting peers. The basic idea is to spread reputation information via specialized intermediary peers called R-AGENTS. Instead of spreading own feedback directly to other peers, a peer buys reputation information from and sells its own experience with other peers to the trustworthy R-agents. While it solves the problem of truthfulness, the scheme exhibits several drawbacks. It requires at least one R-agent to be present in the system at all times, it depends on all R-agents being trustworthy at all times, and it is susceptible to collusion. Also, the scheme suffers from the major disadvantage of establishing truthfulness using payments according to the mechanism design approach: there needs to be a virtual currency which all peers in the system, including the R-agents, accept.

The framework introduced in [67] explicitly benefits from the presence of super-peers. By resorting to threshold cryptography, it focuses on the security aspects of feedback submission among peers. It does not intend to specify a reputation scheme itself, and due to its application-neutral scope, provides no insight into Desktop Grid workflows.

An application-neutral reputation system is introduced in [5]. It is based on solicited first-hand feedback acquired through time-to-live-bounded random walk sampling. Its use is limited because of the expensive polling scheme and the inability to deal with considerable churn. As [81] confirms, a shared interaction history fits large-scale, churn-prone settings better than a witness-only approach.

The reputation mechanism in OURGRID (cf. Section 2.6.2.2) is the *network of favors* [8, 9]. There, accumulated reputation does not decay over time. As with [5], reputation in the network of favors concerns direct witnesses of interactions in OurGrid only which is incompatible with substantial dynamics.

EIGENTRUST creates a global trust estimate in a distributed way, based on the concept of transitive trust [124, 125]. However, EigenTrust relies on pre-trusted peers and is vulnerable to collusion [26].

A form of uncooperative behavior related to free-riding in P2P systems concerns message routing. When super-peers are unwilling to forward or answer queries, the overlay itself may not work as desired. On the basis of the CAN topology but also suitable for use with Chord, [29] introduces a distributed reputation system designed to thwart uncooperative behavior in the context of message propagation.

The incorporation of collaborating peers is justified by a number of studies that model human behavior in situations of social interaction to confirm the de facto existence of reciprocity. [22] reports on an experiment in which individuals in two rooms, A and B, all unknown to each other, interacted. A person in room A sent money to her respective counterpart in room B through an anonymity-preserving channel without any other communication. Each person in room A received 10 US$ and was permitted to share an arbitrary fraction of this amount with her counterpart in room B. The shared amount would triple, and a person in B was then free to send any portion of the tripled amount back to the originator in room A. The Nash equilibrium of this game is for every person in room A to send no money, but in the experiment, 30 out of 32 people sent 5.16 US$ on average, and there was substantial reciprocation from the people in room B. Thus, the majority of players did not choose the rational option which was to defect. This situation can be adapted to Desktop Grids where peers exhibit goodwill by providing resources to others in the face of uncertain reciprocity, but they may wish to limit their risk by constraining the level of donated resources depending on the other peer's reputation. The same game as in [22] but with the addition of reputation information was conducted in another experiment [207]. The findings confirm that a reputation mechanism which provides peers with information about the past behavior of other peers increases the average payoff. In the context of a Desktop Grid, this finding can be interpreted as the effect of a reputation system to increase the overall level of reciprocity.

5.4 Summary

This chapter has assessed the impact of three major behavioral types of peers – altruists, collaborators, and free-riders – on Desktop Grid operations. While altruists share their resources with anyone, free-riders are permanently unwilling to do so. In between these polar opposites, collaborative peers are generally cooperative but do not want their resources to be abused by peers that decline to reciprocate.

Free-riders can act on their own or in collusive groups. Within a group of colluders, free-riders attempt to boost the rating of other free-riders. Colluders act as altruists among themselves but as free-riders in interactions with others. They try to bias the public perception of the colluder group's members through the propagation of forged reputation ratings. The phenomenon of collusion affects all sorts of P2P systems. There is no general, perfectly effective countermeasure, but its effects can be alleviated.

While altruists do not mind being exploited, collaborators do. To this end, a distributed reputation system has been presented that enables collaborators to assess the risk in dealing with other peers, creating the opportunity to choose whether to engage in or to abstain from an interaction with a given remote peer, and generating incentives for peers to adopt reciprocity in their own behavior. The introduction of a similarity measure within this reputation system thwarts the heavily biased ratings submitted by colluding peers, preventing them from influencing the honest and truthful reputation information of cooperative peers. The experiments documented in Section 5.3.3 have shown the reputation system to succeed in deterring free-riders from exploiting computational resources on remote peers.

Major parts of the presented reputation system have been published in [164, 165].

6

The PeerGrid middleware

PEERGRID is a blueprint for a Desktop Grid, its most prominent characteristic being its peculiar super-peer topology. PeerGrid is put into practice through a middleware which every participant executes. This middleware combines low-level network access, Chord overlay management, ChordSPSA, network coordinates, a reputation system, and a workflow engine to provide distributed computing for arbitrary jobs in P2P environments. A prototype of this middleware has been conceived and developed. The following sections present design and implementation aspects of the PeerGrid middleware concept and evaluate the prototype's live performance through demonstration jobs distributed on various testbeds.

6.1   Design overview

The PeerGrid middleware has been conceived to work in large-scale, dynamic, heterogeneous P2P environments, a typical deployment setting of Desktop Grids. Its design has called for scalability, robustness, and flexibility regarding the communication patterns between an initiator and its assigned workers. These goals were pursued to support a wide variety of jobs. The PeerGrid middleware provides auxiliary facilities frequently required by initiators, including overlay broadcast which is essential for initiators to transmit calls for workers.

The PeerGrid middleware follows a layer model of which Figure 6.1 depicts a schematic representation. The lowest layer provides basic reliable unicast messaging for general-purpose point-to-point communications. This messaging is used by a Chord module and a network coordinates provider at the next higher level. On the basis of Chord and

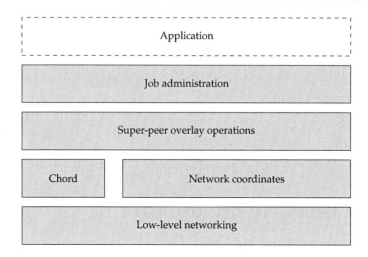

Figure 6.1: Layer architecture model of the PeerGrid middleware

network coordinates, an implementation of ChordSPSA provides super-peer topology operations including maintenance and broadcast services. This layer also cares for edge peers and their switching to the closest known super-peer. The submission and handling of jobs is coordinated on the uppermost layer which also accommodates the reputation system. Since a peer may assume both roles, this layer supports both initiators and workers.

There are two exceptions to the strictly sequential layer architecture. Network coordinates support the Chord core which is located on the same layer by supplying coordinates that can be used to accelerate message forwarding through PIS, PRS and LPRS. Moreover, the job administration layer may want to contact other peers directly (e. g. the initiator of a job). Thus, it requires access to direct unicast connections which is granted through a discrete interface to the lowest layer.

The PeerGrid middleware satisfies the requirements set forth in Section 2.6.1. The job administration layer provides an API to application developers that hides most of the complexity underneath. While configuration parameters can be adjusted manually, the PeerGrid middleware does not require the user to intervene for configuration issues except when initiating a job and when bootstrapping. PeerGrid benefits from the favorable properties of Chord message forwarding including efficient broadcast and constrained broadcast as well as the delay-sensitive message forwarding enhancements presented in Section 4.4.2.3. Moreover, it deploys the ChordSPSA algorithm to maintain a delay-optimized super-peer overlay.

PeerGrid expects jobs to come in two parts: a *controller* which is the job's part that the initiator executes, and a *task* part which is run on every worker. The controller transmits task code and task data to the workers, supervises the distributed computing effort, and gathers the results. The middleware instance running on the initiator needs to be able to execute the controller code, and the middleware instances running on the workers need to be able to execute the task code. One way to achieve both platform independence and sandbox security for task-hosting environments is the deployment of a virtual machine for both the middleware and initiator-defined tasks.

6.2   Implementation aspects

There are no performance-related objections to using Java in the context of high performance computing [239]. Besides addressing platform independence and security issues, Java also facilitates the transfer of code to remote destinations. Thus, the PeerGrid middleware prototype was implemented using Java 6 Standard Edition.

The use of Java fosters portability and safety [73, 239]. With regard to portability, the Java virtual machine is available for a wide variety of host platforms. Its *security manager* can prevent malevolent or faulty tasks from causing harm to the host environment [73, 224]. It does so by enforcing a *security policy* that defines what actions on resources are permissible for the running task to perform.

Java facilitates the development of jobs for distributed computation. Controller code and task code can both be supplied as Java classes; additional class files may be provided at the initiator's discretion. The key idea of this approach is to enable the controller to perform arbitrary operations, constrained only by Java's security manager. The controller class needs to implement a standard controller interface, and the task class needs to implement a standard task interface, both provided by the job administration layer API. Then, on the operator's request, the middleware instance running on the initiator can load the controller class at runtime and execute its code.

Typically, an initiator will want to broadcast a message that calls for worker participation. This operation is provided by the job administration layer which in turn resorts to services implemented by the super-peer overlay operations layer. Upon reception of the call, potential workers are free to contact the controller process directly. The controller then sends task code and data to each worker. Since the task class implements a common interface, the workers' middleware instances know how to execute it and return its results. On the other hand, the task class may use arbitrary other classes that have also been supplied by the initiator via the controller class. This approach ensures maximum flexibility: the middleware instance running on the initiator can dynamically load the controller code at any time. The controller is free to retrieve the task code and data from any location. Task code can consist of any number of classes and implement arbitrary algorithms. In theory, the controller can transmit arbitrary data to the workers, even executable files to be launched as external processes. However, this removes the advantage of platform independence as executable files are machine-dependent unless the source code is transferred to the worker and compiled there upon reception. Besides, the security manager might interfere with the creation of new processes if the security policy lacks an adequate permission.

The remainder of this section highlights implementation aspects that have warranted further investigations in particular because they are likely to be generally relevant for implementations of Desktop Grid middleware.

6.2.1 Network coordinates

Vivaldi was chosen as the network coordinates provider for its inherent dynamic nature and the capability to provide coordinates without the need for an initialization phase. Coordinates have 4 dimensions and are initialized with random values from the interval $[0, 1]$. Periodically, every peer contacts a random super-peer picked from the super-peer list and exchanges messages with the remote peer to complete a Vivaldi cycle.

The Vivaldi cycle period (interval length) is determined in a nonlinear way based on Vivaldi's δ value which is initialized with 1.0 and decreased by 0.025 every time a Vivaldi cycle ends, down to a minimum value of 0.05. [41] In the beginning, there is a need for frequent Vivaldi updates to accrue coordinates accuracy. With time passing, coordinate quality improves while δ decreases. A nonlinear procedure to define the interval between two Vivaldi queries can support this process by slowing down the interval length growth for an extended period of time.

For a point in time at which a value for $\delta \in [\delta_{min}, 1]$ is given (with Vivaldi commonly defining $\delta_{min} = 0.05$), let l be the interval length. It is initialized and bounded below with $l_{min} > 0$. Let there also be an upper bound $l_{max} > l_{min}$. Both bounds may be chosen arbitrarily; PeerGrid uses default values of $l_{min} = 10$ [s] and $l_{max} = 30$ [s]. For any δ with $\delta_{min} \leq \delta \leq 1$, the current value of l is defined in a nonlinear way:

$$f(\delta) = \frac{l_{min}}{\delta^{\log_{\delta_{min}} \frac{l_{min}}{l_{max}}}} \tag{6.1}$$

In contrast, a linear relationship between l and δ can be specified by

---

[41] $1 - \delta$ may be interpreted as the quantified confidence a peer has in the accuracy of its own coordinates.

$$g(\delta) = l_{min} + (1 - \delta) \cdot \frac{l_{max} - l_{min}}{1 - \delta_{min}} \tag{6.2}$$

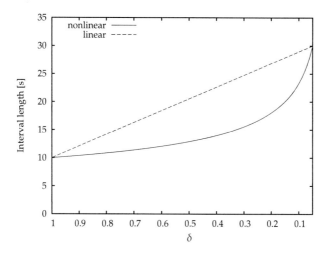

Figure 6.2: Vivaldi interval length with decreasing δ

Figure 6.2 illustrates the difference. With the given parameters, at $\delta = 0.3$, there have been $\frac{1-0.3}{0.025} = 28$ Vivaldi cycles. For $\delta = 0.3$, the nonlinear model from (6.1) maintains an interval length of 15.551 s while the linear model defined in (6.2) has already extended the interval length to 24.737 s at this point. At $\delta = \delta_{min} = 0.05$ however, both approaches yield equal intervals of length l_{max}.

The chosen parameters allow for accurate Vivaldi delay estimates. In a PlanetLab setting, performing as little as one measurement per minute is considered sufficient for reasonable prediction accuracy [139].

6.2.2 Topology coherence

It is generally desirable to keep the topology connected in order to enable broadcasts (in particular, worker requests from initiators and beacons from super-peers) to reach as many peers as possible. Coherence benefits from dampened edge peer dynamics: edge peers should switch to another super-peer only if they are sufficiently certain that the new super-peer is in fact closer. This can be achieved in two ways. Let $d_{current}$ be the estimated delay to the current super-peer and d_{new} the estimated delay to the new super-peer, both computed using network coordinates. If $d_{current} = 0$, the situation is perfect from the edge peer's point of view as no super-peer can offer a smaller delay. Hence, in this situation, the edge peer will not voluntarily switch to another super-peer. If $d_{current} > 0$, let the expected gain of switching be

$$g = 1 - \frac{d_{new}}{d_{current}} \qquad (6.3)$$

If $g \leq 0$, the new super-peer is not closer than the current one, hence the edge peer will not switch. Let $g \in (0, 1]$. One way to inhibit premature switching is to impose a threshold t which must be reached or exceeded by g in order to incent the edge peer to switch. The PeerGrid middleware supports this approach by setting the threshold to a default value of $t = 1\%$. This avoids switching due to tiny prediction errors or delay oscillations. On the other hand, if t is too large, the topology might fail to reach its optimum configuration because one or more edge peers do not switch to closer super-peers because the gain of switching, g, falls short of t. At $t = 1\%$, this risk is sustainable.

In contrast, a stochastic approach treats g as the likelihood of switching. With a uniformly distributed random variable $X \sim U(0, 1)$ and a realization u of X, the edge peer switches to the new super-peer if $u \leq g$. [42] If the edge peer does not switch, it will retry in its subsequent reorganization phase unless network coordinates have changed to make the selected super-peer appear unattractive as a switching target. In the face of positive gain to be attained, the edge peer switches to the closer super-peer in a reorganization round with probability g. The probability p_n that an edge peer with gain g will not switch to the closer super-peer within n rounds is $p_n = (1 - g)^n$. In the asymptotic case, the probability of not switching in the presence of a positive gain is $p_\infty = \lim_{n \to \infty} (1 - g)^n = 0$. Thus, as long as there is positive gain to be had, an edge peer is certain to switch given infinite time. The stochastic approach enables the system to ultimately reach its optimal configuration while alleviating edge-peer switching oscillations.

With regard to super-peer dynamics, the lower bound for ChordSPSA downgrades is set to 1 peer per distinct finger, while the upper bound for ChordSPSA promotions is set to 4 peers per distinct finger. Thus, in a Chord ring with 2^{24} peers, there are 24 distinct fingers to be expected for a super-peer, leading to a theoretical maximum allocation of 96 edge peers per super-peer. The PeerGrid middleware prototype lets super-peers broadcast beacon messages every 30 seconds. Super-peer list entries have a TTL of 4 reorganization phases.

---

[42] For readability's sake, it is assumed here that g remains constant until the edge peer switches. However, the assertion that the edge peer will eventually switch still holds true even if g changes; the single required condition to ensure this behavior is that g remains positive.

6.2.3 Bootstrapping

A common issue of P2P applications is the *bootstrapping* problem [137]. Those wishing to join a P2P system as new peers need to contact a peer which is already part of the system. Although bootstrapping concerns the entire process of joining the overlay, the issue of finding such a peer is at the heart of the problem.

The PeerGrid middleware prototype has followed the assumption that a peer that can be contacted for joining is already known through an exterior source, e.g. the World Wide Web, or a well-known peer that never intends to leave the overlay [137]. Should an assumption of this kind not be justified, alternative solutions include the following:

- If the joining peer had been part of the system before, it can iterate through its most recent super-peer list (or a list of all super-peers that have ever been known), contacting one by another sequentially until a reply arrives or otherwise, all candidates have been tried in vain, and the join attempt fails. This option was preferred by the Desktop Grid implementation presented in [39].

- In a LAN, a UDP broadcast can detect peers which already participate in the overlay [73].

- A bootstrap service which itself is a P2P system is proposed in [53]. Every peer that wants to join a particular P2P system first joins the singleton bootstrap P2P system. Due to the sheer size of the bootstrap P2P system's overlay, a peer in this system could be found by probing random IP ranges. The bootstrap system runs a DHT to store bootstrap information for all served P2P systems. If such a bootstrap system is relied on for bootstrapping, it represents a single point of failure even if its internal organization is distributed.

- Based on statistical properties of IPv4 ranges, a distributed heuristic that generates a stream of IP addresses to be probed as potential entry points is presented in [96]. With the help of DNS information, probing favors IP ranges of organizations to which a disproportionately large fraction of peers belong. While the experiments in [96] have shown this approach to be inferior to iterating over a list of hosts, it is substantially more efficient than a brute-force scan of IP addresses (random probing) which is oblivious to organizational bias.

When the composition of a system's participants is fully dynamic, no participant can be relied on to be always present. Thus, the bootstrapping issue occurs in every system that has no fixed component.

6.2.4 Security issues

It is desirable that tasks running on worker peers can contact their initiator anytime. That way, a task may return its result to the initiator after completion, and may even submit intermediate results as proof-of-work to confirm that the worker has provided the task with computational resources. The results are returned directly by the task running on the worker machine.

Besides untrustworthy foreign code that can safely be executed within a Java sandbox environment controlled by Java's security manager, there are three security-related aspects that have been addressed by previous efforts:

- Selfish super-peers might decide not to forward messages as they do not receive an immediate benefit from doing so. This issue can be tackled in several ways:

  - The FAIRNET solution was proposed in [29]. FairNet was originally conceived for CAN but also works with Chord. It is based on the notion of cooperative peers forwarding messages only to other peers they deem cooperative. Other peers must produce a proof-of-work to earn trust. On the other hand, demanding too many proofs-of-work causes peers to lose reputation. FairNet supports a shared-history reputation system: it piggybacks feedback information on ordinary messages. It tracks the hop sequences between sources and destinations, and if receipts requested from destination peers do not arrive, the cooperativeness ratings of those peers that had been expected to forward the lost message are degraded.

  - With a focus on Pastry but explicitly acknowledged transferability of the results to Chord, secure routing is decomposed into secure identifier assignment, secure routing table maintenance and secure message forwarding in [42]. The latter two approaches work in fully distributed ways: the security of routing table information is ensured by creating a second routing table whose modification underlies strict regulations, while secure forwarding relies on a test of faithfulness. If the test fails, the message is forwarded redundantly along multiple disjoint paths. The major downside of this approach is the way secure identifier assignment is achieved: a trustworthy Certificate Authority (CA) is supposed to issue IP address-based identifiers, signed with its private key. To prevent the assignment of cheap identities to single entities, the CA charges money for its service and/or demand the disclosure of the applicant's true identity. This approach requires a centralized component (the CA) and static IP addresses unless the identifiers issued by the CA are considered transient.

- Network coordinates may be forged to trick peers into connecting to particular super-peers. This issue is pertinent to colluders and was addressed by [122, 123]. Section 3.4 contains a sketch of the proposed approach.

- In Desktop Grids, workers may cheat by choosing not to compute their assigned task but to return arbitrary data. A dishonest worker needs to know the result message's format to fake its contents, requiring it either to intercept messages transmitted by the running task or to retrieve the message format from reengineering the task's code. Both ways entail efforts that exceed the effort of computing the actual task. Additionally, a replication approach might assign the same task to multiple workers and pick the correct result through majority voting. An alternative to a replication approach is QUIZ [243] which assigns a number of tasks to one worker, including a special task of which the submitting peer already knows the result. If this task is processed properly, the worker is assumed to have processed the other tasks properly, too. This sampling method is found to be superior to task replication. It is used in a Desktop Grid scheme which also includes reputation, CLUSTER COMPUTING ON THE FLY (cf. Section 2.6.2.2) [243].

Since these issues have already been solved, the PeerGrid middleware prototype does not explicitly address them, but they need to be taken into account for productive Desktop Grids open to the general public.

6.2.5 Local Power Index computation

To compute the local power index (LPI) of a peer, an appropriate benchmark is required. A single-threaded version of the LINPACK benchmark was selected for this duty [70, 71, 97, 171, 188]. Linpack solves systems of linear equations, a task that is frequently at the core of scientific computing problems [188]. It is floating-point-intensive by nature and delivers the number of floating point operations per second (FLOPS). Linpack is widely used to measure the performance of supercomputers. It is the benchmark of choice to gauge supercomputers for the Top500 list [171].

Given a $n \times n$ matrix of coefficients, Linpack takes $\frac{2}{3} \cdot n^3 + 2 \cdot n^2$ floating-point operations. In practice, no algorithm can do on floating-point operations alone since basic instructions that take care of a program's control flow are not commonly processed by a CPU's floating-point unit. Hence, when measuring a FLOPS rating, it is reasonable to account for the fact that the processing of floating-point operations is accompanied by the processing of integer operations. With regard to the Linpack benchmark, one computes, for a given value of n, the time $t_{\text{Linpack}} [s]$ Linpack took to complete its computation, then divides the number of floating-point operations by t_{Linpack}:

$$p_{\text{Linpack}} = \frac{\frac{2}{3} \cdot n^3 + 2 \cdot n^2}{10^6 \cdot t_{\text{Linpack}}} \ [MFLOPS] \tag{6.4}$$

p_{Linpack} equals the number of millions of floating-point operations per second (MFLOPS). A different quantity is the number of integer operations per time unit, specified in millions of instructions per second (MIPS). The floating-point performance was shown to be positively correlated to the integer performance, so a large MFLOPS value indicates, with high probability, a large MIPS value [97].

The most significant drawback of the MFLOPS measure is the assumption that all floating-point operations are equally expensive. With regard to floating-point instructions, Linpack executes multiplications and additions. If either is computationally more expensive than the other, the resulting MFLOPS value is an average weighted with the frequencies with which the individual floating-point instructions are invoked by Linpack, and cannot serve as a general predictor for floating-point performance with arbitrary instruction mixes. A discussion of Linpack's pros and cons is provided in [171]. In general, Linpack's drawbacks are outweighed by its benefits. An alternative benchmark is the SPECFP benchmark [97, 98] but such a choice would preclude the comparison with performance ratings that refer to Linpack results, such as the Top500 list [171].

6.3   Evaluation

Beyond being a proof of concept, the PeerGrid middleware prototype's purpose is to enable the assessment of performance gains from distributed computing attained in live settings. Unless noted otherwise, all experiments documented in the upcoming sections were repeated 30 times, and all probes were performed on machines running Linux. When a job had to be executed, the initiator broadcasted a *call for workers* message, then waited for 15 seconds in WAN, 3 seconds in LAN settings until it distributed code and data to the workers that had applied in the meantime.

In the evaluated PeerGrid middleware prototype, all components were available except for LPRS and the reputation system. The reputation system requires a large number of jobs to be evaluated, and as the main concern of the prototype middleware implementation was the performance of distributed applications, the reputation system was evaluated by means of the simulations documented in Section 5.3.3.

6.3.1 Overlay connectivity and composition

With respect to the requirements of Desktop Grids, connectivity may be considered the overlay's most important property. Broadcast messages can reach only that part of the overlay in which they have originated, respectively; if the overlay is not connected, peers in other overlay fragments will not receive the message. Since job initiators critically depend on potential workers to receive their job announcement broadcasts, a high degree of connectivity is crucial for Desktop Grid operations.

An experiment to determine the degree of overlay connectivity was performed on PlanetLab nodes, each running an instance of the PeerGrid middleware prototype. First, all peers joined the overlay. One arbitrarily picked peer [43] was selected to act as an observer of the overlay's state in the following way. This peer periodically sent broadcast messages through the overlay, asking the recipients to reply with unicast messages routed through the overlay back to the observer. The replies would arrive only if the respective recipient was connected to the overlay and the broadcast originator did not change its position within the overlay until the replies arrived. This way, complete overlay routing was examined as both the broadcast message and the associated replies were routed through the Chord ring in clockwise direction. This experiment captured the overlay's composition from the broadcast initiator's point of view. Also, since responding peers included their current role (super-peer or edge peer) in the reply message, the current number of super-peers in the overlay could be tracked. [44] In this experiment, overlay connectivity was examined for a 225-node overlay over approximately 9 hours using a sampling frequency of 6/min (i.e. a period of 10 seconds between two samples). In this time, 3, 103 samples were taken. Figure 6.3 depicts the outcome. The figure shows that most of the time, all or almost all of the peers responded to the broadcast queries. In the experiment's beginning, the number of responding peers was steadily increasing. The median number of respondents was 224, the maximum number possible. 224 was also the mode as it occurred in 1, 569 samples (50.56 %); replies from a total number of 223 peers were seen in another 792 samples (25.52 %). The average number of respondents amounted to 218.758 with a standard deviation of 21.843. These results indicate a high level of connectivity which is sustained throughout the entire experiment.

In the same experiment, the number of super-peers was tracked. Figure 6.4 provides a chart of the super-peer number plotted over time. The median number of responding super-peers was 19, the minimum 0 [45] and the maximum 25. Both the minimum and the maximum number were observed only once during the entire experiment, respectively.

---

[43] planetlab2.informatik.uni-goettingen.de

[44] The super-peer/edge peer role of the observer (the broadcast initiator) was disregarded in this context.

[45] The effect of getting no replies occurs when shortly after having sent the broadcast message, the broadcast initiator temporarily disconnects from the overlay due to upgrading, downgrading, or switching to another super-peer, hence it is unable to receive the requested replies.

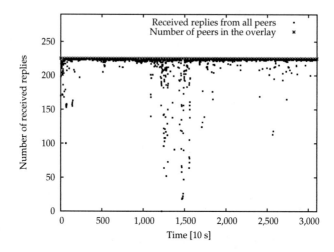

Figure 6.3: Connectivity of a 225-node overlay on PlanetLab

The median number of 19 super-peers, which was also the mode, was observed in 908 samples (29.26 %). The average number of listed super-peers amounted to 18.257 with a standard deviation of 2.21.

A different method to measure the number of super-peers considers the length of the super-peer list. This method was applied in an experiment in Amazon EC2 which ran for slightly more than $2\frac{1}{2}$ days. In this period, 14,750 samples of the super-peer list were recorded. Figure 6.5 depicts the number of super-peer list entries over time. In Amazon EC2, all nodes experience virtually the same network delay to the remaining nodes. Thus, ChordSPSA's delay-based topology optimization was hardly effective. Edge peers switched to other super-peers in anticipation of negligible gains, and super-peers frequently downgraded or promoted edge peers to super-peer level. The minimum observed number was 1 super-peer, the median 21 super-peers, and the maximum 27 super-peers. As before, the median equalled the mode, observed in 4,239 samples (28.74 %). The average number of super-peers in the EC2 setting was 21.355 with a standard deviation of 1.77.

The findings suggest that in both PlanetLab and Amazon EC2 settings, the number of super-peers selected by ChordSPSA is dynamic but varies only slightly over time.

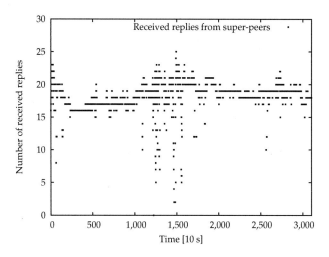

Figure 6.4: Super-peer numbers in a 225-node overlay on PlanetLab

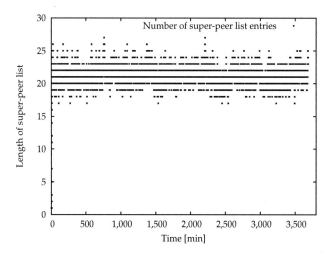

Figure 6.5: Length of the super-peer list in a 250-node overlay on Amazon EC2

6.3.2 Jobs

The PeerGrid middleware prototype was subjected to a series of tests aimed at assessing the performance that can be expected from distributed computing in real-world settings. In this context, a number of experiments involving the distributed computation of various kinds of jobs were conducted. These jobs were selected to represent the vast majority of jobs likely to be submitted to a Desktop Grid. The selection included the following jobs:

- Frequently, jobs perform numerical computations that can be split into portions of independent tasks. This kind of job is common for *parameter-sweep studies* which evaluate sets or ranges of parameters by computing sequences of functions for every parameter value [40, 41, 91]. The MANDELBROT SET was chosen to represent parameter-sweep studies as it is well-known, floating-point-intensive, and its ITA nature matches that of other parameter-sweep applications.

- A secondary ITA job type is an ITA job that contains other ITA jobs within itself, i. e. it is an *Iterated ITA* job. The FLOYD-WARSHALL ALGORITHM that computes all-pairs shortest paths is a representant of this scheme.

- From the CP class of jobs, a *distributed evolutionary algorithm* was chosen to solve a large instance of the BIN PACKING PROBLEM. This combinatorial optimization problem is both practically relevant and NP-hard. The deployed algorithm included all essential building blocks of evolutionary algorithms. In this setting, the major goal was to explore the benefits of inter-worker cooperation.

- Another CP example is a distributed heuristic for the NP-hard TRAVELING SALESMAN PROBLEM. As with bin packing, measuring the benefits of inter-worker cooperation was a key aspect. However, unlike the other jobs, the heuristic was executed on Amazon EC2 nodes, and its performance depended on the interaction of the Java-based PeerGrid middleware prototype and a binary executable that contained the actual heuristic.

Worker availability during the experiments depended on overlay connectivity, message delays, and node load at the time of the initiator's call for workers. In all jobs, available workers connected to the initiator to form a star-shaped topology that lasted for the duration of the respective distributed computation. The experiments and their results are discussed in the remainder of this section.

6.3.2.1 The Mandelbrot Set

A prominent ITA job for distributed computation is the generation of the Mandelbrot set [34]. It represents the vast job class of parameter-sweep studies in which every task consists of the assignment to independently compute results for a specified range of parameters. To obtain the Mandelbrot set, one considers the series

$$z_{n+1} = z_n^2 + c \tag{6.5}$$

given $z_0 = 0$, $z_i \in C$ $\forall i = 0, 1, ..., n$, and an arbitrary $c \in C$. The Mandelbrot set $\mathcal{M}$ is defined as the set of all $c \in C$ whose associated z_n series converges:

$$\mathcal{M} = \{c \in C : |z_n| < \infty, n \to \infty\} \tag{6.6}$$

A subset $\mathcal{G} \subseteq C$ can be graphically tested as to which of its elements belong to $\mathcal{M}$. To do so, $\mathcal{G}$ is mapped to a two-dimensional rasterized display: the real axis is mapped to the display's horizontal dimension while the imaginary axis is mapped to the display's vertical dimension. A criterion to detect divergence for a particular point is to stop iterating once $|z_n| > 2$ [34]. For every available pixel, the matching element of $\mathcal{G}$ is tested for membership in $\mathcal{M}$, and the pixel's color is chosen according to the number of iterations required until the divergence criterion $|z_n| > 2$ is met or the maximum number of iterations is reached.

For the example, the Mandelbrot set was mapped to a graphical display of $1,200 \times 900$ pixels. The maximum number of iterations was set to $2 \cdot 10^6$. The examined subset of C was chosen such that a full shot of the figure became visible:

$$\mathcal{G} = \{(a + ib) \in C \mid -2.02 \le a \le 1.05, -1.45 \le b \le 1.35\} \tag{6.7}$$

Let r peers, $r > 0$, respond to the initiator's call for workers. The initiator splits the computation of the full set of h lines into several tasks, making every task t_i with $i = 1, 2, ..., r - 1$ handle the computation of $\lfloor \frac{h}{r} \rfloor$ lines. Task t_r handles $h - (r - 1) \cdot \lfloor \frac{h}{r} \rfloor$ lines to ensure all lines are computed if $\lfloor \frac{h}{r} \rfloor < \frac{h}{r}$. Figure 6.6 depicts an example that splits the Mandelbrot set vertically into 11 tasks, using the subset $\mathcal{G} \subseteq C$ from (6.7).

A non-discriminating task-assignment scheme would assign the tasks to the workers in a way that does not take the workers' LPI values into account. Assigning the tasks to the workers in *First-Come First-Served* (FCFS) order equals a random assignment that disregards the workers' individual capabilities. Since workers have different capabilities and tasks have different volumes as some lines take longer to compute than others, assigning tasks according to LPI values and task volumes may considerably reduce the makespan. The heuristic that assigns tasks needs to be tailored specifically to the problem at hand to be able to estimate task volumes. Given the subset $\mathcal{G}$ as defined in (6.7), it is helpful to estimate the volume v_i of a task t_i that encompasses computing the lines l_{i1} to

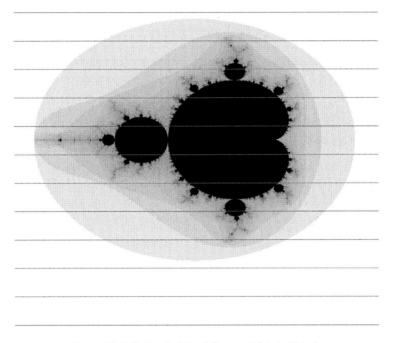

Figure 6.6: Splitting the Mandelbrot set job into 11 tasks

| | | Computation time [s] | |
Platform	Mean	Std. dev.	95% confidence interval
AMD Athlon64 3200+ (2.0 GHz)	5,202.83	28.84	[5,192.061, 5,213.599]
Intel Core2 E6300 (1.86 GHz)	3,795.5	2.18	[3,794.686, 3,796.314]
Intel Pentium D (3.0 GHz)	4,693.5	4.49	[4,691.823, 4,695.177]
PlanetLab (FCFS)	1,162.23	312.84	[1,045.414, 1,279.046]
PlanetLab (LPI)	179.9	41.31	[164.475, 195.325]

Table 6.1: Mandelbrot set time consumption

l_{i2} with $0 \leq l_{i1} \leq l_{i2} \leq h$ as

$$v_i = \sum_{k=l_{i1}}^{l_{i2}} \min(k, h-k) \tag{6.8}$$

since the vertical center is most expensive to compute as many points reach the iteration limit, failing to diverge. On the contrary, in areas close to the vertical edges of the selected subset of $\mathcal{M}$, most points meet the divergence criterion quickly, accelerating the computation of those lines. Given that there are r workers and r tasks, the LPI-observing assignment heuristic sorts worker LPI values and task volumes ascendingly, assigning the j-th task in the volume-sorted task order to the j-th worker in the LPI-sorted worker order, with $j = 1, 2, ..., r$.

In a first experiment, the time required for locally computing the Mandelbrot set in a non-distributed way on various desktop computers, all equipped with 1 GB RAM, running Linux and Java 6, was measured. Moreover, the time required by a distributed computation with 100 PlanetLab nodes (one initiator, up to 99 workers) was recorded. The given time includes the 15-second period the initiator had waited for worker responses before starting the actual distributed computation. The results shown in Table 6.1 indicate that the effects of the LPI-based task-sorting heuristic are tremendous: on PlanetLab, the unoptimized version with random task assignment took 6.4 times as long. On average, the optimized version took less than 3 minutes to complete. In solitary computation on various CPUs, computing the Mandelbrot set with the given parameters took longer than one hour. Compared to solitary computation on an Athlon64 3200+ CPU, the distributed Mandelbrot set computation with tasks sorted by LPI on PlanetLab experienced a speedup of 29.061 on average.

When the LPI-based sorting heuristic was tested, there were 81.87 workers per run on average with a standard deviation of 12.24, yielding a 95% confidence interval for the mean number of workers of $[77.300, 86.440]$. When the FCFS strategy was tested, there were 75.1 workers per run on average with a standard deviation of 6.64. The 95 % confidence interval for the mean number of workers in this case was $[72.609, 77.590]$. Since the intervals overlapped, there was no significant difference in the number of workers at the 95 % confidence level.

In the example, all tasks consisted of the same number of lines. A stronger version of the heuristic presented here might adapt the task sizes, i.e. tasks have varying number of lines, and the tasks need not consist of ranges but can contain arbitrary sets of lines instead. In summary, the outcome of the Mandelbrot set experiment suggests that parameter-sweep studies benefit from distributed computing. They benefit particularly if a heuristic matches a task's volume to a worker's individual capabilities.

6.3.2.2 All-pairs shortest paths in graphs

The computation of shortest paths between all pairs of vertices of a given graph $G = (V, E)$ is a common problem in graph theory. Using dynamic programming, the Floyd-Warshall algorithm solves this problem efficiently in $O(|V|^3)$ time [54, 84, 227].

The Floyd-Warshall algorithm expects a $|V| \times |V|$ matrix $D = (d_{ij})$ which contains the known initial distances between all $n = |V|$ vertices, with the main diagonal carrying zeros and all other elements being non-negative. Unavailable links are marked with ∞. The algorithm's key idea is to iteratively add intermediate vertices from the graph to the known shortest path between two vertices until all the graph's vertices have been considered for adding.

Formally, let the vertices $v \in V$ be enumerated as $1, 2, ..., n$. Also, let d_{ij}^p be the shortest distance between i and j that uses only vertices from the set $\{1, 2, \ldots, p\}$ as intermediate hops. ($d_{ij}^0 = d_{ij}$ gives the initially known distance between i and j that uses no intermediate vertices from the graph.) The algorithm performs n iterations and examines every pair of vertices (i, j) in each iteration, testing whether a path leading from i to j via k is shorter than the currently known distance d_{ij}^{k-1}. If so, the path length d_{ij}^k is updated to $d_{ik}^{k-1} + d_{kj}^{k-1}$. Otherwise, d_{ij}^k is set to d_{ij}^{k-1}. Every iteration maintains the invariant that d_{ij}^{k-1} is an optimal partial solution in that it is the shortest path's distance between vertices i and j that contains only intermediate vertices from the set $\{1, 2, \ldots, k-1\}$.

In the k-th iteration, vertex k is considered for insertion into the currently known shortest path between i and j. Let the path between i and j be split into two separate paths, p_1 leading from i to k and p_2 from k to j. By construction, both paths contain intermediate vertices from 1 to $k-1$ only. If it is beneficial to add k to the shortest path, the condition $d_{ij}^{k-1} > d_{ik}^{k-1} + d_{kj}^{k-1}$ holds. In this case, p_1 and p_2 share no intermediate vertex. If they did, joining p_1 and p_2 at an intermediate vertex would preclude the indirection via k. Since k iterates over all vertices, all vertices are tested for inclusion into shortest paths. Also, k is always inserted at the best position by using the shortest path from the source i to k, p_1, and from there, the shortest path to the destination, j. The algorithm's k-th iteration either refrains from changing d_{ij}^k if including k does not shorten the currently known shortest distance between i and j (using only vertices up to k as intermediate path elements), or updates d_{ij}^k to the path length obtained when passing through k. This observation yields a recursive relationship for the computation of d_{ij}^k:

$$d_{ij}^k = \min(d_{ij}^{k-1}, d_{ik}^{k-1} + d_{kj}^{k-1}) \qquad (6.9)$$

The first argument in (6.9) retains the previous iteration's shortest distance from i to j if the addition of k yields no benefit. Otherwise, k is inserted into the path from i and j. The formulation of (6.9) also ensures that $d_{ij}^0, d_{ij}^1, ..., d_{ij}^k$ is a non-increasing sequence.

(6.9) bears the useful property that neither d_{ik}^k nor d_{kj}^k are modified at any time during the k-th iteration. Adding k as the final intermediate vertex to a path leading from i to k or as the first intermediate vertex on a path leading from k to j will not modify the path length since by assumption, $d_{ii}^k = 0 \ \forall \ i, \ k \in 1, 2, ..., n$; adding it in other places would violate the invariant, and will therefore not be considered by the algorithm. When accessing elements from the matrix' k-th row or k-th column in the k-th iteration, three cases can be distinguished:

- $i = k \wedge j = k$:
  $d_{kk}^k = \min(d_{kk}^{k-1}, d_{kk}^{k-1} + d_{kk}^{k-1}) = \min(d_{kk}^{k-1}, 2 \cdot d_{kk}^{k-1}) = \min(0, 0) = 0 = d_{kk}^{k-1}$

- $i \neq k \wedge j = k$:
  $d_{ik}^k = \min(d_{ik}^{k-1}, d_{ik}^{k-1} + d_{kk}^{k-1}) = \min(d_{ik}^{k-1}, d_{ik}^{k-1} + 0) = d_{ik}^{k-1}$

- $i = k \wedge j \neq k$:
  $d_{kj}^k = \min(d_{kj}^{k-1}, d_{kk}^{k-1} + d_{kj}^{k-1}) = \min(d_{kj}^{k-1}, 0 + d_{kj}^{k-1}) = d_{kj}^{k-1}$

The first case conserves the elements along the main diagonal: the distance of a vertex to itself is zero through all iterations. The other cases address the fact that adding k as an intermediate hop leaves the shortest distance unchanged, so no modification is carried out with regard to d_{ik}^k and d_{kj}^k, respectively. Hence, throughout the k-th iteration, both the k-th column and the k-th row remain constant. This property will be exploited shortly for the purpose of distributed computation. Furthermore, the matrix D may be modified in-place since there will be no future access to $d_{ij}^{k-1}, d_{ij}^{k-2}, ..., d_{ij}^0$ once d_{ij}^k is written: in iteration $k + 1$, d_{ij}^{k+1} will be computed using results from the preceding iteration only.

A pseudocode formulation of the Floyd-Warshall algorithm is given as Algorithm 6 [54].

Algorithm 6 Floyd-Warshall

---

1   **for** $k = 1$ to n **do**
2   **for** $i = 1$ to n **do**
3   **for** $j = 1$ to n **do**
4            $d_{ij} = \min(d_{ij}, d_{ik} + d_{kj})$
5   **end for**
6   **end for**
7   **end for**

The algorithm variant discussed here computes shortest distances. Beyond that, if the actual vertices that make up the individual shortest paths for all node pairs are required, they can be obtained with an extension that does not affect the algorithm's essential properties [54].

The execution of the pseudocode assignment in line 4 of Algorithm 6 requires $O(1)$ time. Additionally, exploiting the fact that the k-th column and k-th row remain constant throughout the k-th iteration, both inner loops are fully independent from each other and from previous iterations of themselves, so assignments to matrix elements d_{ij} may be carried out in arbitrary order. In contrast, the outermost loop needs to be executed in strictly sequential order as updating the matrix elements during the $(k + 1)$-th iteration depends on results obtained through the k-th iteration.

In the Floyd-Warshall algorithm, the independence of assignments to d_{ij}^k enables parallelized computation. Given n^2 worker units available for parallel computation, each of them can update one matrix element in $O(1)$ time per iteration, effectively replacing both inner loops with a single instruction that takes $O(1)$ time to execute under ideal conditions.

In workflow terms, the outermost loop creates an ITA job in each of its n iterations. Thus, the Floyd-Warshall algorithm constitutes an *Iterated ITA* problem. The initiator assigns a set of matrix elements for computation to every worker. Once all workers have returned the updated elements, the initiator may assemble the partial results into the result matrix at the end of iteration k. As with other ITA jobs, the initiator will need to wait for the slowest worker to deliver its results. This issue is magnified here because the initiator will need to wait for the slowest worker in every single iteration. In heterogeneous environments, faster workers remain idle in the meantime as they cannot proceed to the $(k + 1)$-th iteration until column $k + 1$ has been completed in the k-th iteration. Since computing d_{ij}^k entails the same effort for all values of i, j and k, it is expected that a distributed variant of the Floyd-Warshall algorithm will minimize the idle time if workers have homogeneous capabilities, or if the number of elements to be computed is adjusted to the computational resources of the individual worker.

Since every iteration of the Floyd-Warshall algorithm's outer loop basically constitutes an ITA job of its own, the distributed computation is I/O intensive as each iteration requires transferring substantial parts of the matrix even with I/O minimization measures in effect. I/O load may be minimized by transmitting parts of D only instead of the full matrix. A worker that is supposed to update a set of matrix elements in the k-th iteration requires only the matrix elements from these lines, the k-th row, and the k-th column of D. Conversely, when the worker has completed its computation in the k-th iteration, it is sufficient to return the updated matrix elements only. Still, the distributed computation is expected to require substantial transfers of matrix information back and forth between the initiator and its workers until the final matrix is obtained.

An experiment was conducted with a matrix containing random distances between $1,000$ nodes. All matrix elements were non-negative, and the main diagonal consisted of zeroes. In this experiment, 4 stand-alone computers with a conventional, single-threaded Floyd-Warshall implementation were compared to each other and to a distributed, I/O-minimized implementation of the Floyd-Warshall algorithm that was executed on the DAG cluster with one initiator and up to 4 workers. 30 runs were conducted in all probed configurations.

| | *Computation time [s]* | | |
Platform	Mean	Std. dev.	95 % confidence interval
Intel Xeon E5420 (2.5 GHz)	2.752	0.004	[2.751, 2.754]
Intel Core 2 E6300 (1.86 GHz)	4.798	0.013	[4.793, 4.803]
Intel Pentium 4 (2.8 GHz)	16.027	0.294	[15.917, 16.136]
AMD Athlon64 3200+ (2.0 GHz)	24.771	0.154	[24.713, 24.828]
Distributed — 1 worker	180.8	1.789	[180.132, 181.468]
Distributed — 2 workers	125.1	3.021	[123.972, 126.228]
Distributed — 3 workers	119.3	2.756	[118.271, 120.392]
Distributed — 4 workers	198.033	6.886	[195.462, 200.605]

Table 6.2: Execution times of the Floyd-Warshall algorithm computation

Table 6.2 contains this experiment's outcome. The results unveil architectural differences in floating-point processing as the slowest unit, the AMD Athlon64 3200+, takes approximately 9 times as long as the fastest unit, the Intel Xeon E5420, despite being clocked only 20% slower.

From the figures in the table, it can also be observed that the distributed computation approach taken in this setting was not justified by potential savings in processing time. In every distributed configuration, the computation time was substantially higher than in any of the local configurations. In particular, the distributed case with a single worker revealed the I/O burden placed on the network. While the worker's computational

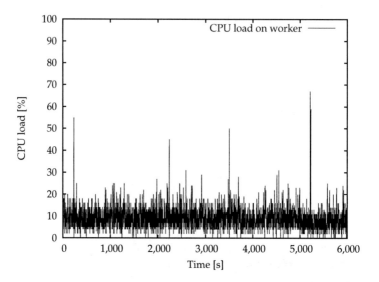

Figure 6.7: CPU load on a worker node while executing the parallelized Floyd-Warshall algorithm

resources were identical to the Intel Xeon E5420 stand-alone configuration, the initiator needed to hand out every matrix instance to the worker, and the worker needed to return its intermediate results, repeating this procedure 1, 000 times in the algorithm's outermost loop. This made for an approximately 65-fold increase in computation time. The situation improved with 2 and 3 workers: here, the savings attained through parallel computing started to make up for network I/O efforts. Still, local computation was considerably faster. With 4 workers, computation time started to increase again. This was due to several causes: additional network I/O, administrative overhead at the initiator, and the sensitivity to makespan issues as the rising number of workers could cause more delays at the end of each iteration. Consequently, workers spent more time running idle. This is illustrated by Figure 6.7 which depicts the fraction of actual load on a single worker node during the 30-runs distributed computation of the Floyd-Warshall algorithm. A sample was taken approximately every 2 seconds. The CPU load is given as the percentage of a single core's maximum load on an Intel Xeon E5420 CPU. Apart from processing the Floyd-Warshall workload, the core was idle. The figure shows that CPU load on the worker was generally low, with an average load of 8.6 % and a 75 % percentile of 11 %. The worker process spent most of its lifetime waiting for I/O operations to complete. This included waiting for the initiator to transmit the upcoming iteration's data.

Due to the I/O intensity, the Floyd-Warshall algorithm cannot be effectively distributed in this way. Since the apparent bottleneck is network bandwidth, a parallel implementation of this algorithm with workers that have fast access to shared memory, such as multiple execution units on modern CPUs, multi-processor systems, GPUs, or FPGAs can ignore this limitation and deliver substantial performance gains over serial execution [30, 106, 127, 175, 181]. Since distributed Floyd-Warshall computation time even on a LAN high-performance cluster system is unsatisfactory, no additional WAN-based studies were conducted in this context. The results confirm in a Desktop Grid context the prediction of poor performance for cluster computing applications that frequently access shared memory [21].

6.3.2.3 The bin packing problem

The bin packing problem is an NP-hard combinatorial optimization problem that can be stated as an integer program [52, 95, 156]. It is concerned with minimizing the number of identical bins required to store a given set of n indivisible items with different but strictly positive weights. The weights can alternatively be interpreted as sizes [52].

The bin packing problem has a number of practical applications. For instance, given a collection of files, the number of DVDs to store these files is to be minimized. In another example, the number of trucks transporting equipment to a construction site should be kept as low as possible.

Bin packing is related to the KNAPSACK problem, another NP-hard combinatorial optimization problem that addresses a packing issue [156]. Given a set X of n items, indexed $1, \ldots, n$, a weight $w_i > 0$ for item i, a value $v_i \geq 0$ for item i, and a knapsack that can hold a maximum weight of c, the solution to the knapsack problem is the value-maximizing subset of X whose items' cumulative weights do not exceed the knapsack's weight limit, c. Both knapsack and bin packing represent packing problems, but with a different focus. In bin packing, all items can be considered of equal value, and the number of knapsacks (bins) to stow them all is to be minimized. In the knapsack problem, items have varying values but there is only a single bin available. Thus, in bin packing, the number of bins is variable but the set of packed items is constant, while in the knapsack problem, the number of bins is fixed (to 1) and the set of packed items is variable.

While the knapsack problem has many practical applications, it has not been chosen as a demonstration job for PeerGrid as exact solutions are easily attainable with standard desktop hardware for instances containing hundreds of thousands of items. For this reason, knapsack instances for which distributed computation in a Desktop Grid is conceivable are likely to contain millions of items. However, transferring instance data for such large numbers of items exceeds the capabilities of an initiator with moderate upstream bandwidth. For instance, with $1,200,000$ items and 4 byte to specify an item (16 bits each for weight and utility), an initiator would need to transmit 4.8 MByte of instance data alone. In the unicast case, this amount is multiplied by the number of workers. While this can be alleviated by multicast through the overlay, it is considered too heavy a load.

Unlike the knapsack problem, exact solutions for bin packing problems can be computed in reasonable time with desktop-level equipment for small instances only. Already the computation of lower bounds through LP relaxation is costly. For solving the LP relaxation of a $3,500$-item bin packing instance with a bin capacity of $1,000,000$ units and item sizes randomly drawn from a uniform distribution with bounds $[200,000; 350,000]$, glpsol from the GNU LINEAR PROGRAMMING KIT took 12 hours, 31 minutes and 7 seconds of CPU time on an Intel Xeon E5420 CPU while requiring 11.675 GByte of RAM for this effort. A survey of various LP formulations for the bin packing problem is available in [63], which also discusses bin packing as a special case of the vehicle routing problem. These LP formulations are useful for delivering bounds in exact algorithms.

The following sections first present an integer program and lower bounds for the bin packing problem. Subsequently, non-distributed and distributed heuristics that approximate optimal solutions are discussed.

6.3.2.3.1 An integer program and lower bounds

Let there be $n \geq 1$ items with arbitrary positive weights. Every bin can carry at least the heaviest item. [46] Given that every bin can store at least one item, the maximum number of bins required is n. Conversely, at least one bin is required to store all items no matter the bin capacities and item weights. This provides simple upper and lower bounds: the minimum number of required bins, OPT, is contained in the set $\{1, ..., n\}$. Let s_i be the weight of item i and $bincap$ the positive capacity of a single bin. A stronger lower bound is based on the relaxation that all items are divisible [156], yielding

$$LB_{\text{Divisible}} = \left\lceil \frac{\sum_{i=1}^{n} s_i}{bincap} \right\rceil \qquad (6.10)$$

With $i, j \in 1, \ldots, n$, let the binary variable x_j be set to 1 iff bin j is in use, and let the binary variable y_{ij} be set to 1 iff item i is stored in bin j. With these prerequisites, an integer program that captures the bin packing problem is stated below [156]:

---

[46]This assumption ensures that a bin can hold any item. Hence, infeasible configurations where items whose weight exceeds the capacity of the bins cannot be stored are avoided.

$$\min Z = \sum_{j=1}^{n} x_j \tag{6.11}$$

subject to $\quad\displaystyle\sum_{i=1}^{n} y_{ij} \cdot s_i \le x_j \cdot bincap \qquad \forall\, j = 1,\ldots,n \tag{6.12}$

$$\sum_{j=1}^{n} y_{ij} = 1 \qquad\qquad \forall\, i = 1,\ldots,n \tag{6.13}$$

$$x_j \ge x_{j+1} \qquad\qquad \forall\, j = 1,\ldots,n-1 \tag{6.14}$$

$$x_j \in \{0,1\} \qquad\qquad \forall\, i,j = 1,\ldots,n \tag{6.15}$$

$$y_{ij} \in \{0,1\} \qquad\qquad \forall\, i,j = 1,\ldots,n \tag{6.16}$$

The objective function (6.11) sums up the flags of bins in use. Constraints (6.12) ensure that no bin exceeds its capacity, and that x_j is set to 1 if bin j is in use. Constraints (6.13) guarantee that every item is assigned to exactly one bin.

Constraints (6.14) enforce the usage of bins in the order specified by the bin index. It is implicitly assumed in [156]. However, its explicit inclusion into the model can accelerate an IP solver's progress by a substantial margin as the solution space is shrunk. Let Z^* be the minimum number of bins required to store n items. Then $\binom{n}{Z^*}$ optimal solutions exist. Constraints (6.14) reduce this to a single optimal solution that occupies the first Z^* bins. For example, if $Z^* = 3$ and $n = 20$, there are $\binom{20}{3} = 1,140$ optimal solutions that include, for instance, the bin combinations $2,8,9$ and $1,3,6$. Since bins are identical, these solutions are equivalent, and it is therefore sufficient to consider the sequence $1,2,3$. Also, items with zero weight can be excluded from the actual problem as they may be safely added to any bin without violating its capacity constraint.

6.3.2.3.2 Heuristics

There are various heuristics for the bin packing problem [52, 95, 156]. Let the available bins be indexed $B_1, B_2, \ldots, B_n$.

The NEXT FIT (NF) heuristic is a 2-approximation of the optimal solution and has $O(n)$ time complexity. It traverses the sequence of given items and opens bins in sequence, while only the currently considered bin is modified. Previous bins remain closed. NF assigns item 1 to B_1 and sets the current bin to B_1. Subsequently, for the j-th item ($j \in \{2,\ldots,n\}$), NF checks if the current bin's remaining capacity suffices to hold item j. Otherwise, NF opens a new bin, closes the current bin, and the new bin becomes the current bin. Item j is assigned to the current bin and the next item is fetched.

Unlike NF which handles only one bin at a time, the FIRST FIT (FF) heuristic considers all bins opened in the past for adding item j. Item j is placed in the lowest-index bin that has sufficient remaining capacity. While a straightforward implementation has a time complexity on the order of $O(n^2)$, FF can be implemented to run in $O(n \cdot \log n)$ time [52]. FF improves upon NF as it is a 1.7-approximation of the optimal solution.

The BEST FIT (BF) heuristic differs from FF only in that it adds item j to the previously opened bin with the lowest remaining residual capacity which is still sufficient for holding item j. Thus, the lowest-index choice made by FF is replaced by BF's more complex choice of considering all open bins for addition. The solutions found by BF can be substantially better or substantially worse than those found by FF [52]. However, like FF, BF is a 1.7-approximation, and it can be implemented to run in $O(n \cdot \log n)$ time.

NF, FF and BF are improved by sorting the items according to their weights in a descending way first [52]. The resulting heuristics are NEXT FIT DECREASING (NFD), FIRST FIT DECREASING (FFD) and BEST FIT DECREASING (BFD), respectively. BFD performs better than FFD when no item has a weight below $\frac{bincap}{6}$, but can create worse allocations if this criterion is not met. Both BFD and FFD are $\frac{11}{9}$-approximations, while NFD is a 1.691-approximation. All can be implemented to run in $O(n \cdot \log n)$ time [52].

6.3.2.3.3 An evolutionary algorithm

Distributed evolutionary algorithms form an important class of CP jobs. The term *evolutionary algorithm* encompasses various types of algorithms that are based on imitating nature's evolution process. As a particular kind of evolutionary algorithms, *genetic algorithms* (GA) perform randomized hill-climbing searches on multi-element populations to optimize the value of a given *fitness function* [173]. Every element of a population, called an *individual*, represents a solution whose quality can be rated with the fitness function.

A GA modifies its population through the use of *operators*. Common operators include *mutation* which randomly modifies a single individual, *selection* which filters sets of individuals by favoring better individuals over worse ones according to their fitness, and *crossover* that creates new individuals (children) from existing ones (parents) by merging the parents' genetic information into one or more children. Thus, the population evolves, supposedly to the end of improving the values returned by the fitness function.

As a population can be split into several smaller populations (known as *demes* [173], *islands* [230], or *subpopulations* [230]) that are evolved separately but with an exchange of individuals between the partial populations, GAs lend themselves to distributed computation [173]. The distribution of subpopulations over the workers corresponds to the *island model* [230]. In the island model, every worker executes a GA on its local island of individuals. Individuals are exchanged between the islands to enable inter-worker cooperation.

For the bin packing problem, the heuristics discussed in Section 6.3.2.3.2 can be combined with a GA to yield a distributed hybrid algorithm for solving bin packing instances [196]. This evolutionary approach represents a vast body of CP approaches that could be submitted to a Desktop Grid as it maintains populations, implements mutation, crossover and selection operators, and exchanges individuals with other workers to the end of solving a combinatorial optimization problem in a distributed context. Additionally, it cooperates with a problem-specific heuristic. In the case of an n-item bin packing instance, a GA with n-ary coding is coupled with the FF heuristic [196]. The key idea is to let a GA create permutations of the item order. In the order prescribed by the GA, the items are then assigned to bins using FF. It was shown that when used in combination with the proposed GA, FF performs better than BF for large instances [196].

As with other GAs, every individual in the hybrid GA's population represents a solution to the problem. The fitness of an individual could be assessed by the number of bins that it occupies, but this would not suffice to distinguish between solutions that have identical bin counts. Hence, a more fine-grained fitness function is required. For a given individual, let C_i be the occupied capacity of bin i and N the number of bins used by the individual. With this, a fitness function $f(s)$ that evaluates an individual s is given by [196]

$$f(S) = \frac{\sum_{i=1}^{N} C_i^2}{N \cdot bincap^2} \in [0,1] \tag{6.17}$$

In every iteration of the hybrid GA, two individuals are randomly picked for crossover. The random picking process adopts a *roulette wheel* mechanism that specifies an individual's likelihood of being picked as its normalized fitness function value (i.e. for an individual s from a population P, the probability $p_{crossover}$ of picking s for crossover is $p_{crossover} = \frac{f(s)}{\sum_{t \in P} f(t)}$) [173].

The C1 operator was chosen for crossover as it preserves the feasibility of solutions [196]. With two parent individuals, C1 determines two offspring as follows. A crossover point c is randomly drawn with uniform probability from the set $\{1, \ldots, n-1\}$. C1 performs crossover by letting the i-th offspring keep the i-th parent's elements at index positions $\{1, \ldots, c\}$, and sequentially filling the remaining positions with the elements from the other parent that have not been copied from the i-th parent. The elements from the other parent are retrieved in the order they occur in that parent. For example, in a bin packing instance with $n = 6$ items, parents $p_1 = (4,3,2,5,6,1)$ and $p_2 = (2,3,5,1,4,6)$, and the crossover point at $c = 3$, C1 copies the three leftmost elements in each parent to the respective offspring and fills the remaining positions with the missing items from the other parent. Thus, offspring o_1 becomes $o_1 = (4, 3, 2, 5, 1, 6)$ while offspring o_2 becomes $o_2 = (2, 3, 5, 4, 6, 1)$. After an evaluation of both offspring with (6.17), the better one replaces the worst individual in the population. The other offspring is discarded.

In each round, after the C1 operator has been applied, every individual is considered for mutation. The mutation operator swaps the positions of two randomly picked items within a mutated individual's item ordering. The probability $p_{\text{mutation}}(s)$ of picking individual s for mutation is $p_{\text{mutation}}(s) = \min(1 - f(s) + b, 1)$, where $b \in [0, 1]$ is a mutation acceleration bonus initialized with 0 and increased by 0.01 up to the maximum value of 1 whenever 20 rounds without improvement of the best known fitness value have elapsed. Thus, in the extreme case of $b = 1$, every individual is guaranteed to be mutated. When a new best known fitness value is recorded, b is reset to zero. This approach adapts the mutation rate to the progress the hybrid GA makes while moving through the solution space. If C1 crossover is sufficient to keep up improvements, the impact of mutation will be negligible, but if crossover alone does not manage to improve the population, mutation gradually gains importance.

The hybrid GA was evaluated with the $3,500$-item bin packing instance described in Section 6.3.2.3. For this instance, the FFD solution required $1,034$ bins. According to the $LB_{\text{Divisible}}$ lower bound defined in (6.10), the optimal solution had at least 962 bins, while the instance's LP relaxation led to a lower bound at 961.471 bins.

The distributed setting was composed of 100 PlanetLab nodes providing up to 99 workers. Each worker carried a population of 50 individuals which was initialized with the FFD solution and 49 randomly generated solutions. Thus, the algorithm could not fare worse than FFD. The hybrid GA was executed 30 times for half an hour each and its progress recorded. The experiment was performed once with cooperating workers and another time with isolated workers to assess the gain arising from cooperation. In the cooperative configuration, once a worker found a new best known solution, the solution was transmitted to the initiator that notified the remaining workers. A worker that received a new best known solution from the initiator replaced the worst-rated individual in its local population with the received solution. In contrast, in the isolated case, every worker computed on its own. New best known solutions were transmitted to the initiator but the initiator refrained from passing the news on to the other workers.

The results are depicted in Figure 6.8 which contains error bars representing 95 % confidence intervals for the mean. The figure shows that cooperation produces significantly better results than isolated computation. Overall solution quality benefits from the exchange of intermediate solutions among the workers. The best found solution required 998 bins. It was encountered in the cooperative configuration only. A solution requiring

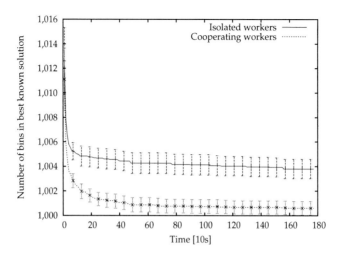

Figure 6.8: Performance of the hybrid genetic algorithm on a 3,500-item bin packing instance

this number of bins was found in 2 out of the 30 runs. In contrast, the best solution found by the isolated configuration occupied 1,000 bins, and it was found in a single run only.

At the 95 % confidence level, there was no significant difference in the number of workers between the two configurations. In the cooperative configuration, there were 48.94 workers per run on average with a standard deviation of 10.907. In contrast, the isolated configuration saw 54.2 workers per run on average with a standard deviation of 11.012. With a 95 % confidence interval for the means' difference of $[-10.835, 0.310]$, a Welch test did not reject the null hypothesis of equal worker numbers.

When set up in the isolated configuration for half an hour, a single run found a solution that required 1,003.8 bins on average (median 1,004 bins, maximum 1,009 bins). This is worse than the cooperative setting as a run in that configuration found a solution with 1,000.6 bins on average (median 1,000.5 bins, maximum 1,005 bins). These results indicate that cooperative computation which shares intermediate results among all workers is beneficial to solving the bin packing problem, and it is likely to benefit other CP approaches as well.

6.3.2.4 The Traveling Salesman Problem

The TRAVELING SALESMAN PROBLEM (TSP) is an NP-hard combinatorial optimization problem in graphs [65, 95, 111]. In the TSP, a salesman wishes to visit n cities. He intends to visit each city exactly once, and after having visited all cities, he wants to return to the city in which his tour had started. The TSP has a wide number of practical applications beyond finding shortest tours for salesmen, such as drilling problems and genome sequencing [13, 111].

6.3.2.4.1 An integer program

Given a directed, strongly connected graph $G = (V, E)$ with a distance function $d(i, j)$ that assigns weights to every edge $(v_i, v_j) \in E$, one seeks a permutation $(v_{\pi(1)}, v_{\pi(2)}, \dots, v_{\pi(|V|)})$ of the nodes in V that minimizes the value of Z in (6.18):

$$\min Z = \left(\sum_{i=1}^{|V|-1} d(v_{\pi(i)}, v_{\pi(i+1)}) \right) + d(v_{\pi(|V|)}, v_{\pi(1)}) \tag{6.18}$$

Besides the formulation with a permutation operator in (6.18), an integer program for the TSP can be stated as follows. Let the binary variable x_{ij} be set to 1 iff the edge (v_i, v_j) is used in the shortest tour. The integer program is then formulated as [65]

$$\min T = \sum_{\substack{i=1}}^{n} \sum_{\substack{j=1 \\ j \neq i}}^{n} d(i, j) \cdot x_{ij} \tag{6.19}$$

subject to

$$\sum_{\substack{j=1 \\ j \neq i}}^{n} x_{ij} = 1 \qquad \forall\, i \in V \tag{6.20}$$

$$\sum_{\substack{i=1 \\ j \neq i}}^{n} x_{ij} = 1 \qquad \forall\, j \in V \tag{6.21}$$

$$\sum_{v_i, v_j \in S}^{n} x_{ij} \leq |S| - 1 \qquad \forall\, S \subset V,\, |S| \geq 2 \tag{6.22}$$

$$x_{ij} \in \{0, 1\} \qquad \forall\, i, j \in V \tag{6.23}$$

A valid tour requires every node to have an out-degree and an in-degree of both 1 with respect to the subgraph induced by the tour. These requirements are enforced by constraints (6.20) and (6.21), respectively. Since these constraints cannot prevent the creation of disjoint subtours (cycles of length strictly less than $|V|$), constraints (6.22) see to it that a single tour which contains all vertices is computed.

6.3.2.4.2 Heuristics

Each of the $n!$ permutations of the n vertices (cities) specifies a valid tour. Since any city may serve as the starting point for a tour, there are n permutations which refer to the same tour. Thus, there are $\frac{n!}{n} = (n-1)!$ unique tours. Under these circumstances, an enumerative approach ("brute-force") to find the shortest tour is intractable for all but tiny instances. More sophisticated exact algorithms can solve instances of modest size but need considerable computational resources for such efforts [111].

Large instances can only be tackled by heuristics in reasonable time. As with other combinatorial problems, there are heuristics that construct initial solutions and others that attempt to improve existing ones. Also, there are composite heuristics that include both construction and improvement subroutines. A simple greedy construction method is NEAREST-NEIGHBOR [111]. It starts with an arbitrary city. Unless all cities have been visited, the algorithm greedily adds the closest remaining city for the next hop. This approach suffers from the observation that while in the beginning, short edges are included into the tour, long distances prevail in the end.

A different way to construct an initial tour is the QUICK-BORŮVKA algorithm [12, 83]. Given a geometric instance, the algorithm processes the instance's cities in the order which is obtained by sorting them according to one of their coordinates. In each of the at most two iterations, an adjacent edge is added to every city which has a degree of less than two in the partial tour. The edge selected for addition is the least costly edge which neither causes a subtour to be created nor is adjacent to a city of degree two.

A simple improvement heuristic is the 2-OPT algorithm [111]. It starts with an arbitrary tour and proceeds iteratively. In every iteration, it replaces two edges from the current tour with two edges not used in the current tour such that a shorter tour results. The algorithm terminates once no more improvements can be attained. The 2-opt algorithm is a special case of the K-OPT algorithm which, in every iteration, replaces k edges with k others in the current tour until a (presumably non-global) optimum is reached. A tour which cannot be improved through replacement of k edges is k-optimal. However, this approach requires $O(n^k)$ evaluations per iteration for a n-city instance [111].

The situation improves with the LIN-KERNIGHAN (LK) algorithm [12, 13, 111, 148]. In every iteration of LK, the value of k is adjusted. Like k-opt, LK iteratively performs a sequence of exchanges until no more improvement is attainable. LK resorts to backtracking for finding sequences of edges to be exchanged, and in contrast to k-opt, temporarily permits the inclusion of edge exchanges which worsen the current solution in order to escape local optima. A number of requirements on the edges to be exchanged apply. These requirements are defined along with an algorithmic specification of LK in [111, 148].

A major improvement of LK was the introduction of *kicks* to perturb a tour found by LK and re-apply LK on the kicked tour [12, 13]. This modification yielded the CHAINED LIN-KERNIGHAN (CLK) algorithm. Its standard kick is the *double-bridge move*, a particular 4-opt edge exchange. CLK usually finds good solutions for large instances, but often fails to find the shortest tours for moderately-sized instances [13].

Besides CLK, LK has been improved by Keld Helsgaun in 2000 to yield the LIN-KERNIGHAN-HELSGAUN (LKH) algorithm [13, 111]. Every LKH run consists of a series of trials, each of which is initialized with a tour found by an arbitrary construction heuristic. [47] LKH's key building block is the *1-tree*, a spanning tree augmented with one additional edge. Since every tour is a 1-tree, the sought shortest tour's length is bounded below by the length of a minimum 1-tree. With a minimum 1-tree of the original graph, LKH estimates the chances of a link to be part of the shortest tour. LKH uses candidate lists to select the edges to be included within a k-opt move. These edges are chosen based on a *nearness* measure that reflects the length increment of a minimum 1-tree which is forced to incorporate the particular edge. LKH performs 5-opt exchanges with edges selected according to their nearness [111]. LKH is more time-consuming than CLK, but empirical findings suggest that the average tour length benefits substantially.

6.3.2.4.3 Distributed computation

Because of the outstanding quality that solutions produced by LKH generally feature, a distributed version of LKH was evaluated. [48] The distributed variant, DISTLKH, created a star-shaped overlay of workers with the initiator at the center. The initiator maintained a list of announcements. Every time a worker found a new best known solution, it announced the event to the initiator along with the local file name, the tour length, a timestamp, and its network address. Moreover, each worker queried the initiator every 10 seconds for the latest announcement. If the retrieved announcement referred to a better solution than the querying worker had, the better solution was downloaded from the worker that found it.

The TSP instance $E316k.0$ with $316,228$ nodes served as input. [49] As PlanetLab nodes

---

[47] In this context, the Quick-Borůvka heuristic is frequently preferred for the construction of the initial tour [13].

[48] The LKH implementation and a stand-alone execution framework were provided by Prof. Dr. Peter Merz.

[49] The shortest known tour's length for this instance is tracked on
    http://www.akira.ruc.dk/~keld/research/LKH/DIMACS_results.html. Currently, it is at $401,307,462$ units.

could not satisfy LKH's memory requirements, 250 Amazon EC2 nodes had been leased to form the evaluation testbed. In every run, DistLKH was set up to perform 15 trials. After the second and every subsequent trial, the LKH implementation provided the resulting tour as a file for download by remote workers. The initial tour was computed by the Quick-Borůvka heuristic.

To assess the benefit of cooperation, two configurations were compared. In the *cooperative* setting, all peers behaved as described. In the *isolated* setting, the initiator denied inter-worker cooperation by refraining from publishing announcements of new best known tours, effectively isolating the workers from each other. In both configurations, 30 runs were conducted. Each run lasted for 2 hours. Tour lengths were recorded by the initiator every 10 seconds after the first time a worker had reported a solution. This event occurred after approximately 20 minutes.

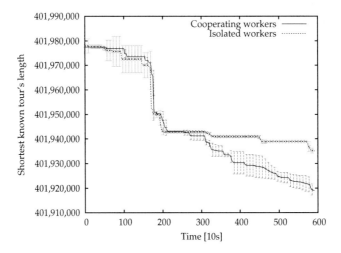

Figure 6.9: Lengths of tours produced by the distributed LKH algorithm on Amazon EC2 nodes

The results of this experiment are depicted in Figure 6.9. The tours initially found by the workers in the isolated configuration were slightly better on average than their counterparts from the cooperative configuration, but the difference was not significant at the 95 % confidence level. Shortly after $t = 2,560\,s$, the majority of workers completed their first two LKH runs and started to exchange solutions in the cooperative configuration. With time passing, the gains of the cooperative configuration accumulated. The figure shows that the cooperative configuration achieved significant improvements over the isolated setting, supporting the expectation that cooperation is beneficial for distributed optimization heuristics.

At the 95 % confidence level, there was no significant difference in the number of workers between the two probed configurations. In the isolated configuration, there were 239
workers on average with a standard deviation of 9.316, while the cooperative configuration saw an average of 237 workers with a standard deviation of 5.436. With a p-value of
0.315, the null hypothesis of equal worker numbers was not rejected.

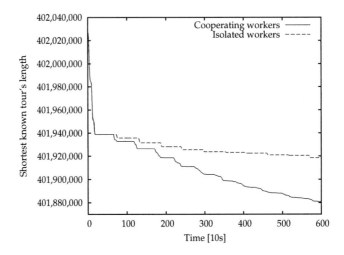

Figure 6.10: Lengths of tours produced by the distributed LKH algorithm on the DAG
cluster

The experiment was repeated on the DAG cluster with 8 PeerGrid instances on each of the
6 nodes. Otherwise, the configuration (including the instance, *E316k.0*) was identical to
the EC2 setting. Initialization and the first two LKH runs took approximately 20 minutes
after which the nodes started exchanging tours. In each of the 30 runs, for both the
cooperative and the isolated configuration, the maximum possible 47 workers joined the
effort. Figure 6.10 shows the outcome, confirming that cooperation led to significantly
better solutions than isolated computation in this setting, too. [50]

Although there were less peers in the system than with EC2 (48 instead of 250), the
computational capabilities of each peer were considerably more pronounced than those
of an EC2 SMALL node. It is for this reason that the average shortest known tour found

---

[50] The confidence interval indicators (error bars) were omitted in Figure 6.10 due to the comparatively small standard
deviations in the samples (the mean standard deviation per recorded sample amounted to 1493.94 in the cooperative
configuration and to 261.53 in the isolated configuration). The resulting exceedingly narrow confidence intervals
would have collapsed into the plotted curves.

in the cooperative DAG cluster configuration was shorter than the average shortest known tour found in the cooperative EC2 configuration ($401, 880, 702$ length units vs. $401, 919, 060$ length units, both quantities rounded to integer boundaries).

In summary, much like the hybrid GA that tackled the bin packing problem, the distributed LKH computation experienced benefits from the exchange of solutions among the workers. The best tours found in the cooperative configuration were substantially shorter than those found when workers computed independently from each other.

6.4 Summary

This chapter has addressed the design and implementation aspects of the PeerGrid middleware, which, when run on every participating peer, organizes and maintains a fully distributed Desktop Grid. The middleware is built in a layer-oriented fashion, with point-to-point network I/O at the lowest and job administration at the highest level. Portability and security properties benefit from resorting to the Java platform.

To evaluate the performance of distributed applications with a PeerGrid middleware prototype in live settings, four jobs that represent the vast majority of jobs likely to be submitted to Desktop Grids were developed and experimentally assessed. There were two ITA problems (the Mandelbrot set computation and the Floyd-Warshall algorithm) and two CP jobs (the Bin Packing and Traveling Salesman combinatorial optimization problems). These experiments have yielded the result that unless the network represents an I/O bottleneck, the PeerGrid middleware prototype succeeds in leveraging idle CPU time from the participating resources. In the evolutionary algorithms, it was observed that cooperation led to better results than isolated work. A considerable speedup over single-node computation was achieved in all cases except for the Floyd-Warshall algorithm which strongly depends on fast shared memory in order to perform well in a distributed setting.

In summary, while jobs need to be carefully assessed with regard to their fitness for Desktop Grids, the middleware prototype has empirically shown the cumulative potential of idle peers that can be unleashed in a distributed way.

7

Conclusion

Similar to Computational Grids but without the administrative overhead and fixed components, Desktop Grids leverage the idle resources of online desktop computers for distributed computing. Their distributed nature, high dynamics, heterogeneous composition, and inherent need for scalability not only fit the properties of P2P systems but also distinguish Desktop Grids from more tightly coupled forms of distributed computing, including parallel, cluster, volunteer, and Grid computing. This work has explored the requirements of Desktop Grids with particular regard to the communications infrastructure. It has proposed distributed algorithms to create and maintain super-peer topologies optimized for both end-to-end delay and super-peer load, incorporated network coordinates into the topology optimization effort, examined the adverse effects of selfish behavior, consolidated the findings into a blueprint for a novel type of Desktop Grid, PeerGrid, and documented the setup and outcome of experiments with a middleware prototype that enabled a Desktop Grid of the proposed kind.

This thesis provides the following contributions to the current state of the art:

- The hypercube method, designed to yield good results already in low-dimensional spaces, is introduced to solve the individual problem in GNP. It is considerably more accurate than the Simplex Downhill algorithm which it replaces. In addition, the split-force improvement noticeably accelerates the progress of the Vivaldi algorithm.

- Super-peer topologies are identified as the most promising candidate for a communications infrastructure that satisfies a Desktop Grid's needs. Under the objectives of minimizing the average end-to-end delay and the load a super-peer bears, an exact model for constructing a topology with a fully meshed super-peer core is derived from a Hub Location problem. The related problem of selecting a subset of peers to form the super-peer core and subsequentially performing the assignment of edge peers to the super-peers makes up the Super-Peer Selection Problem (SPSP). The goal of minimizing a super-peer's load is met by establishing $\sqrt{n}$ super-peers and assigning $\sqrt{n} - 1$ edge peers to each super-peer in a n-peer overlay.

- As the SPSP cannot be solved exactly under realistic conditions due to its computational complexity and the requirement of a global view, the Super-Peer Selection Algorithm (SPSA) is introduced which heuristically solves the SPSP in a distributed, self-organized way. SPSP adapts the load of super-peers dynamically by creating new super-peers and downgrading existing ones as required. Network coordinates support edge peers in finding their closest super-peer, and super-peers in determining the most suitable edge peer for replacement or promotion.

- Since the full mesh forces super-peers to maintain connections to all other super-peers, the ChordSPSA algorithm replaces the fully meshed super-peer core with a Chord ring. Based on SPSA but equipped with a number of modifications to adopt the new super-peer interconnection structure, ChordSPSA maintains SPSA's properties of being distributed, self-organizing, and topology-optimizing. With the Chord-based super-peer topology, efficient broadcast (both ordinary full and constrained broadcast) requires every forwarding peer to transmit only $O(\log n)$ instead of $O(\sqrt{n})$ messages in an n-peer overlay. The super-peer list can be maintained by periodic beacon messages or deterministic gossip, a dissemination scheme that exploits the Chord finger structure to remove stochastic uncertainty from the gossip concept.

- Chord identifier assignment is improved through PIS which benefits from the presence of the super-peer list and network coordinates. With PIS, a peer chooses its Chord ID such that the cumulative delay to its finger destinations is minimized. In message forwarding, PRS greedily chooses the finger which incurs the least delay per covered unit of the identifier space. Under the assumption of all finger tables being populated properly, the more sophisticated LPRS scheme reconstructs the finger tables of all super-peers from the information provided by the super-peer list into a unified graph, then executes Dijkstra's single-source shortest-path algorithm to determine the next hop for every super-peer destination. PIS, PRS and LPRS all work in a distributed environment, run in polynomial time, and do not require extra messages. Experiments have shown the average end-to-end message delay to diminish vastly in comparison to pure Chord.

- Delivering a proof of concept, a middleware prototype was developed to implement the proposed PeerGrid concept along with four jobs that intend to demonstrate the capabilities of the prototype in three different testbeds. Aside from the performance aspect, the prototype has also maintained a high degree of overlay connectivity throughout the experiments.

This thesis has placed its focus on the algorithmic aspects of P2P Desktop Grid middleware design, and evaluated its proposed approach with a prototype-supported performance assessment in live environments. Beyond this, two promising fields have been left to future research.

One direction would pursue the extension of the super-peer selection metric to consider additional aspects of peer heterogeneity. Besides the link delay estimated through network coordinates, metrics such as recent CPU load, CPU speed, bandwidth, and lifetime can yield meaningful information on a peer's fitness for performing in a super-peer role. Moreover, the inclusion of reputation information could prevent colluders from becoming super-peers (cf. Section 5.2.1). Incorporating these clues into the promotion processes of SPSA and ChordSPSA could further increase the stability and reliability of the super-peer core.

A possible second direction concerns overlay dynamics that cause peers to change their locations, temporarily disconnecting them. Clearly, messages destined for disconnected peers cannot be delivered and are eventually dropped. A DHT-supported scheme of *persistent addresses* can solve this issue. In such a scheme, every peer assigns itself, in addition to other addresses (such as the IP address and Chord ID), a persistent address which is a unique address that never changes. The Chord super-peer core serves as a DHT. Every peer hashes its persistent address to a DHT peer with which it registers a mapping from its persistent address to the Chord ID at which it can currently be reached (for edge peers, this is their respective super-peer's Chord ID). Peers which change their location in the overlay update the registered mapping within the DHT to reflect the new situation. Persistent addresses become the sole kind of destination addresses for all messages to be routed through the overlay. The proposed scheme resembles DNS in that it requires persistent addresses to be resolved to overlay addresses before an actual message is sent. With this scheme, workers and initiators could communicate anytime without the need to maintain direct connections. It would work even for peers operating from behind firewalls in the face of high overlay dynamics.

There have been numerous attempts at tapping the idle resources of online desktop computers. However, all existing schemes lack desirable properties. Computational Grids entail extensive administrative effort and are not designed to handle a large, highly dynamic pool of desktop computers with significant administrative autonomy. Moreover, the setup of Computational Grids contains a single point of failure such as a centralized scheduler. In volunteer computing, a single, unchanging initiator submits jobs of a pre-defined kind which are processed by workers that donate their idle cycles for no return. This client/server approach lacks reciprocity, the ability to support arbitrary jobs, and the freedom to permit arbitrary participants to become initiators. Existing Desktop Grids feature a centralized instance (a single point of failure and a potential point of censorship), are built on an unstructured topology (which is prone to scalability issues), do not consider the benefits of topology optimization (which misses the opportunity to accelerate message forwarding), assume peers to be altruistic (which fosters exploitation by free-riders), or require modifications to the runtime environment such as a tweaked Java virtual machine (which endangers the system's acceptance with the intended target audience). PeerGrid exhibits none of these issues. With desktop computers becoming increasingly powerful, Desktop Grids built according to the PeerGrid blueprint contribute to satisfying the ever-growing need for computational power in a scalable, topology-optimized, fully distributed way.

Appendix A

CPUs in PlanetLab nodes

CPU type	Clock rate [GHz]	Count	Total
AMD Athlon	unspecified	2	
AMD Athlon XP 1900+	1.60	1	
AMD Athlon XP 2000+	1.67	1	
AMD Athlon XP 2500+	1.83	2	
AMD Athlon XP 2600+	1.92	1	
AMD Athlon XP 2800+	2.08	2	
AMD Athlon subtotal			**9**
AMD Athlon 64 3200+	2.00	6	
AMD Athlon64 subtotal			**6**
AMD Athlon 64 X2 5200+	2.60	1	
AMD Athlon64 X2 subtotal			**1**
AMD Opteron 246	2.00	1	
AMD Opteron Dual-Core 285	2.60	2	
AMD Opteron Dual-Core 1222	3.00	2	
AMD Opteron subtotal			**5**
Intel Pentium 3	unspecified	3	
Intel Pentium 3	1.27	8	
Intel Pentium 3	1.40	1	
Intel Pentium 3 subtotal			**12**
Intel Celeron	2.93	1	
Intel Celeron subtotal			**1**

(Continued on the next page)

CPU type	Clock rate [GHz]	Count	Total
Intel Pentium 4	1.50	4	
Intel Pentium 4	1.70	1	
Intel Pentium 4	1.80	22	
Intel Pentium 4	2.00	3	
Intel Pentium 4	2.40	22	
Intel Pentium 4	2.53	1	
Intel Pentium 4	2.66	11	
Intel Pentium 4	2.80	24	
Intel Pentium 4	3.00	17	
Intel Pentium 4	3.06	8	
Intel Pentium 4	3.20	10	
Intel Pentium 4	3.40	16	
Intel Pentium 4	3.60	2	
Intel Pentium 4 subtotal			**141**
Intel Pentium D	2.80	7	
Intel Pentium D	3.00	18	
Intel Pentium D	3.20	41	
Intel Pentium D	3.40	3	
Intel Pentium D subtotal			**69**
Intel Pentium Dual E2180	2.00	2	
Intel Pentium Dual subtotal			**2**
Intel Core 2 Duo E4600	2.40	4	
Intel Core 2 Duo E6420	2.13	2	
Intel Core 2 Duo E6550	2.33	76	
Intel Core 2 Duo E6600	2.40	1	
Intel Core 2 Duo E6700	2.66	2	
Intel Core 2 Duo E7200	2.53	2	
Intel Core 2 Duo E8200	2.66	2	
Intel Core 2 Duo E8400	3.00	2	
Intel Core 2 Duo E8500	3.16	2	
Intel Core 2 Quad Q6600	2.40	4	
Intel Core 2 Quad Q6700	2.66	1	
Intel Core 2 Quad X6800	2.93	2	
Intel Core 2 subtotal			**100**
Intel Xeon	2.20	2	

(Continued on the next page)

CPU type	Clock rate [GHz]	Count	Total
Intel Xeon	2.40	16	
Intel Xeon	2.66	1	
Intel Xeon	2.80	16	
Intel Xeon	3.00	18	
Intel Xeon	3.06	1	
Intel Xeon	3.20	4	
Intel Xeon	3.40	6	
Intel Xeon E3040	1.86	5	
Intel Xeon E3050	2.13	2	
Intel Xeon E3060	2.40	35	
Intel Xeon E3070	2.66	2	
Intel Xeon E3075	2.66	13	
Intel Xeon E3110	3.00	4	
Intel Xeon E5140	2.33	2	
Intel Xeon E5150	2.66	2	
Intel Xeon E5420	2.50	8	
Intel Xeon E5430	2.66	2	
Intel Xeon X3210	2.13	3	
Intel Xeon X3220	2.40	12	
Intel Xeon X3320	2.50	1	
Intel Xeon X3323	2.50	3	
Intel Xeon X3350	2.66	2	
Intel Xeon X3363	2.83	2	
Intel Xeon subtotal			**162**
Unidentified Intel processor	unspecified	1	
Intel unidentified subtotal			**1**
Examined processors total			**509**

Table A.1: CPUs in PlanetLab nodes

References

[1] Karl Aberer, Luc Onana Alima, Ali Ghodsi, Sarunas Girdzijauskas, Seif Haridi, and Manfred Hauswirth. The Essence of P2P: A Reference Architecture for Overlay Networks. *Proceedings of the 5th IEEE International Conference on Peer-to-Peer Computing*, pages 11–20, 2005.

[2] Karl Aberer, Anwitaman Datta, and Manfred Hauswirth. P-Grid: Dynamics of Self-Organizing Processes in Structured Peer-to-Peer Systems. In Ralf Steinmetz and Klaus Wehrle, editors, *Peer-to-Peer Systems and Applications*, pages 137–153. Springer, 2005.

[3] Ittai Abraham and Dahlia Malkhi. Compact routing on Euclidian metrics. In *Proceedings of the 23rd Annual ACM Symposium on Principles of Distributed Computing*, pages 141–149, 2004.

[4] Eytan Adar and Bernardo A. Huberman. Free Riding on Gnutella. *First Monday*, 5(10), 2000.

[5] Emmanuelle Anceaume and Aina Ravoaja. Incentive-Based Robust Reputation Mechanism for P2P Services. In *Proceedings of the 10th International Conference on Principles of Distributed Systems*, pages 305–319, 2006.

[6] David P. Anderson. SETI@home. In Andy Oram, editor, *Peer-to-Peer: Harnessing the Benefits of a Disruptive Technology*, pages 67–76. O'Reilly, 2001.

[7] David P. Anderson, Jeff Cobb, Eric Korpela, Matt Lebofsky, and Dan Werthimer. SETI@home: an experiment in public-resource computing. *Communications of the ACM*, 45(11):56–61, 2002.

[8] Nazareno Andrade, Francisco Vilar Brasileiro, Walfredo Cirne, and Miranda Mowbray. Discouraging Free Riding in a Peer-to-Peer CPU-Sharing Grid. In *Proceedings of the 13th International Symposium on High-Performance Distributed Computing*, pages 129–137, 2004.

[9] Nazareno Andrade, Francisco Vilar Brasileiro, Walfredo Cirne, and Miranda Mowbray. Automatic grid assembly by promoting collaboration in Peer-to-Peer grids. *Journal of Parallel and Distributed Computing*, 67(8):957–966, 2007.

[10] Nazareno Andrade, Walfredo Cirne, Francisco Vilar Brasileiro, and Paulo Roisenberg. OurGrid: An Approach to Easily Assemble Grids with Equitable Resource Sharing. In *Proceedings of the 9th International Workshop on Job Scheduling Strategies for Parallel Processing*, pages 61–86, 2003.

[11] Cosimo Anglano, John Brevik, Massimo Canonico, Daniel Nurmi, and Richard Wolski. Fault-aware scheduling for Bag-of-Tasks applications on Desktop Grids. In *Proceedings of the 7th IEEE/ACM International Conference on Grid Computing*, pages 56–63, 2006.

[12] David Applegate, William Cook, and André Rohe. Chained Lin-Kernighan for Large Traveling Salesman Problems. *INFORMS Journal on Computing*, 15(1):82–92, 2003.

[13] David L. Applegate, Robert E. Bixby, Vasek Chvatal, and William J. Cook. *The Traveling Salesman Problem: A Computational Study*. Princeton University Press, 2007.

[14] Marc Sánchez Artigas, Pedro García López, and Antonio F. Gómez-Skarmeta. A Comparative Study of Hierarchical DHT Systems. In *Proceedings of the 32nd Annual IEEE Conference on Local Computer Networks*, pages 325–333, 2007.

[15] Marc Sánchez Artigas, Pedro García López, and Antonio F. Gómez-Skarmeta. On the Feasibility of Dynamic Superpeer Ratio Maintenance. In *Proceedings of the 4th IEEE International Conference on Peer-to-Peer Computing*, pages 333–342, 2008.

[16] Robert Axelrod. *The evolution of cooperation*. Basic Books, 1984.

[17] Nadia Ben Azzouna and Fabrice Guillemin. Experimental analysis of the impact of peer-to-peer applications on traffic. *European transactions on Telecommunications: Special issue on P2P networking and P2P services*, 15(6):511–522, 2004.

[18] Hari Balakrishnan, M. Frans Kaashoek, David R. Karger, Robert Morris, and Ion Stoica. Looking up data in P2P systems. *Communications of the ACM*, 46(2):43–48, 2003.

[19] Michael Barbehenn. A Note on the Complexity of Dijkstra's Algorithm for Graphs with Weighted Vertices. *IEEE Transactions on Computers*, 47(2):263, 1998.

[20] Ingmar Baumgart, Bernhard Heep, and Stephan Krause. OverSim: A Flexible Overlay Network Simulation Framework. In *Proceedings of the 10th IEEE Global Internet Symposium*, pages 87–88, 2007.

[21] Gordon Bell and Jim Gray. What's next in high-performance computing? *Communications of the ACM*, 45(2):91–95, 2002.

[22] Joyce Berg, John Dickhaut, and Kevin McCabe. Trust, Reciprocity, and Social History. *Games and Economic Behavior*, 10(1):122–142, 1995.

[23] Francine Berman, Geoffrey Fox, and Anthony J. G. Hey. The Grid: Past, Present, Future. In Francine Berman, Geoffrey Fox, and Anthony J. G. Hey, editors, *Grid Computing: Making the Global Infrastructure a Reality*, pages 9–50. Wiley, 2005.

[24] Francine Berman, Richard Wolski, Henri Casanova, Walfredo Cirne, Holly Dail, Marcio Faerman, Silvia M. Figueira, Jim Hayes, Graziano Obertelli, Jennifer M. Schopf, Gary Shao, Shava Smallen, Neil T. Spring, Alan Su, and Dmitrii Zagorodnov. Adaptive Computing on the Grid Using AppLeS. *IEEE Transactions on Parallel and Distributed Systems*, 14(4):369–382, 2003.

[25] Philip A. Bernstein. Middleware: A Model for Distributed System Services. *Communications of the ACM*, 39(2):86–98, 1996.

[26] Thomas Bocek, Wang Kun, Fabio Victora Hecht, David Hausheer, and Burkhard Stiller. PSH: A Private and Shared History-Based Incentive Mechanism. In *Proceedings of the 2nd International Conference on Autonomous Infrastructure, Management and Security*, pages 15–27, 2008.

[27] Thomas Bocek, Michael Shann, David Hausheer, and Burkhard Stiller. Game theoretical analysis of incentives for large-scale, fully decentralized collaboration networks. In *Proceedings of the 22nd IEEE International Symposium on Parallel and Distributed Processing*, pages 1–8, 2008.

[28] John Bohannon. Grassroots Supercomputing. *Science*, 308(5723):810–813, 2005.

[29] Klemens Böhm and Erik Buchmann. Free riding-aware forwarding in Content-Addressable Networks. *The VLDB Journal*, 16(4):463–482, 2007.

[30] Uday Bondhugula, Ananth Devulapalli, Joseph Fernando, Pete Wyckoff, and P. Sadayappan. Parallel FPGA-based All-Pairs Shortest-Paths in a Directed Graph. In *Proceedings of the 20th IEEE International Parallel and Distributed Processing Symposium*, page 90, 2006.

[31] Miguel L. Bote-Lorenzo, Yannis A. Dimitriadis, and Eduardo Gómez-Sánchez. Grid Characteristics and Uses: A Grid Definition. In *Proceedings of the European Across Grids Conference*, pages 291–298, 2003.

[32] Andrew Brampton, Andrew MacQuire, Idris A. Rai, Nicholas J. P. Race, and Laurent Mathy. Stealth distributed hash table: a robust and flexible super-peered DHT. In *Proceedings of the 2006 ACM CoNEXT conference*, pages 1–12, 2006.

[33] Ulrik Brandes, Patrick Kenis, Jürgen Lerner, and Denise van Raaij. Network Analysis of Collaboration Structure in Wikipedia. In *Proceedings of the 18th International World Wide Web Conference*, pages 731–740, 2009.

[34] Bodil Branner. The Mandelbrot Set. In Robert L. Devaney and Linda Keen, editors, *Chaos and Fractals - The Mathematics Behind the Computer Graphics*, pages 75–105. AMS, 1989.

[35] R. Buyya, D. Abramson, and J. Giddy. Nimrod/G: An Architecture of a Resource Management and Scheduling System in a Global Computational Grid. In *Proceedings of the 4th International Conference on High Performance Computing in Asia-Pacific Region*, pages 283–289, 2000.

[36] Brad Calder, Andrew A. Chien, Ju Wang, and Don Yang. The Entropia virtual machine for desktop grids. In *Proceedings of the 1st International Conference on Virtual Execution Environments*, pages 186–196, 2005.

[37] James F. Campbell. Hub location and the p-hub median problem. *Operations Research*, 44(6):923–935, 1996.

[38] James F. Campbell, Andreas T. Ernst, and Mohan Krishnamoorthy. Hub Location Problems. In Zvi Drezner and Horst W. Hamacher, editors, *Facility Location: Applications and Theory*, pages 373–407. Springer, 2002.

[39] Denis Caromel, Alexandre di Costanzo, and Clément Mathieu. Peer-to-Peer for Computational Grids: Mixing Clusters and Desktop Machines. *Parallel Computing*, 33(4–5):275–288, 2007.

[40] Henri Casanova and Francine Berman. Parameter sweeps on the Grid with APST. In Francine Berman, Geoffrey Fox, and Anthony J. G. Hey, editors, *Grid Computing: Making the Global Infrastructure a Reality*, pages 773–787. Wiley, 2005.

[41] Henri Casanova, Dmitrii Zagorodnov, Francine Berman, and Arnaud Legrand. Heuristics for Scheduling Parameter Sweep Applications in Grid Environments. *Proceedings of the 9th Heterogeneous Computing Workshop*, pages 349–363, 2000.

[42] Miguel Castro, Peter Druschel, Ayalvadi Ganesh, Antony Rowstron, and Dan S. Wallach. Secure routing for structured peer-to-peer overlay networks. *ACM SIGOPS Operating Systems Review*, 36:299–314, 2002.

[43] Miguel Castro, Peter Druschel, Y. Charlie Hu, and Antony Rowstron. Topology-Aware Routing in Structured Peer-to-Peer Overlay Networks. In *Future Directions in Distributed Computing*, volume 2584 of *Lecture Notes in Computer Science*, pages 103–107, 2003.

[44] Arjav J. Chakravarti, Gerald Baumgartner, and Mario Lauria. The organic grid: self-organizing computation on a Peer-to-Peer network. *IEEE Transactions on Systems, Man, and Cybernetics, Part A*, 35(3):373–384, 2005.

[45] Alice Cheng and Eric Friedman. Sybilproof reputation mechanisms. In *Proceedings of the 2005 ACM SIGCOMM workshop on Economics of Peer-to-Peer systems*, pages 128–132, 2005.

[46] Andrew A. Chien. Architecture of a commercial enterprise desktop Grid: the Entropia system. In Francine Berman, Geoffrey Fox, and Anthony J. G. Hey, editors, *Grid Computing: Making the Global Infrastructure a Reality*, pages 337–350. Wiley, 2005.

[47] Andrew A. Chien. Computing Elements. In Ian Foster and Carl Kesselman, editors, *The Grid: Blueprint for a New Computing Infrastructure*, pages 567–591. Morgan Kaufmann, 2007.

[48] Andrew A. Chien. Massively Distributed Computing: Virtual Screening on a Desktop Grid. In Ian Foster and Carl Kesselman, editors, *The Grid: Blueprint for a New Computing Infrastructure*, pages 147–155. Morgan Kaufmann, 2007.

[49] John Chuang. Designing incentive mechanisms for peer-to-peer systems. In *Proceedings of the 1st IEEE International Workshop on Grid Economics and Business Models*, pages 67–81, 2004.

[50] Brent Chun, David Culler, Timothy Roscoe, Andy Bavier, Larry Peterson, Mike Wawrzoniak, and Mic Bowman. PlanetLab: an overlay testbed for broad-coverage services. *Computer Communication Review*, 33(3):3–12, 2003.

[51] David Clark. Face-to-Face with Peer-to-Peer Networking. *IEEE Computer*, 34(1):18–21, 2001.

[52] Edward G. Coffman, Michael R. Garey, and David S. Johnson. Approximation algorithms for bin packing: A survey. In Dorit Hochbaum, editor, *Approximation algorithms*, pages 46–93. PWS Publishing Company, 1997.

[53] Michael Conrad and Hans-Joachim Hof. A Generic, Self-organizing, and Distributed Bootstrap Service for Peer-to-Peer Networks. In *Proceedings of the 2nd International Workshop on Self-Organizing Systems*, pages 59–72, 2007.

[54] Thomas Cormen, Charles Leiserson, Ronald Rivest, and Clifford Stein. *Introduction to Algorithms*. MIT Press, 2001.

[55] Manuel Costa, Miguel Castro, Antony Rowstron, and Peter Key. PIC: Practical Internet Coordinates for Distance Estimation. In *Proceedings of the 24th International Conference on Distributed Computing Systems*, pages 178–187, 2004.

[56] George Coulouris, Jean Dollimore, and Tim Kindberg. *Distributed Systems: Concepts and Design*. Addison-Wesley, 2005.

[57] Russ Cox, Frank Dabek, M. Frans Kaashoek, Jinyang Li, and Robert Morris. Practical, distributed network coordinates. *Computer Communication Review*, 34(1):113–118, 2004.

[58] Joel M. Crichlow. *An introduction to distributed and parallel computing*. Prentice Hall, 1988.

[59] Jon Crowcroft, Tim Moreton, Ian Pratt, and Andrew Twigg. Peer-to-Peer Technologies. In Ian Foster and Carl Kesselman, editors, *The Grid: Blueprint for a New Computing Infrastructure*, pages 593–622. Morgan Kaufmann, 2007.

[60] Frank Dabek, Russ Cox, M. Frans Kaashoek, and Robert Morris. Vivaldi: a decentralized network coordinate system. In *Proceedings of ACM SIGCOMM*, pages 15–26, 2004.

[61] Frank Dabek, Jinyang Li, Emil Sit, James Robertson, M. Frans Kaashoek, and Robert Morris. Designing a DHT for Low Latency and High Throughput. In *Proceedings of the 1st Symposium on Networked Systems Design and Implementation*, pages 85–98, 2004.

[62] Vasilios Darlagiannis. Self-Organization in Peer-to-Peer Systems. In Ralf Steinmetz and Klaus Wehrle, editors, *Peer-to-Peer Systems and Applications*, pages 353–366. Springer, 2005.

[63] José M. Valério de Carvalho. LP models for bin packing and cutting stock problems. *European Journal of Operational Research*, 141(2):253–273, 2002.

[64] Alan J. Demers, Daniel H. Greene, Carl Hauser, Wes Irish, John Larson, Scott Shenker, Howard E. Sturgis, Daniel C. Swinehart, and Douglas B. Terry. Epidemic Algorithms for Replicated Database Maintenance. In *Proceedings of the 6th Annual ACM Symposium on Principles of Distributed Computing*, pages 1–12, 1987.

[65] Martin Desrochers and Gilbert Laporte. Improvements and extensions to the Miller-Tucker-Zemlin subtour elimination constraints. *Operations Research Letters*, 10:27–36, 1991.

[66] Edsger W. Dijkstra. A note on two problems in connexion with graphs. *Numerische Mathematik*, 1:269–271, 1959.

[67] Tassos Dimitriou, Ghassan Karame, and Ioannis T. Christou. SuperTrust - A Secure and Efficient Framework for Handling Trust in Super Peer Networks. In *Proceedings of the 9th International Conference on Distributed Computing and Networking*, pages 350–362, 2008.

[68] Andreas Dinges, Björn Wagner, and Paul Müller. Dynamic Overlay Networks for Image Processing Grids. In *Proceedings of the 7th International Conference on Hybrid Intelligent Systems*, pages 362–365, 2007.

[69] Roger Dingledine, Michael J. Freedman, and David Molnar. Accountability. In Andy Oram, editor, *Peer-to-Peer: Harnessing the Benefits of a Disruptive Technology*, pages 271–340. O'Reilly, 2001.

[70] Jack J. Dongarra. The LINPACK benchmark: an explanation. In *Proceedings of the 1st International Conference on Supercomputing*, pages 456–474, 1988.

[71] Jack J. Dongarra, Piotr Luszczek, and Antoine Petitet. The LINPACK Benchmark: Past, Present, and Future. *Concurrency and Computation: Practice and Experience*, 15:1–18, 2003.

[72] John R. Douceur. The Sybil Attack. In *Proceedings of the 1st International Workshop on Peer-to-Peer systems*, pages 251–260, 2002.

[73] Niels Drost, Rob van Nieuwpoort, and Henri Bal. Simple Locality-Aware Co-allocation in Peer-to-Peer Supercomputing. In *Proceedings of the 6th IEEE International Symposium on Cluster Computing and the Grid*, page 14, 2006.

[74] Jörg Eberspächer and Rüdiger Schollmeier. First and Second Generation of Peer-to-Peer Systems. In Ralf Steinmetz and Klaus Wehrle, editors, *Peer-to-Peer Systems and Applications*, pages 35–56. Springer, 2005.

[75] Jörg Eberspächer and Rüdiger Schollmeier. Past and Future. In Ralf Steinmetz and Klaus Wehrle, editors, *Peer-to-Peer Systems and Applications*, pages 17–23. Springer, 2005.

[76] Sameh El-Ansary, Luc Onana Alima, Per Brand, and Seif Haridi. Efficient Broadcast in Structured P2P Networks. In *Proceedings of the 2nd International Workshop on Peer-to-Peer Systems*, pages 304–314, 2003.

[77] Wolfgang Emmerich. Software engineering and middleware: a roadmap. In *Proceedings of the 22nd International Conference on Software Engineering*, pages 117–129, 2000.

[78] Amy K. Erickson. Idle computers get busy screening drug targets for cancer. In *Nature Medicine*, volume 11, page 584, 2005.

[79] Patrick Eugster and Rachid Guerraoui. Probabilistic Multicast. In *Proceedings of the 2002 International Conference on Dependable Systems and Networks*, pages 313–324, 2002.

[80] Michal Feldman and John Chuang. Overcoming free-riding behavior in Peer-to-Peer systems. *ACM SIGecom Exchanges*, 5(4):41–50, 2005.

[81] Michal Feldman, Kevin Lai, Ion Stoica, and John Chuang. Robust incentive techniques for Peer-to-Peer networks. In *Proceedings of the 5th ACM Conference on Electronic Commerce*, pages 102–111, 2004.

[82] Michal Feldman, Christos H. Papadimitriou, John Chuang, and Ion Stoica. Free-riding and whitewashing in Peer-to-Peer systems. *IEEE Journal on Selected Areas in Communications*, 24(5):1010–1019, 2006.

[83] Thomas Fischer and Peter Merz. A Distributed Chained Lin-Kernighan Algorithm for TSP Problems. In *Proceedings of the 19th International Parallel and Distributed Processing Symposium*, 2005.

[84] Robert W. Floyd. Algorithm 97: Shortest path. *Communications of the ACM*, 5(6):345, 1962.

[85] Ian Foster and Adriana Iamnitchi. On Death, Taxes, and the Convergence of Peer-to-Peer and Grid Computing. In *Proceedings of the 2nd International Workshop on Peer-to-Peer Systems*, pages 118–128, 2003.

[86] Ian Foster and Carl Kesselman. Concepts and Architecture. In Ian Foster and Carl Kesselman, editors, *The Grid: Blueprint for a New Computing Infrastructure*, pages 37–63. Morgan Kaufmann, 2007.

[87] Ian Foster, Carl Kesselman, and Steven Tuecke. The Anatomy of the Grid - Enabling Scalable Virtual Organizations. *International Journal of Supercomputer Applications*, 15:200–222, 2001.

[88] Geoffrey Fox and Shrideep Pallickara. NaradaBrokering: an event-based infrastructure for building scalable durable peer-to-peer Grids. In Francine Berman, Geoffrey Fox, and Anthony J. G. Hey, editors, *Grid Computing: Making the Global Infrastructure a Reality*, pages 579–600. Wiley, 2005.

[89] Eric J. Friedman and Paul Resnick. The Social Cost of Cheap Pseudonyms. *Journal of Economics & Management Strategy*, 10(2):173–199, 2001.

[90] Drew Fudenberg and Jean Tirole. *Game Theory*. MIT Press, 1991.

[91] Noriyuki Fujimoto and Kenichi Hagihara. A Comparison among Grid Scheduling Algorithms for Independent Coarse-Grained Tasks. In *Proceedings of the 2004 Symposium on Applications and the Internet Workshops*, pages 674–680, 2004.

[92] Prasanna Ganesan, Krishna Gummadi, and Hector Garcia-Molina. Canon in G Major: Designing DHTs with Hierarchical Structure. In *Proceedings of the 24th International Conference on Distributed Computing Systems*, pages 263–272, 2004.

[93] Luis Garcés-Erice, Ernst W. Biersack, Pascal Felber, Keith W. Ross, and Guillaume Urvoy-Keller. Hierarchical Peer-to-Peer Systems. In *Proceedings of the 9th International Euro-Par Conference*, pages 1230–1239, 2003.

[94] Luis Garcés-Erice, Keith W. Ross, Ernst W. Biersack, Pascal Felber, and Guillaume Urvoy-Keller. Topology-Centric Look-Up Service. In *Proceedings of the 5th International Workshop on Networked Group Communications*, pages 58–69, 2003.

[95] Michael R. Garey and David S. Johnson. *Computers and intractability*. W.H. Freeman and Company, 1979.

[96] Chris GauthierDickey and Christian Grothoff. Bootstrapping of Peer-to-Peer Networks. In *Proceedings of the 2008 International Symposium on Applications and the Internet*, pages 205–208, 2008.

[97] Ran Giladi. Evaluating the Mflops Measure. *IEEE Micro*, 16(4):69–75, 1996.

[98] Ran Giladi and Niv Ahituv. SPEC as a Performance Evaluation Measure. *IEEE Computer*, 28(8):33–42, 1995.

[99] Philippe Golle, Kevin Leyton-Brown, and Ilya Mironov. Incentives for sharing in peer-to-peer networks. In *Proceedings of the 3rd ACM Conference on Electronic Commerce*, pages 264–267, 2001.

[100] Li Gong. JXTA: A Network Programming Environment. *IEEE Internet Computing*, 5(3):88–95, 2001.

[101] Stefan Götz, Simon Rieche, and Klaus Wehrle. Selected DHT Algorithms. In Ralf Steinmetz and Klaus Wehrle, editors, *Peer-to-Peer Systems and Applications*, pages 95–117. Springer, 2005.

[102] Jabeom Gu, Jaehoon Nah, Hyeokchan Kwon, Jongsoo Jang, and Sehyun Park. Random Visitor: Defense against Identity Attacks in P2P Networks. *IEICE Transactions*, 91-D(4):1058–1073, 2008.

[103] Krishna P. Gummadi, Ramakrishna Gummadi, Steven D. Gribble, Sylvia Ratnasamy, Scott Shenker, and Ion Stoica. The impact of DHT routing geometry on resilience and proximity. In *Proceedings of ACM SIGCOMM*, pages 381–394, 2003.

[104] Krishna P. Gummadi, Stefan Saroiu, and Steven D. Gribble. King: Estimating Latency between Arbitrary Internet End Hosts. *Proceedings of the 2nd ACM SIGCOMM Workshop on Internet measurement*, pages 5–18, 2002.

[105] Mordechai Haklay and Patrick Weber. OpenStreetMap: User-Generated Street Maps. *IEEE Pervasive Computing*, 7(4):12–18, 2008.

[106] Pawan Harish and P. J. Narayanan. Accelerating Large Graph Algorithms on the GPU Using CUDA. In *Proceedings of the 14th International Conference on High Performance Computing*, pages 197–208, 2007.

[107] John A. Hartigan. *Clustering algorithms*. Wiley, 1975.

[108] M. Hassaballah, Saleh Omran, and Youssef B. Mahdy. A Review of SIMD Multimedia Extensions and their Usage in Scientific and Engineering Applications. *The Computer Journal*, 51(6):630–649, 2008.

[109] Brian Hayes. Cloud computing. *Communications of the ACM*, 51(7):9–11, 2008.

[110] Michael Heidt, Tim Dörnemann, Kay Dörnemann, and Bernd Freisleben. Omnivore: Integration of Grid Meta-Scheduling and Peer-to-Peer Technologies. In *Proceedings of the 8th IEEE International Symposium on Cluster Computing and the Grid*, pages 316–323, 2008.

[111] Keld Helsgaun. An Effective Implementation of the Lin-Kernighan Traveling Salesman Heuristic. *European Journal of Operational Research*, 126(1):106–130, 2000.

[112] Francis Heylighen. The science of self-organization and adaptivity. *The Encyclopedia of Life Support Systems*, pages 253–280, 2002.

[113] Markus Hillenbrand and Paul Müller. Web Services and Peer-to-Peer. In Ralf Steinmetz and Klaus Wehrle, editors, *Peer-to-Peer Systems and Applications*, pages 207–224. Springer, 2005.

[114] Quirin Hofstätter, Stefan Zöls, Maximilian Michel, Zoran Despotovic, and Wolfgang Kellerer. Chordella - A Hierarchical Peer-to-Peer Overlay Implementation for Heterogeneous, Mobile Environments. In *Proceedings of the 8th IEEE Conference on Peer-to-Peer Computing*, pages 75–76, 2008.

[115] Feng Hong, Minglu Li, Xinda Lu, Jiadi Yu, Yi Wang, and Ying Li. HP-Chord: A Peer-to-Peer Overlay to Achieve Better Routing Efficiency by Exploiting Heterogeneity and Proximity. In *Proceedings of the 3rd International Conference on Grid and Cooperative Computing*, pages 626–633, 2004.

[116] Samuel Jacoby, Janusz Kowalik, and Joseph Pizzo. *Iterative methods for nonlinear optimization problems*. Prentice Hall, 1972.

[117] Gian Paolo Jesi, Alberto Montresor, and Özalp Babaoglu. Proximity-Aware Superpeer Overlay Topologies. In Alexander Keller and Jean-Philippe Martin-Flatin, editors, *Proceedings of the 2nd IEEE International Workshop on Self-Managed Networks, Systems and Services*, pages 43–57. Springer, 2006.

[118] Junjie Jiang, Ruoyu Pan, Changyong Liang, and Weinong Wang. BiChord: An Improved Approach for Lookup Routing in Chord. In *Proceedings of the 9th East European Conference on Advances in Databases and Information Systems*, pages 338–348, 2005.

[119] Audun Josang and Roslan Ismail. The Beta Reputation System. In *Proceedings of the 15th Bled Electronic Commerce Conference*, 2002.

[120] Joshy Joseph and Craig Fellenstein. *Grid computing*. Prentice Hall, 2004.

[121] Radu Jurca and Boi Faltings. An Incentive Compatible Reputation Mechanism. In *Proceedings of the IEEE Conference on E-Commerce*, pages 285–292, 2003.

[122] Mohamed Ali Kaafar, Laurent Mathy, Chadi Barakat, Kave Salamatian, Thierry Turletti, and Walid Dabbous. Securing Internet coordinate embedding systems. In *Proceedings of ACM SIGCOMM*, pages 61–72, 2007.

[123] Mohamed Ali Kaafar, Laurent Mathy, Thierry Turletti, and Walid Dabbous. Virtual networks under attack: disrupting Internet coordinate systems. In *Proceedings of the 2006 ACM CoNEXT conference*, pages 1–12, 2006.

[124] Sepandar D. Kamvar, Mario T. Schlosser, and Hector Garcia-Molina. Incentives for Combatting Freeriding on P2P Networks. In *Proceedings of the 9th International Euro-Par Conference*, pages 1273–1279, 2003.

[125] Sepandar D. Kamvar, Mario T. Schlosser, and Hector Garcia-Molina. The EigenTrust algorithm for reputation management in P2P networks. In *Proceedings of the 12th International World Wide Web Conference*, pages 640–651, 2003.

[126] Gene Kan. Gnutella. In Andy Oram, editor, *Peer-to-Peer: Harnessing the Benefits of a Disruptive Technology*, pages 94–122. O'Reilly, 2001.

[127] Gary J. Katz and Joseph T. Kider. All-pairs shortest-paths for large graphs on the GPU. In *Proceedings of the 23rd ACM SIGGRAPH/EUROGRAPHICS Symposium on Graphics Hardware*, pages 47–55, 2008.

[128] Leonard Kaufman and Peter J. Rousseeuw. *Finding groups in data*. John Wiley & Sons, 1989.

[129] Sebastian Kaune, Konstantin Pussep, Gareth Tyson, Andreas Mauthe, and Ralf Steinmetz. Cooperation in P2P Systems through Sociological Incentive Patterns. In *Proceedings of the 3rd International Workshop on Self-Organizing Systems*, pages 10–22, 2008.

[130] Jon Kleinberg. The Small-World Phenomenon: An Algorithmic Perspective. In *Proceedings of the 32nd ACM Symposium on Theory of Computing*, pages 163–170, 2000.

[131] Michael Kleis, Eng Keong Lua, and Xiaoming Zhou. Hierarchical Peer-to-Peer Networks Using Lightweight SuperPeer Topologies. In *Proceedings of the 10th IEEE Symposium on Computers and Communications*, pages 143–148, 2005.

[132] Florian Kolter. Jobverarbeitung in Super-Peer-basierten Desktop Grids unter besonderer Berücksichtigung von Fairness. Diploma thesis, University of Kaiserslautern, 2008.

[133] Derrick Kondo, Michela Taufer, Charles L. Brooks, Henri Casanova, and Andrew A. Chien. Characterizing and Evaluating Desktop Grids: An Empirical Study. In *Proceedings of the 18th International Parallel and Distributed Processing Symposium*, 2004.

[134] Klaus Krauter, Rajkumar Buyya, and Muthucumaru Maheswaran. A taxonomy and survey of grid resource management systems for distributed computing. *Software: Practice and Experience*, 32(2):135–164, 2001.

[135] Gerald Kunzmann, Robert Nagel, Tobias Hoßfeld, Andreas Binzenhöfer, and Kolja Eger. Efficient Simulation of Large-Scale P2P Networks: Modeling Network Transmission Times. In *Proceedings of the 15th Euromicro International Conference on Parallel, Distributed and Network-Based Processing*, pages 475–481, 2007.

[136] Hsin-Chuan Kuo, Jiang-Ren Chang, and Kai-Shun Shyu. A hybrid algorithm of evolution and simplex methods applied to global optimization. *Journal of Marine Science and Technology*, 12(4):280–289, 2004.

[137] Roman Kurmanowytsch, Engin Kirda, Clemens Kerer, and Schahram Dustdar. OMNIX: A Topology-Independent P2P Middleware. In *Proceedings of the 15th Conference on Advanced Information Systems Engineering*, 2003.

[138] Jeffrey C. Lagarias, James A. Reeds, Margaret H. Wright, and Paul E. Wright. Convergence properties of the Nelder-Mead simplex method in low dimensions. *SIAM Journal on Optimization*, 9(1):112–147, 1998.

[139] Jonathan Ledlie, Peter Pietzuch, and Margo I. Seltzer. Stable and accurate network coordinates. In *Proceedings of the 26th International Conference on Distributed Computing Systems*, page 74, 2006.

[140] Craig Lee and Domenico Talia. Grid programming models: current tools, issues and directions. In Francine Berman, Geoffrey Fox, and Anthony J. G. Hey, editors, *Grid Computing: Making the Global Infrastructure a Reality*, pages 555–578. Wiley, 2005.

[141] Sung-Ju Lee, Puneet Sharma, Sujata Banerjee, Sujoy Basu, and Rodrigo Fonseca. Measuring Bandwidth Between PlanetLab Nodes. In *Proceedings of the 6th International Passive and Active Network Measurement Workshop*, pages 292–305, 2005.

[142] Richard Lethin. Reputation. In Andy Oram, editor, *Peer-to-Peer: Harnessing the Benefits of a Disruptive Technology*, pages 341–353. O'Reilly, 2001.

[143] Brian Neil Levine, Clay Shields, and N. Boris Margolin. A Survey of Solutions to the Sybil Attack. Technical Report 2006-052, University of Massachusetts, Amherst, 2006.

[144] Jinyang Li, Jeremy Stribling, Robert Morris, M. Frans Kaashoek, and Thomer M. Gil. A performance vs. cost framework for evaluating DHT design tradeoffs under churn. In *Proceedings of IEEE INFOCOM*, pages 225–236, 2005.

[145] Qiao Lian, Yu Peng, Mao Yang, Zheng Zhang, Yafei Dai, and Xiaoming Li. Robust incentives via multi-level Tit-for-Tat. *Concurrency and Computation: Practice and Experience*, 20(2):167–178, 2008.

[146] Jian Liang, Rakesh Kumar, and Keith W. Ross. The FastTrack overlay: A measurement study. *Computer Networks Journal*, 50(6):842–858, 2006.

[147] Hyuk Lim, Jennifer C. Hou, and Chong-Ho Choi. Constructing Internet coordinate system based on delay measurement. In *Proceedings of ACM SIGCOMM*, pages 129–142, 2003.

[148] Shen Lin and Brian W. Kernighan. An Effective Heuristic Algorithm for the Travelling-Salesman Problem. *Operations Research*, 21(2):498–516, 1973.

[149] Virginia Lo, Daniel Zappala, Dayi Zhou, Yuhong Liu, and Shanyu Zhao. Cluster Computing on the Fly: P2P Scheduling of Idle Cycles in the Internet. In *Proceedings of the 3rd International Workshop on Peer-to-Peer Systems*, pages 227–236, 2004.

[150] Virginia Lo, Dayi Zhou, Yuhong Liu, Chris GauthierDickey, and Jun Li. Scalable Supernode Selection in Peer-to-Peer Overlay Networks. In *Proceedings of the 2nd International Workshop on Hot Topics in Peer-to-Peer Systems*, pages 18–27, 2005.

[151] Thomas Locher, Stefan Schmid, and Roger Wattenhofer. eQuus: A Provably Robust and Locality-Aware Peer-to-Peer System. In *Proceedings of the 6th IEEE International Conference on Peer-to-Peer Computing*, pages 3–11, 2006.

[152] Eng Keong Lua, Jon Crowcroft, Marcelo Pias, Ravi Sharma, and Steven Lim. A survey and comparison of peer-to-peer overlay network schemes. *Communications Surveys & Tutorials, IEEE*, 7:72–93, 2005.

[153] Eng Keong Lua, Timothy Griffin, Marcelo Pias, Han Zheng, and Jon Crowcroft. On the accuracy of embeddings for Internet coordinate systems. In *Proceedings of the Internet Measurement Conference*, pages 125–138, 2005.

[154] Dahlia Malkhi, Moni Naor, and David Ratajczak. Viceroy: a scalable and dynamic emulation of the butterfly. In *Proceedings of the 21st Annual Symposium on Principles of Distributed Computing*, pages 183–192, 2002.

[155] Gurmeet Singh Manku, Mayank Bawa, and Prabhakar Raghavan. Symphony: Distributed Hashing in a Small World. In *Proceedings of the 4th USENIX Symposium on Internet Technologies and Systems*, pages 127–140, 2003.

[156] Silvano Martello and Paolo Toth. *Knapsack problems: algorithms and computer implementations*. Wiley, 1990.

[157] Cecilia Mascolo, Licia Capra, and Wolfgang Emmerich. An XML-based Middleware for Peer-to-Peer computing. In *Proceedings of the 1st IEEE International Conference on Peer-to-Peer Computing*, pages 69–74, 2001.

[158] Andreas Mauthe and Oliver Heckmann. Distributed Computing – GRID Computing. In Ralf Steinmetz and Klaus Wehrle, editors, *Peer-to-Peer Systems and Applications*, pages 193–206. Springer, 2005.

[159] MaxMind. GeoLite City. http://www.maxmind.com/app/geolitecity.

[160] Petar Maymounkov and David Mazières. Kademlia: A Peer-to-Peer Information System Based on the XOR Metric. In *Proceedings of the 1st International Workshop on Peer-to-Peer Systems*, pages 53–65, 2002.

[161] Hermann De Meer and Christian Koppen. Characterization of Self-Organization. In Ralf Steinmetz and Klaus Wehrle, editors, *Peer-to-Peer Systems and Applications*, pages 227–246. Springer, 2005.

[162] Hermann De Meer and Christian Koppen. Self-Organization in Peer-to-Peer Systems. In Ralf Steinmetz and Klaus Wehrle, editors, *Peer-to-Peer Systems and Applications*, pages 247–266. Springer, 2005.

[163] Peter Merz and Katja Gorunova. Efficient Broadcast in P2P Grids. In *Proceedings of the 5th International Symposium on Cluster Computing and the Grid*, pages 237–242, 2005.

[164] Peter Merz, Florian Kolter, and Matthias Priebe. Free-Riding Prevention in Super-Peer Desktop Grids. In *Proceedings of the 3rd International Multi-Conference on Computing in the Global Information Technology*, pages 297–302, 2008.

[165] Peter Merz, Florian Kolter, and Matthias Priebe. A Distributed Reputation System for Super-Peer Desktop Grids. *IARIA International Journal on Advances in Security*, 2(1):30–41, 2009.

[166] Peter Merz and Matthias Priebe. A New Iterative Method to Improve Network Coordinates-Based Internet Distance Estimation. In *Proceedings of the 6th International Symposium on Parallel and Distributed Computing*, pages 169–176, 2007.

[167] Peter Merz, Matthias Priebe, and Steffen Wolf. A Simulation Framework for Distributed Super-Peer Topology Construction Using Network Coordinates. In *Proceedings of the 16th Euromicro Conference on Parallel, Distributed and Network-based Processing*, pages 491–498, 2008.

[168] Peter Merz, Matthias Priebe, and Steffen Wolf. Super-Peer Selection in Peer-to-Peer Networks using Network Coordinates. In *Proceedings of the 3rd International Conference on Internet and Web Applications and Services*, pages 385–390, 2008.

[169] Peter Merz, Jan Ubben, and Matthias Priebe. On the Construction of a Super-Peer Topology underneath Middleware for Distributed Computing. In *Proceedings of the 8th IEEE International Symposium on Cluster Computing and the Grid*, pages 590–595, 2008.

[170] Peter Merz, Steffen Wolf, Dennis Schwerdel, and Matthias Priebe. A Self-Organizing Super-Peer Overlay with a Chord Core for Desktop Grids. In *Proceedings of the 3rd International Workshop on Self-Organizing Systems*, pages 23–34, 2008.

[171] Hans Werner Meuer. The TOP500 Project: Looking Back Over 15 Years of Supercomputing Experience. *Informatik Spektrum*, 31(3):203–222, 2008.

[172] Su-Hong Min, Joanne Holliday, and Dong-Sub Cho. Optimal Super-peer Selection for Large-scale P2P System. In *Proceedings of the 2006 International Conference on Hybrid Information Technology*, pages 588–593, 2006.

[173] Tom M. Mitchell. *Machine Learning*. McGraw Hill, 1997.

[174] Alper Tugay Mizrak, Yuchung Cheng, Vineet Kumar, and Stefan Savage. Structured Superpeers: Leveraging Heterogeneity to Provide Constant-Time Lookup. In *Proceedings of the 3rd IEEE Workshop on Internet Applications*, pages 104–111, 2003.

[175] Pat Morin. Coarse Grained Parallel Computing on Heterogeneous Systems. In *Proceedings of the 13th ACM Symposium on Applied Computing*, pages 628–634, 1998.

[176] S. Naicken, A. Basu, B. Livingston, and S. Rodhetbhai. A Survey of Peer-to-Peer Network Simulators. In *Proceedings of The 7th Annual Postgraduate Symposium, Liverpool*, 2006.

[177] S. Naicken, B. Livingston, A. Basu, S. Rodhetbhai, I. Wakeman, and D. Chalmers. The state of peer-to-peer simulators and simulations. *Computer Communication Review*, 37(2):95–98, 2007.

[178] John A. Nelder and Roger Mead. A simplex method for function minimization. *Computer Journal*, 7:308–313, 1965.

[179] T. S. Eugene Ng and Hui Zhang. Predicting Internet Network Distance with Coordinates-Based Approaches. In *Proceedings of IEEE INFOCOM*, pages 170–179, 2002.

[180] T. S. Eugene Ng and Hui Zhang. A Network Positioning System for the Internet. In *Proceedings of the USENIX Annual Technical Conference*, pages 141–154, 2004.

[181] John Nickolls, Ian Buck, Michael Garland, and Kevin Skadron. Scalable Parallel Programming with CUDA. *ACM Queue*, 6(2):40–53, 2008.

[182] Seth James Nielson, Scott Crosby, and Dan S. Wallach. A Taxonomy of Rational Attacks. In *Proceedings of the 4th International Workshop on Peer-to-Peer Systems*, pages 36–46, 2005.

[183] Morton E. O'Kelly. A quadratic integer program for the location of interacting hub facilities. *European Journal of Operational Research*, 32(3):393–404, 1987.

[184] Morton E. O'Kelly, Darko Skorin-Kapov, and Jadranka Skorin-Kapov. Lower Bounds for the Hub Location Problem. *Management Science*, 41(4):713–721, 1995.

[185] David L. Oppenheimer, Brent N. Chun, David A. Patterson, Alex C. Snoeren, and Amin Vahdat. Service Placement in a Shared Wide-Area Platform. In *Proceedings of the USENIX Annual Technical Conference*, pages 273–288, 2006.

[186] Venkata N. Padmanabhan and Lakshminarayanan Subramanian. An investigation of geographic mapping techniques for Internet hosts. In *Proceedings of ACM SIGCOMM*, pages 173–185, 2001.

[187] Charles E. Perkins and Pravin Bhagwat. Highly Dynamic Destination-Sequenced Distance-Vector Routing (DSDV) for mobile computers. In *Proceedings of ACM SIGCOMM*, pages 234–244, 1994.

[188] Antoine Petitet, Henri Casanova, Jack J. Dongarra, Yves Robert, and R. Clinton Whaley. Parallel and Distributed Scientific Computing: A Numerical Linear Algebra Problem Solving Environment Designer's Perspective. In Jacek Blazewicz, editor, *Handbook on Parallel and Distributed Processing*, pages 464–504. Springer, 2000.

[189] Peter Pietzuch, Jonathan Ledlie, Michael Mitzenmacher, and Margo I. Seltzer. Network-Aware Overlays with Network Coordinates. In *Proceedings of the 1st Workshop on Dynamic Distributed Systems*, 2006.

[190] Peter Pietzuch, Jonathan Ledlie, and Margo I. Seltzer. Supporting network coordinates on PlanetLab. In *Proceedings of the 2nd Conference on Real, Large Distributed Systems*, pages 19–24, 2005.

[191] Young June Pyun and Douglas S. Reeves. Constructing a Balanced, (log(N)/log log(N))-Diameter Super-Peer Topology for Scalable P2P Systems. In *Proceedings of the 4th IEEE International Conference on Peer-to-Peer Computing*, pages 210–218, 2004.

[192] Michael J. Quinn. *Parallel computing: theory and practice*. McGraw-Hill, 1994.

[193] Sylvia Ratnasamy, Paul Francis, Mark Handley, Richard M. Karp, and Scott Shenker. A scalable content-addressable network. In *Proceedings of ACM SIGCOMM*, pages 161–172, 2001.

[194] Sylvia Ratnasamy, Mark Handley, Richard M. Karp, and Scott Shenker. Topologically-Aware Overlay Construction and Server Selection. In *Proceedings of IEEE INFOCOM*, pages 1190–1199, 2002.

[195] M. Venkateswara Reddy, A. Vijay Srinivas, Tarun Gopinath, and D. Janakiram. Vishwa: A reconfigurable P2P middleware for Grid Computations. In *Proceedings of the International Conference on Parallel Processing*, pages 381–390, 2006.

[196] Colin Reeves. Hybrid Genetic Algorithms for Bin-packing and Related Problems. *Annals of Operations Research*, 63:371–396, 1993.

[197] Paul Resnick, Ko Kuwabara, Richard Zeckhauser, and Eric Friedman. Reputation systems. *Communications of the ACM*, 43(12):45–48, 2000.

[198] Sean Rhea, Dennis Geels, Timothy Roscoe, and John Kubiatowicz. Handling Churn in a DHT. In *Proceedings of the USENIX Annual Technical Conference*, pages 127–140, 2004.

[199] Daniel Ridge, Donald Becker, Phillip Merkey, and Thomas Sterling. Beowulf: harnessing the power of parallelism in a pile-of-PCs. In *Proceedings of the IEEE Aerospace Conference*, pages 79–91, 1997.

[200] Matei Ripeanu and Ian Foster. Mapping the Gnutella Network: Macroscopic Properties of Large-Scale Peer-to-Peer Systems. In *Proceedings of the 1st International Workshop on Peer-to-Peer systems*, pages 85–93, 2002.

[201] Timothy Roscoe. The PlanetLab Platform. In Ralf Steinmetz and Klaus Wehrle, editors, *Peer-to-Peer Systems and Applications*, pages 567–581. Springer, 2005.

[202] David De Roure, Mark A. Baker, Nicholas R. Jennings, and Nigel R. Shadbolt. The evolution of the Grid. In Francine Berman, Geoffrey Fox, and Anthony J. G. Hey, editors, *Grid Computing: Making the Global Infrastructure a Reality*, pages 65–100. Wiley, 2005.

[203] Antony Rowstron and Peter Druschel. Pastry: Scalable, Decentralized Object Location, and Routing for Large-Scale Peer-to-Peer Systems. In *Proceedings of the IFIP/ACM International Conference on Distributed Systems Platforms*, pages 329–350, 2001.

[204] Stefan Savage, Andy Collins, Eric Hoffman, John Snell, and Thomas E. Anderson. The End-to-End Effects of Internet Path Selection. In *Proceedings of ACM SIGCOMM*, pages 289–299, 1999.

[205] Robert R. Schaller. Moore's law: past, present and future. *IEEE Spectrum*, 34(6):52–59, 1997.

[206] Detlef Schoder, Kai Fischbach, and Christian Schmitt. Application Areas. In Ralf Steinmetz and Klaus Wehrle, editors, *Peer-to-Peer Systems and Applications*, pages 25–32. Springer, 2005.

[207] Stephan Schosser, Klemens Böhm, Rainer Schmidt, and Bodo Vogt. Incentives engineering for structured P2P systems - a feasibility demonstration using economic experiments. In *Proceedings of the 7th ACM Conference on Electronic Commerce*, pages 280–289, 2006.

[208] Ayman Shaker and Douglas S. Reeves. Self-Stabilizing Structured Ring Topology P2P Systems. In *Proceedings of the 4th IEEE International Conference on Peer-to-Peer Computing*, pages 39–46, 2005.

[209] Yuval Shavitt and Tomer Tankel. Big-bang simulation for embedding network distances in Euclidean space. *IEEE/ACM Transactions on Networking*, 12(6):993–1006, 2004.

[210] Clay Shirky. Listening to Napster. In Andy Oram, editor, *Peer-to-Peer: Harnessing the Benefits of a Disruptive Technology*, pages 21–37. O'Reilly, 2001.

[211] Michael Shirts and Vijay S. Pande. Screen Savers of the World Unite! *Science*, 290:1903–1904, 2000.

[212] Atul Singh and Mads Haahr. Creating an adaptive network of hubs using Schelling's model. *Communications of the ACM*, 49(3):69–73, 2006.

[213] Krishnakanth Sistla, Alan D. George, and Robert W. Todd. Experimental Analysis of a Gossip-Based Service for Scalable, Distributed Failure Detection and Consensus. *Journal of Cluster Computing*, 6(3):237–251, 2003.

[214] Patrick Smith. *Client/server computing*. SAMS, 1992.

[215] William Spendley, George R. Hext, and Francis R. Himsworth. Sequential Application of Simplex Designs in Optimization and Evolutionary Operation. *Technometrics*, 4:441–461, 1962.

[216] Mudhakar Srivatsa, Li Xiong, and Ling Liu. TrustGuard: countering vulnerabilities in reputation management for decentralized overlay networks. In *Proceedings of the 14th International Conference on the World Wide Web*, pages 422–431, 2005.

[217] Ralf Steinmetz and Klaus Wehrle. What Is This "Peer-to-Peer" About? In Ralf Steinmetz and Klaus Wehrle, editors, *Peer-to-Peer Systems and Applications*, pages 9–16. Springer, 2005.

[218] Thomas L. Sterling, Daniel Savarese, Donald J. Becker, John E. Dorband, Udaya A. Ranawake, and Charles V. Packer. BEOWULF: A Parallel Workstation for Scientific Computation. In *Proceedings of the 24th International Conference on Parallel Processing*, pages 11–14, 1995.

[219] Ion Stoica, Robert Morris, David Karger, Frans M. Kaashoek, and Hari Balakrishnan. Chord: A scalable Peer-to-Peer lookup service for Internet applications. In *Proceedings of ACM SIGCOMM*, pages 149–160, 2001.

[220] Domenico Talia and Paolo Trunfio. Toward a Synergy Between P2P and Grids. *IEEE Internet Computing*, 7(4):94–96, 2003.

[221] Andrew S. Tanenbaum. *Computer networks*. Prentice Hall, 2003.

[222] Liying Tang and Mark Crovella. Virtual landmarks for the Internet. In *Proceedings of the Internet Measurement Conference*, pages 143–152, 2003.

[223] Hongsuda Tangmunarunkit, Ramesh Govindan, Scott Shenker, and Deborah Estrin. The Impact of Routing Policy on Internet Paths. In *Proceedings of IEEE INFOCOM*, pages 736–742, 2001.

[224] Ian J. Taylor. *From P2P to Web Services and Grids*. Springer, 2005.

[225] Douglas Thain, Todd Tannenbaum, and Miron Livny. Condor and the Grid. In Francine Berman, Geoffrey Fox, and Anthony J. G. Hey, editors, *Grid Computing: Making the Global Infrastructure a Reality*, pages 299–336. Wiley, 2005.

[226] Dimitrios K. Vassilakis and Vasilis Vassalos. Modelling Real P2P Networks: The Effect of Altruism. In *Proceedings of the 7th IEEE International Conference on Peer-to-Peer Computing*, pages 19–26, 2007.

[227] Stephen Warshall. A Theorem on Boolean Matrices. *Journal of the ACM*, 9(1):11–12, 1962.

[228] Klaus Wehrle, Stefan Götz, and Simon Rieche. Distributed Hash Tables. In Ralf Steinmetz and Klaus Wehrle, editors, *Peer-to-Peer Systems and Applications*, pages 79–93. Springer, 2005.

[229] Aaron Weiss. Computing in the clouds. *ACM netWorker*, 11(4):16–25, 2007.

[230] Darrell Whitley, Soraya Rana, and Robert B. Heckendorn. The Island Model Genetic Algorithm: On Separability, Population Size and Convergence. *Journal of Computing and Information Technology*, 7:33–47, 1998.

[231] Steffen Wolf. On the Complexity of the Uncapacitated Single Allocation *p*-Hub Median Problem with Equal Weights. Technical Report 363/07, University of Kaiserslautern, 2007.

[232] Steffen Wolf and Peter Merz. Evolutionary Local Search for the Super-Peer Selection Problem and the *p*-Hub Median Problem. In *Proceedings of the 4th International Workshop on Hybrid Metaheuristics*, pages 1–15, 2007.

[233] Bernard Wong, Aleksandrs Slivkins, and Emin Gün Sirer. Meridian: a lightweight network location service without virtual coordinates. In *Proceedings of ACM SIGCOMM*, pages 85–96, 2005.

[234] Theodore Wong. Performance. In Andy Oram, editor, *Peer-to-Peer: Harnessing the Benefits of a Disruptive Technology*, pages 203–241. O'Reilly, 2001.

[235] Li Xiao, Zhenyun Zhuang, and Yunhao Liu. Dynamic Layer Management in Superpeer Architectures. *IEEE Transactions on Parallel and Distributed Systems*, 16(11):1078–1091, 2005.

[236] Zhichen Xu, Chunqiang Tang, and Zheng Zhang. Building topology-aware overlays using global soft-state. In *Proceedings of the 23rd International Conference on Distributed Computing Systems*, pages 500–508, 2003.

[237] Beverly Yang and Hector Garcia-Molina. Designing a Super-Peer Network. In *Proceedings of the 19th International Conference on Data Engineering*, pages 49–62, 2003.

[238] Mao Yang, Zheng Zhang, Xiaoming Li, and Yafei Dai. An Empirical Study of Free-Riding Behavior in the Maze P2P File-Sharing System. In *Proceedings of the 4th International Workshop on Peer-to-Peer Systems*, pages 182–192, 2005.

[239] Shuo Yang, Ali Raza Butt, Xing Fang, Y. Charlie Hu, and Samuel P. Midkiff. A Fair, Secure and Trustworthy Peer-to-Peer Based Cycle-Sharing System. *Journal of Grid Computing*, 4(3):265–286, 2006.

[240] Weishuai Yang, Nael Abu-Ghazaleh, and Michael J. Lewis. Automatic Clustering for Self-Organizing Grids. In *Proceedings of the 2006 IEEE International Conference on Cluster Computing*, pages 1–9, 2006.

[241] Ben Y. Zhao, Yitao Duan, Ling Huang, Anthony D. Joseph, and John Kubiatowicz. Brocade: Landmark Routing on Overlay Networks. In *Proceedings of the 1st International Workshop on Peer-to-Peer Systems*, pages 34–44, 2002.

[242] Ben Y. Zhao, Ling Huang, Jeremy Stribling, Sean C. Rhea, Anthony D. Joseph, and John D. Kubiatowicz. Tapestry: A Resilient Global-scale Overlay for Service Deployment. *IEEE Journal on Selected Areas in Communications*, 22:41–53, 2004.

[243] Shanyu Zhao, Virginia Lo, and Chris GauthierDickey. Result Verification and Trust-Based Scheduling in Peer-to-Peer Grids. In *Proceedings of the 5th IEEE International Conference on Peer-to-Peer Computing*, pages 31–38, 2005.

[244] Han Zheng, Eng Keong Lua, Marcelo Pias, and Timothy G. Griffin. Internet Routing Policies and Round-Trip-Times. In *Proceedings of the Passive and Active Network Measurement Workshop*, pages 236–250, 2005.

[245] Dayi Zhou and Virginia Lo. Cluster Computing on the Fly: resource discovery in a cycle sharing peer-to-peer system. In *Proceedings of the 4th IEEE International Symposium on Cluster Computing and the Grid*, pages 66–73, 2004.

[246] Dayi Zhou and Virginia Lo. Wave Scheduler: Scheduling for Faster Turnaround Time in Peer-Based Desktop Grid Systems. In *Proceedings of the 11th International Workshop on Job Scheduling Strategies for Parallel Processing*, pages 194–218, 2005.

[247] Stefan Zöls, Zoran Despotovic, and Wolfgang Kellerer. Cost-Based Analysis of Hierarchical DHT Design. In *Proceedings of the 6th IEEE International Conference on Peer-to-Peer Computing*, pages 233–239, 2006.

[248] Stefan Zöls, Zoran Despotovic, and Wolfgang Kellerer. On hierarchical DHT systems – An analytical approach for optimal designs. *Computer Communications*, 31(3):576–590, 2008.

Author's publications

The author's publications are listed below in reverse chronological order:

- Dennis Schwerdel, Matthias Priebe, Paul Müller, and Peter Merz. ChordNet: Protocol Specification and Analysis. Technical Report 371/09, University of Kaiserslautern, 2009.

- Peter Merz, Florian Kolter, and Matthias Priebe. A Distributed Reputation System for Super-Peer Desktop Grids. *IARIA International Journal on Advances in Security*, 2(1):30–41, 2009.

- Peter Merz, Steffen Wolf, Dennis Schwerdel, and Matthias Priebe. A Self-Organizing Super-Peer Overlay with a Chord Core for Desktop Grids. In *Proceedings of the 3rd International Workshop on Self-Organizing Systems*, pages 23–34, 2008.

- Peter Merz, Florian Kolter, and Matthias Priebe. Free-Riding Prevention in Super-Peer Desktop Grids. In *Proceedings of the 3rd International Multi-Conference on Computing in the Global Information Technology*, pages 297–302, 2008. *Best Paper Award.*

- Peter Merz, Matthias Priebe, and Steffen Wolf. Super-Peer Selection in Peer-to-Peer Networks using Network Coordinates. In *Proceedings of the 3rd International Conference on Internet and Web Applications and Services*, pages 385–390, 2008.

- Peter Merz, Jan Ubben, and Matthias Priebe. On the Construction of a Super-Peer Topology underneath Middleware for Distributed Computing. In *Proceedings of the 8th IEEE International Symposium on Cluster Computing and the Grid*, pages 590–595, 2008.

- Peter Merz, Matthias Priebe, and Steffen Wolf. A Simulation Framework for Distributed Super-Peer Topology Construction Using Network Coordinates. In *Proceedings of the 16th Euromicro Conference on Parallel, Distributed and Network-based Processing*, pages 491–498, 2008.

- Peter Merz and Matthias Priebe. A New Iterative Method to Improve Network Coordinates-Based Internet Distance Estimation. In *Proceedings of the 6th International Symposium on Parallel and Distributed Computing*, pages 169–176, 2007.

Curriculum vitae

Full name	Matthias Priebe
Date of birth	January 15, 1979
Place of birth	Darmstadt, Germany
Nationality	German

1989–1998	Georg-Büchner-Schule Darmstadt Secondary school education, completed with the Abitur
1998–1999	Civilian service
1999–2005	Student at Technische Universität Darmstadt Course of studies: Information systems (Wirtschaftsinformatik)
2004	Semester abroad Technische Universiteit Eindhoven, The Netherlands
2005	Graduation in Information Systems (Dipl.-Wirtsch.-Inform.) Diploma awarded by Technische Universität Darmstadt
2006–2009	Research assistant with the Distributed Algorithms Group Department of Computer Science Technische Universität Kaiserslautern
2008–present	PhD candidate under the supervision of Prof. Dr. Peter Merz